Mandy
Sacher

Unfussy Eaters Club

murdoch books
Sydney | London

Contents

PART TWO: THE FOOD

Introduction

As a paediatric nutritionist and mum of two, I know firsthand that the world of baby food and feeding can be overwhelming and filled with conflicting advice. It can feel like there's so much to get right, and the pressure to 'do it perfectly' can quickly turn what should be an enjoyable feeding adventure into a stressful and anxious time. This book is here to give you the tools to feel supported and confident as you embark on this special phase with your child.

Through these pages, the greatest gift I hope to share with you is the transformative power of starting your baby on wholefoods. My philosophy is that there is no such thing as 'kiddies' food'. From day one, the best way to introduce solids is by sharing family meals and focusing on REAL FOOD, setting the stage for your little one to eat what you eat, at the table with everyone else. This approach not only makes mealtimes easier but also prompts positive role modelling. When your baby sees you enjoying real, wholesome food, they are more likely to develop a positive relationship with food themselves.

Whether you're starting solids, dealing with a fussy toddler who is struggling with new textures, or simply looking for inspiration for family meals that everyone can enjoy, this book is for you. I hope it will be your one-stop children's nutrition bible and trusted kitchen companion as your little one grows.

The journey ahead will have its challenges, but you've already shown your deep commitment to nourishing your child well. Keep trusting in yourself and the process. This real-food approach is one of the most powerful ways to shape your child's relationship with food for life.

I believe that healthy eating is a lifelong journey, and it all begins with those first bites. Join the Unfussy Eaters Club and make this an exciting, stress-free experience for both you and your little ones.

Warmest,

Mandy Sacher

How to use this book

Allergens and dietaries

Look out for these icons to determine whether the recipes are suitable for your family. On the recipe pages, you will see allergen icons crossed out, indicating that the recipe is free from the allergen. These labels are based on ingredients used in the recipe, but always check packaging, as some products might carry 'may contain' warnings because they're processed in facilities that also handle allergens, such as peanuts or wheat. 'Peanut free' means no peanuts, although the recipe may still contain other nuts, such as almond or cashew. Find out more on pages 30–34.

Age ranges

The minimum age at which to serve a dish is shown at the top of the recipe. But keep in mind, all the recipes can be adapted for the whole family – after all, who has time to cook a different meal for everyone? Keep an eye out for the bold text in the recipe methods, which will explain how to prep the dish for younger and older children.

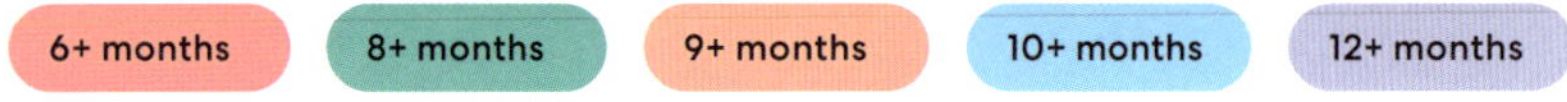

Serving sizes: one doesn't fit all

Serving sizes in this book are designed to be flexible and family friendly. How much each member eats will naturally vary depending on age, appetite and stage of development. Here's a rough guide to help you gauge portions:

- **Babies (6–12 months)** Start small – a tablespoon or two is plenty. Gradually increase to ½ cup of food per meal or more.
- **Toddlers (1–3 years:** Toddlers often eat around a quarter to half the amount of an adult. Their appetite may change day to day – that's completely normal.
- **Young children (4–8 years)** May eat about half to two-thirds of an adult portion, depending on the meal and their individual needs.
- **Older children (9–13 years)** Can need similar portions to adults – or even larger ones during growth spurts, especially of filling foods, such as grains and healthy fats.
- **Teenagers** Their bodies are growing fast and their appetites often reflect that. Expect adult-sized servings, and sometimes more!

Don't worry about sticking to exact portions. Some days your child might be hungrier, other days less – that's okay. Offer balanced meals, let them decide how much they need, and know that variety, consistency and a relaxed atmosphere go a long way.

See page 27 for signs of hunger and fullness.

Serving suggestions

Some ingredient lists include optional serving suggestions. Always check the method to see which are appropriate for your baby's age, and how they should be prepared.

Sugar and salt

The base recipes don't use salt or sodium-rich ingredients, such as tamari and soy sauce. It's fine to season the dishes for older family members. If you want to add salt to your child's meal, you can do so sparingly if they are older than 12 months, keeping the recommended daily intakes for sodium in mind:

- **1–3 years** 200–400 mg
- **4–8 years** 300–600 mg
- **9–13 years** 400–800 mg

The same goes for sugar. While these recipes are sugar-free, you can sweeten them for over 2s. Find suggestions for which sweeteners (free from added sugars) to use in the 'Make it ...' boxes.

When I say sugar-free, I mean free from refined or added sugars (see page 14).

'Make it ...' boxes

The 'Make it ...' boxes will guide you on easy swaps and ways to cater for particular allergies (such as **dairy free**, **gluten free** and **egg free**) and on what to do when you might be missing an ingredient (e.g. **seasonal** and **pantry friendly**). **Boosted** gives you ideas to get even more nutrition into the dish. **Family friendly** – for 2+ years up to adults – provides ideas to make the recipes delicious for older tastebuds too. And **school friendly** highlights what food packs well in a lunch box and for a nut-free school environment. Note: Some suggestions may alter the allergen profile of the recipe, so check icons and ingredients choices carefully.

Batch-cooking basics

You don't need to cook fresh meals every day. A well-stocked freezer is your friend during the weaning journey and busy mealtimes. The basics are simple: choose two or three recipes to cook each week, double or triple them, then portion and freeze immediately.

When your baby is first starting solids, sweet potato, carrot, apple and pumpkin (squash) purées are excellent for batch cooking. From 6 months on, each week aim to prepare one protein dish (once introduced), one vegetable-based meal, one baked item and one grain dish (once introduced).

My top tips

- Cook multiple dishes simultaneously.
- Prep all vegetable and fruit purées at once.
- Share the load with a friend, so you're only cooking two to three meals per week.
- Ensure you have plenty of freezer space.
- Use ice cube trays for small portions.
- Freeze in 2–4 tablespoon portions for older babies.
- Always label with date and contents.
- Once frozen, use within 3 months.

PART ONE

The foundations

Step 1: The Real Food mindset

While the first 1000 days are a foundational window for shaping your child's health, research shows it's never too late to make impactful changes.

Even children aged 4–12 experience significant improvements in gut health and reduced inflammation simply by increasing fibre and reducing ultra-processed foods (UPFs; see page 247). This means that, no matter the age of your child, making small shifts toward real food can positively influence their gut, immunity, mood and long-term wellbeing. Your efforts truly count, no matter when you begin.

This is the first baby food book to directly address the dangers of UPFs and offer a clear, practical solution. UPFs are recognised as the biggest source of hidden sugars, salt and harmful additives in children's diets, with Australian studies confirming they dominate children's food choices and contribute to nearly half of their daily sodium intake. UPFs are designed to hijack children's bodies and brains. A 2024 British Medical Journal review links high UPF intake to increased risks of obesity, type 2 diabetes, heart disease, cancer, depression, anxiety, and even early death. Babies and toddlers are especially vulnerable, with developing brains, guts, and immune systems that need real nourishment, not artificial ingredients. This book will give you the power to stop that cycle before it starts.

Real food is as simple as it sounds. It's food that's close to its natural state, minimally processed and free from artificial additives, flavours and preservatives. Think fresh fruits and vegetables, wholegrains, pasture-raised meats, eggs, wild-caught, low-mercury fish and dairy with minimal ingredients. It's also about avoiding added sugars until after the age of 2 (see pages 14–15). Tooth decay is the most common chronic condition in children worldwide, with excess sugar identified as the leading cause – even in children under 6. Plus, the first 1000 days of life represent the most critical window for developing a robust gut microbiome, with important development continuing through to age 3.

Real food isn't about being perfect. It's about nourishing your family with the best food possible while being realistic and flexible. Small changes, like swapping white bread for wholemeal or choosing unsweetened yoghurt over flavoured, can make a big difference (see page 16 for my guide to easy swaps). When starting out, take small steps to prepare for feeding the newest member of your family, and you'll soon achieve your goal.

The many benefits of the gut-brain connection

Gut health influences so much more than just digestion. The gut-brain connection – the remarkable two-way communication system between your baby's digestive system and their developing brain – helps explain why.

Mood regulation Your little one's gut bacteria actually help produce serotonin and other feel-good compounds.

Brain development A balanced microbiome supports crucial neural connections forming in their brain.

Emotional resilience The state of your baby's gut directly impacts how they process and respond to daily stress.

Immune training Early gut colonisation helps train your baby's immune system to sort the good guys from the troublemakers.

Allergy prevention A diverse, balanced microbiome reduces the risk of food allergies and autoimmune conditions by promoting immune tolerance to common foods.

The family meal reset: A quick guide

Introducing solids isn't just a milestone for your baby, it's a powerful opportunity to reset your entire family's approach to eating. Whether this is your first baby or your fourth, welcoming a new family member offers the perfect catalyst for positive change. It's never too late to reset, even if you have older children who were raised differently or processed foods have become the norm in your household.

The family meal reset means critically examining what's on everyone's plate and choosing foods as close to their natural state as possible – foods your grandparents would recognise, without lengthy ingredient lists or artificial additives. This isn't about perfection or deprivation, it's about making wholesome, nutrient-dense options the default, and reducing or eliminating ultra-processed foods (UPFs) when possible. By eliminating the idea of 'adult food' and 'baby food', you create one inclusive food culture that benefits everyone's health while significantly reducing mealtime stress. When you prepare a vibrant sweet-potato mash for your baby, why not roast extra for the family dinner? When you introduce iron-rich meat to your little one, perhaps it's time to source better quality proteins for the whole family.

And there are so many benefits. Research consistently shows that children who share family meals and aren't restricted to 'kid foods' develop and maintain healthier relationships with food, and experience better nutritional outcomes into adulthood. It's strong evidence that how we eat together matters as much as what we eat.

There's also a powerful ripple effect beyond nutrition. Research demonstrates that regular family meals with shared foods foster better academic performance, improved self-esteem and greater resilience in children of all ages.

By embracing real food now, you're nourishing your child's growing body, and establishing the foundation for your entire family's lifelong relationship with food. You're creating rituals and connections that will sustain them far beyond the highchair years.

What if my child is older?

If you didn't start this way, please don't worry. It's never too late to make positive changes. Whether your child is 3 or 13, small and consistent shifts towards more wholefoods can make a big difference.

According to research, even diet changes made later can help reduce the risk of ADHD symptoms, obesity, diabetes and fatty liver in children, especially when reducing UPFs and increasing wholefoods.

Start by introducing just one or two nourishing swaps each week. Perhaps swap store-bought muffins for homemade banana oat ones, or offer veggie sticks with hummus after school. Get your child involved in choosing or preparing food and focus on creating positive, low-pressure experiences at mealtimes. Children are incredibly adaptable, especially when they feel included, supported and inspired.

Here's how to reset your family's eating habits to align with a Real Food philosophy.

Purge and restock

Take a close look at your pantry, fridge and freezer. Read the labels, and remove items loaded with added sugars, artificial colours, flavours and preservatives (see page 14). Replace them with wholefood alternatives. For example, swap:

- sugary breakfast cereals for rolled oats;
- processed sauces for simple, natural ones;
- refined bread and pasta for wholemeal versions.

See page 16 for more ideas.

Focus on labels

While making everything from scratch is ideal, it's not always practical. Learning to read labels (see page 14) is essential when buying products to ensure they align with your Real Food philosophy. There are plenty that have my Real Food stamp of approval, so eating Real Food is possible for even the busiest of parents. On page 16, you'll find a list of easy real-food swaps.

Ignore marketing claims

Claims like 'natural', 'real fruit', 'no artificial flavours' and 'no added cane sugar' can be misleading. Always check the ingredients list and nutrition panel to verify the product's quality. Don't rely on the Health Star Rating either; it's a government-backed system, but at this stage it doesn't take additives or processing into account. Many UPFs still score 4 or even 5 stars despite containing minimal real food. While this system is specific to Australia and New Zealand, the same caution applies to other front-of-pack labels worldwide, such as the UK's traffic-light system and the US's 'heart-healthy' symbols. These systems often give UPFs an undeserved health halo, so always look beyond the front label.

Recent analysis shows that 85 per cent of commercial toddler foods contain added sugars, ultra-processed ingredients or misleading marketing, often with images of whole fruit but no actual fruit inside. This creates a false sense of trust for parents trying to do the right thing.

That's why I've included a section on how to read ingredient lists and nutrition labels confidently. Head to page 14 for a quick guide to spotting red flags and decoding the fine print. This is where you'll find the truth about what's really in your family's food, not just the marketing spin.

Plan simple, balanced meals

Build your meals around wholefoods, focusing on a mix of fresh vegetables, quality proteins, healthy fats and wholegrains. Keep it simple – your baby doesn't need fancy recipes, just wholesome, minimally processed foods.

How to read a nutrition label

Knowing what's in your food is one of the most important skills you can develop as a parent. Here's what to look out for when choosing packaged foods. The top image is an example of a healthy option, while the bottom image shows a product with additives, colours and preservatives, too much sugar and sodium, and low fibre.

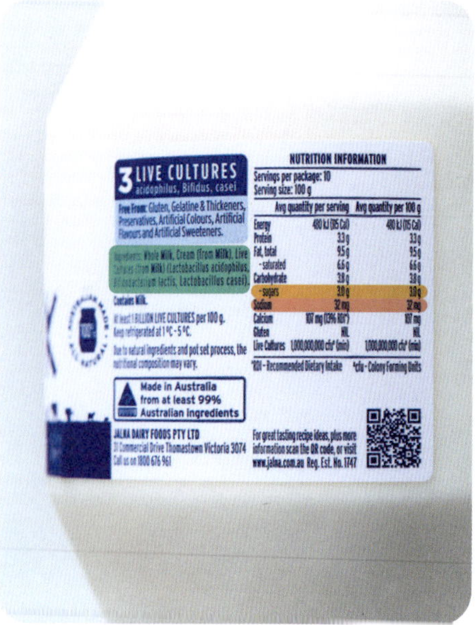

BEST BEFORE:

NUTRITION INFORMATION			
Servings Per Package: 8		Serving Size: 71 g	
	Quantity Per Serving	% Daily Intake* Per Serving	Quantity Per 100 g
Energy	888 kJ 212 Cal	10%	1250 kJ 299 Cal
Protein	6.1 g	12%	8.6 g
Fat, total	6.2 g	9%	8.8 g
- saturated	3.2 g	13%	4.5 g
Carbohydrate	31.2 g	10%	43.9 g
- sugars	2.1 g	2%	3.0 g
Dietary Fibre	2.4 g	8%	3.4 g
Sodium	631 mg	27%	889 mg

Quantities stated above are averages only.

* Percentage Daily Intakes are based on an average adult diet of 8700kJ. Your daily intakes may be higher or lower depending on your energy needs.

Ingredients: Wheat flour (62%) (thiamine, folic acid), water, vegetable oil, mineral salts (450, 500), iodised salt, sugar, spinach & herb seasoning [(0.9%), colours (102, 133)], emulsifier (471) (**soy**), acidity regulator (297), vegetable gums (412, 466), preservatives (282, 200), processing aids (**wheat**).

Contains: wheat, gluten, soy.

Ingredients Look for short, simple ingredient lists with recognisable foods. Ingredients at the beginning of the list are the main ones in the product.

Sugar To find out how much sugar there is, look at the per 100 g column. Foods with **low sugar** (≤ 5 g/ ⅛ oz per 100 g) are ideal for everyone, particularly young children; **moderate sugar** (5–10 g/⅛–⅓ oz per 100 g) is okay occasionally for older children and adults; and **high sugar** (>10 g/⅓ oz per 100 g) is best limited, especially for kids. Hidden sugars go by many names (see opposite).

> The above figures apply to added sugars, not naturally occurring sugars found in whole fruit, veg or plain dairy. These natural sugars come packaged with fibre and nutrients, and aren't harmful in the same way. If a product contains fruit or milk, expect the amounts to be higher.

Sodium Babies' kidneys can't handle high levels of salt. Watch for it listed as a top ingredient. Look at the per 100 g (3½ oz) column to determine if a product is considered low or high in sodium. Use the per serve to work out how much your child is likely to have in one sitting. Opt for items with less than 120 mg sodium per 100 g (3½ oz) for babies and young children. For older children and adults, aim for low (120 mg) or moderate (400 mg) where possible. Products with 400 mg+ – especially closer to 600 mg – have too much sodium for young children and people needing to limit salt intake.

Fibre High-fibre options are great for the whole family. Look for 3 g (⅛ oz) or more per serve in items like bread or snacks; 4–5 g+ is excellent.

Numbers Steer clear of potentially harmful additives, such as artificial colours and chemical preservatives, especially for babies and toddlers. Even seemingly innocent products, such as wraps, may contain emulsifiers, propionates, sorbates, thickeners or artificial colours. Many of these are banned in baby foods under FSANZ regulations but allowed in general foods. Additives such as tartrazine and MSG are banned in baby foods because they can be harmful when it comes to breathing, behaviour, digestion and blood oxygen.

Sweeteners and hidden sugars in packaged foods

These are the different names for sweeteners and sugars that are often listed on packaged foods:

- Agave
- Cane sugar
- Cassava syrup
- Coconut sugar
- Corn syrup
- Date sugar
- Demerara sugar
- Dextrose
- Disaccharides
- Evaporated cane juice
- Fruit concentrate
- Fruit extract
- Fructose
- Galactose
- Glucose
- Golden syrup
- Granulated sugar
- Grape sugar
- High-fructose corn syrup
- High-maltose corn syrup
- Honey
- Icing (confectioners') sugar
- Invert sugar
- Lactose
- Lo han (monk fruit)
- Malt
- Maltodextrin
- Maltose
- Mannitol
- Maple syrup
- Molasses
- Monosaccharides
- Muscovado sugar
- Palm sugar (jaggery)
- Panela
- Raw sugar
- Refined sugar
- Rice syrup
- Soft brown sugar
- Sorbitol
- Stevia
- Sucrose
- Treacle
- Turbinado sugar
- White (granulated) sugar
- Xylitol

Easy real-food swaps

Making the shift to real food doesn't have to be overwhelming. Even one or two swaps can make a big difference – you'll reduce the unnecessary sugars, salts and additives in your family's diet while increasing nutrient-dense wholefoods. See my top suggestions in the table overleaf.

Tip Look for these key words on packaging – they indicate whole/real foods: wholegrain, wholemeal, whole wheat, unhulled or hulled barley, stoneground, brown rice, oats, oatmeal, wheatberries, buckwheat, quinoa, amaranth and whole spelt.

Type of food	Avoid or limit	Choose
Baby purées	Jars or pouches with added sugars, thickeners or concentrates (see opposite for more details)	100 per cent vegetable purées or vegetable combos with beef, chicken or fish – or make your own (see page 71). Use store-bought fruit purées sparingly, as they are sweeter than natural fruits, and are best used to sweeten baked goods, pancakes and other goodies, as they replace the processed sugars
Bread	White bread or bread with additives	100 per cent wholemeal, spelt or sourdough bread with no added sugar or preservatives
Cereal and porridge	Pre-flavoured or sweetened instant baby porridge and cereals	Plain rolled oats, millet porridge or quinoa flakes. Flavour with ground cinnamon, mashed banana or homemade fruit purées (see page 76–7) or steamed veggies (for savoury porridge)
Cheese	Processed cheese slices, cheese spreads with additives or preservatives and high-sodium cheeses	Full-cream, low-sodium block cheese, shredded organic cheese or white cheese made from real ingredients with no additives
Cooking oils and fats	Refined seed or vegetable oils, such as canola, safflower or sunflower oils, margarine and non-dairy spreads	Extra virgin olive oil, virgin unrefined coconut oil, cold-pressed unrefined avocado oil, cold-pressed sesame seed oil (in moderation), cold-pressed macadamia oil, unsalted butter or ghee
Crackers and puffed snacks	Crackers or snacks with added salt, sugar or artificial flavours	Wholegrain crackers made from brown rice, quinoa or spelt. For puffed snacks, look for unsweetened puffed brown rice, quinoa or smashed chickpeas
Dips	Dips high in sodium and additives	Hummus, tzatziki, beetroot dip and bean dip with no additives or vegetable oils that are low in sodium. For babies, homemade dips are always best (see pages 224 and 238)
Dried fruit	Dried fruit with added sugar or sulphur dioxide. For example, bright orange apricots	Organic, unsweetened, sulphur-free dried fruit, such as dates, figs, apricots or raisins. These are better for snacking or as a natural sweetener in recipes (see page 208)
Muesli bars	Baby muesli bars with glucose syrup, artificial flavours or sugary coatings	Bars made with nuts, seeds, oats and natural sweeteners, such as dates, apple and pear. Better yet, make your own. Make sure they are baby friendly (soft and chewy)
Pasta	White pasta	Wholemeal, spelt or lentil-based pasta
Pasta sauce	Jarred sauces with added sugar and/or that are high in sodium	Tomato-based sauces that are homemade from tomato passata (puréed tomatoes), olive oil and fresh herbs
Nut and seed spreads	Artificial spreads with added sugar, vegetable oil and preservatives, such as BHA	Low-sodium natural nut and seed butters with no added sugar, preservatives or vegetable oils
Yoghurt	Flavoured yoghurt, low-fat varieties and those with artificial sweeteners. Avoid the convenient squeezable yoghurts marketed to babies – they often hide surprising amounts of sugar	Full-fat Greek-style or natural yoghurt. For babies, offer goat's or sheep milk yoghurt first and choose unsweetened. It's an excellent way to familiarise them with yoghurt's natural 'sour' taste. Look for options with added probiotics to support gut health and immunity

What's the problem with baby-food pouches?

While commercial baby-food pouches may seem convenient, relying on them as your baby's primary source of nutrition can have long-term implications for their eating habits and development.

Babies introduced to commercial purées early miss exposure to the natural flavours and textures of homemade food. One batch of homemade carrot purée may be sweet and smooth, while the next may be less sweet and more lumpy. These differences help babies to accept variety in their meals. As well, the ultra-high heat used to make pouches shelf-stable not only alters the taste of the food but diminishes the nutritional content.

Another factor that may make it difficult for babies to transition to more textured foods, leading to food rejection and fussy eating, is that sucking purée directly from pouches doesn't encourage chewing or texture exploration, limiting opportunities to develop oral motor skills.

Babies accustomed to pouches also miss out on the important sensory and visual connection with real food, as they learn to associate food with packaging rather than its natural form.

Pouches often contain more than 3 teaspoons of sugar, and flavoured yoghurts marketed at toddlers can contain more sugar than a chocolate bar!

Tip Whenever possible, offer fresh, whole foods. They remain the gold standard for your baby's nutrition and long-term relationship with food. However, realistic goals and flexibility matter too.

When pouches are okay

As a mum, I deeply understand how exhausting and overwhelming those early months can be, especially when you're sleep-deprived, juggling multiple responsibilities or simply having one of those 'just got to get through it' kind of days. Sometimes, baby food pouches can be a real lifeline, and that's okay. They can also be incredibly helpful during travel and emergencies. They can be great for sugar-free baking too; unsweetened 100 per cent pure apple or pear purée can go a long way in sweetening baby muffins or banana bread that's refined sugar free.

If you choose to use pouches occasionally, opt for ones that meet the following criteria:

- **High vegetable or protein content** Ensure the primary ingredients are nutrient-dense vegetables or protein, rather than fruit.
- **Fruit listed towards the end of the ingredients** Avoid pouches where fruit is the dominant ingredient to reduce exposure to excessive natural sugars and help avoid conditioning babies to prefer sweet foods.
- **Organic** Choose pouches made from organic ingredients to minimise exposure to pesticides.
- **BPA-free packaging** Ensure the pouch is free from harmful plastics when possible.
- **No added sugars or fruit concentrates** Avoid products that include unnecessary sweeteners or concentrates, such as sweetened yoghurt or custard pouches, which can condition your baby to prefer overly sweet flavours.
- **Transparent ingredient lists** Look for simple, recognisable ingredients, without additives or preservatives (see page 14).

Try to serve the purée in a bowl or squeeze it onto a spoon so your baby can still interact with their food in a meaningful way.

Should I go organic?

During your child's early years, choosing organic foods can offer significant benefits. Babies and young children have developing organs and immature detoxification systems, making them more vulnerable to environmental chemicals. Research shows that babies have lower natural levels of the enzymes needed to process pesticide residues. Given the volume of vegetables and fruit they consume relative to their body weight, they are often more exposed to these chemicals than adults. By prioritising organic foods during this critical developmental stage, you can help reduce their exposure to pesticides and other harmful substances.

That said, I know organic options aren't always accessible or affordable. Ensuring adequate fruit and vegetable intake remains paramount, and any fruits and vegetables are better than none. Conventional produce properly washed and prepared remains nutritious and valuable. Focus first on variety and freshness, then on organic for frequently consumed items from the Dirty Dozen list (see below).

Beyond fruit and vegetables, it is best to choose organic, pasture-raised chicken and eggs (to ensure the chickens that produced them are free from antibiotics) and organic dairy (as it's higher in nutrients).

Making smart choices using the EWG's lists

It can be overwhelming to balance health goals with a family budget. That's where the American Environmental Working Group (EWG) lists come in. They rank fruits and vegetables based on their pesticide residue levels. The Dirty Dozen highlights the produce that's most important to buy organic where possible, while the Clean Fifteen identifies those with the lowest pesticide levels, even when conventionally grown. I used them as a guide for my own starting solids journey and balanced conventional options from the clean list with organic options from the dirty list. These lists, and the science around organic foods, are updated every year, so stay informed.

Dirty dozen

Priority for organic

- ○ Spinach
- ○ Strawberries
- ○ Kale, collard and mustard greens
- ○ Grapes
- ○ Peaches
- ○ Cherries
- ○ Nectarines
- ○ Pears
- ○ Apples
- ○ Blackberries
- ○ Blueberries
- ○ Potatoes

Clean fifteen

Less essential for organic

- ○ Pineapples
- ○ Sweet corn (fresh or frozen)
- ○ Avocados
- ○ Papayas
- ○ Onions
- ○ Sweet peas (frozen)
- ○ Asparagus
- ○ Cabbages
- ○ Watermelons
- ○ Cauliflowers
- ○ Bananas
- ○ Mangoes
- ○ Carrots
- ○ Mushrooms
- ○ Kiwis

Money-saving tips for organic shopping

In-season buying Seasonal fruit and veg are often more affordable and fresher than those bought out of season.

Check freezer options Frozen organic produce can be cheaper and just as nutritious.

Visit farmers' markets Shop near closing time for discounts on organic goods.

Join co-ops or buying groups Pool resources with other families to buy in bulk.

Grow your own Simple herbs and greens can be grown at home with minimal effort.

Compare prices Check local stores, smaller grocers and markets for better deals.

Shopping guide

A well-stocked pantry is the foundation of real-food living. These wholefood staples make it easier to prepare quick, nourishing meals for the whole family. Choose organic where possible (see opposite).

Fresh produce

- ○ **Alliums** Garlic, leek, onion, spring onion (scallion)
- ○ **Cruciferous veg** Broccoli, brussels sprouts, white/purple cabbage, cauliflower
- ○ **Leafy greens** Bok choy (pak choy), kale, rocket, spinach, watercress
- ○ **Root veg** Beetroot, celeriac, parsnip, orange/purple/white sweet potato, Japanese/kent/butternut pumpkin (squash), carrot
- ○ **Tubers and starches** Artichoke, Jerusalem artichoke, jicama
- ○ **Soft summer veg** Zucchini (courgette), yellow squash, cucumber, tomato, eggplant (aubergine)
- ○ **Sweet, colourful veg** Capsicum (pepper), corn, mushroom, peas, snow peas
- ○ **Miscellaneous greens** Asparagus, celery, fennel, okra
- ○ **Citrus** Grapefruit, lemon, lime, orange, mandarin
- ○ **Tropical** Kiwi, mango, papaya, pineapple, passionfruit
- ○ **Stone fruit** Apricot, nectarine, peach, plum
- ○ **Core fruit** Apple, pear
- ○ **Berries** Mixed (fresh/frozen), strawberry, mulberry, raspberry, blackberry, blueberry
- ○ **Dried fruit** Naturally sundried, sugar- and sulphur-free apricot, cranberry, dates, goji berry, fig
- ○ **Other fruit** Guava, rhubarb, pomegranate, apple, mango

Natural sweeteners

For 2+ years

- ○ Banana, date or apple purée
- ○ Date syrup or date paste
- ○ Coconut sugar
- ○ Raw honey (dangerous for under 12 months)
- ○ Pure maple syrup
- ○ Unprocessed stevia

Meat and poultry

Organic

- ○ Beef (grass-fed)
- ○ Lamb (grass-fed)
- ○ Chicken (pasture-raised)
- ○ Duck (pasture-raised)
- ○ Turkey (pasture-raised)
- ○ Pork (grass-fed)
- ○ Organ meats (such as liver and bone marrow) in small amounts

Seafood

Low-mercury, sustainably sourced

- ○ Anchovy
- ○ Atlantic mackerel
- ○ Cod
- ○ Sardines
- ○ Wild salmon
- ○ Trout
- ○ Flathead
- ○ Haddock
- ○ Clams
- ○ Scallops
- ○ Small shrimp
- ○ Skipjack tuna, canned in springwater

Dairy

Unsweetened, low-salt, full-cream

- ○ A2 or organic milk
- ○ Sheep's milk
- ○ Goat's milk
- ○ Butter (grass-fed, unsalted)
- ○ Fresh cream
- ○ Ghee (grass-fed)
- ○ Yoghurt (unsweetened, natural, cow/goat/sheep)
- ○ Greek-style yoghurt (natural unsweetened, cow/goat/sheep)
- ○ Yellow cheese (mozzarella/Swiss/cheddar/parmesan sparingly)
- ○ White cheese (goat/ricotta)
- ○ Quark

Dairy alternatives

Unsweetened, organic

- ○ Soy milk
- ○ Almond milk
- ○ Coconut milk
- ○ Coconut yoghurt (natural)
- ○ Rice milk (for baking only)
- ○ Seed milk (hemp)

Plant proteins

Non-GMO

- ○ Tofu (organic)
- ○ Tempeh (organic)
- ○ Legumes and beans (see below)
- ○ Quinoa
- ○ Nuts and seeds (see below)

Legumes and beans

Dried/BPA-free cans

- ○ Adzuki beans
- ○ Black beans
- ○ Kidney beans
- ○ Navy beans
- ○ Pinto beans
- ○ Green/red/brown lentils
- ○ Split peas
- ○ Chickpeas

Nuts and seeds

Store in fridge/freezer

- ○ Almonds
- ○ Brazil nuts
- ○ Cashews
- ○ Hazelnuts
- ○ Macadamias
- ○ Pecans
- ○ Chia seeds
- ○ Flaxseeds
- ○ Hemp seeds
- ○ Pine nuts
- ○ Pepitas (pumpkin seeds)
- ○ Sesame seeds
- ○ Sunflower seeds

Grains

- ○ Amaranth
- ○ Basmati rice
- ○ Brown rice
- ○ Buckwheat
- ○ Millet
- ○ Oats
- ○ Quinoa
- ○ Teff
- ○ Barley
- ○ Kamut
- ○ Rye
- ○ Spelt

Fresh or dried herbs

- ○ Basil
- ○ Bay leaf
- ○ Dill
- ○ Flat-leaf parsley
- ○ Coriander (cilantro)
- ○ Mint
- ○ Rosemary
- ○ Sage
- ○ Oregano
- ○ Thyme

Ground spices

- ○ Black pepper
- ○ Cardamom
- ○ Cinnamon
- ○ Cloves
- ○ Cumin
- ○ Curry powder (mild)
- ○ Garlic (fresh or ground)
- ○ Ginger (fresh or ground)
- ○ Nutmeg
- ○ Paprika
- ○ Turmeric

Oils and fats

- ○ Avocado oil (cold-pressed)
- ○ Extra virgin olive oil
- ○ Macadamia oil (cold-pressed)
- ○ Sesame oil (cold-pressed)
- ○ Flaxseed oil
- ○ Coconut oil (virgin, cold-pressed)
- ○ Lard (grass-fed)
- ○ Beef tallow (grass-fed)

Baking and flours

- ○ Almond flour
- ○ Coconut flour
- ○ Brown rice flour
- ○ Oat flour
- ○ Quinoa flour
- ○ Arrowroot or tapioca flour
- ○ Baking powder (aluminium-free)
- ○ Bicarbonate of soda (baking soda)
- ○ Whole wheat flour
- ○ Whole spelt flour
- ○ Millet flour
- ○ Buckwheat flour

Step 2: Starting solids

4–6 months

See pages 64–6 for age-appropriate meal plans.

The first tastes your baby experiences are vital in shaping their future food preferences. Babies have a natural preference for sweet foods, and it's our job to encourage them to enjoy other flavours, such as bitter and sour. This early food journey is not only about nutrition, but also about teaching your baby to enjoy eating and exploring new tastes.

Signs baby is ready for solids

Each baby is unique, and will be ready to start solids at different times. These signs together show that your baby is ready.

- **Good head and neck control** Your baby can hold their head up steadily.
- **Sits with support** They don't need to sit fully independently but should be able to sit upright with minimal assistance.
- **Loss of or less pronounced tongue-thrust reflex** They no longer automatically push food out of their mouth with their tongue.
- **Shows interest in food** They watch you eat, reach for your food or open their mouth when food is offered.
- **Coordinates hand-to-mouth movements** They can pick up objects and bring them to their mouth with control.
- **Increased appetite** They seem hungrier than usual, even after full milk feeds.
- **Opens mouth when food is offered** They show anticipation or excitement.

Will introducing solids early help my baby sleep?

Some parents wonder whether introducing solids at 4 or 5 months will help their baby sleep. The short answer is no. At this stage, food is not meant to replace their primary source of nutrition (breastmilk or formula), but is introduced for practice, taste exploration and to help with their motor development. The small amount of food you offer them is unlikely to make your baby feel fuller or sleep longer. Sleeping through the night is a developmental issue rather than a satiety issue. Additionally, introducing solids too early can sometimes cause digestive discomfort, such as gas or constipation, which may disrupt sleep rather than enhance it.

Timing first bites

Try introducing new foods earlier in the day to reduce worry and ensure medicare support is available if needed. It's best to avoid offering new foods in the evening, as any reactions are likely to show up a few hours later.

Once you've introduced a new food and observed no adverse reactions (see page 30), you can offer it at any time of the day with confidence. However, always be mindful of your baby's cues, and avoid feeding them when they are overly tired or irritable. Each baby is unique and will be ready at different times, so trust your instincts and consult your paediatrician if you have any concerns or questions.

Should I start with rice cereal?

Iron-fortified rice cereal was traditionally offered as a baby's first food because it's easy to digest and a low allergy risk. However, I encourage you to start with vegetable purées, which are more balanced and nutrient dense. They also introduce your baby to a broader range of flavours. Thankfully, this approach is now aligned with mainstream advice. This early exposure helps shape healthier food preferences and may reduce the risk of fussy eating later on.

There are a few drawbacks of rice cereal too:

- It often relies on refined white rice, which has been stripped of its natural nutrients. It's also low in fibre and not nutrient dense.
- Many commercial varieties are fortified with synthetic forms of iron that can be harder to absorb and may contribute to constipation – a common issue when starting solids.
- Commercial varieties often contain hidden sugars.

Introducing new foods: Step-by-step

When it comes to baby's first foods, my approach is to introduce one food at a time, using real, whole foods puréed to a thin texture. We cover exactly how to do this in the Purées chapter (see page 71). Vegetables and fruit can be offered from 4 months, and proteins, grains and allergens from 6 months. Opposite, you'll find my recommended order of introduction.

While current guidelines support offering one new food per day if no reactions occur, I often recommend a more gradual start if your baby is less than 6 months of age. If offering solids at:

- **4 months old** Stick with a slower pace, repeating foods for two days in a row, for two to three weeks.
- **5 months old** You can usually try a new food daily after the first week. If you prefer to go more slowly, it's fine to stick to one food every two days for up to two weeks.

This gives you time to monitor for any sensitivities and build your confidence. It also lets your baby become familiar with each new flavour.

If starting out at **6 months old,** going at a faster pace and introducing one new food per day is perfectly okay if well tolerated, as your baby's digestive system and oral motor skills are more robust than when they were younger.

Introduce one new allergen (see page 30) at a time during a meal, in an age-appropriate form. If no reaction occurs, keep offering it at least twice per week to maintain tolerance. Some parents prefer to wait 2–3 days between introducing new allergens, especially in high-risk babies, but this isn't essential. Always consult your healthcare professional if you have concerns.

Tip Under 6 months of age, breastmilk or formula is still your baby's most important source of nutrients. Offer milk before food and do not replace any milk feeds with solids. After 6 months, you can begin to offer food first at certain times of the day.

1. Vegetables

In Australia, only one in twenty children eat the recommended amount of vegetables per day. Starting with fresh vegetables, which are naturally less sweet, helps your baby develop a palate that appreciates a wide range of flavours. I have found that bubs who are introduced to a wider variety of veggies as their first foods have a wider repertoire in their diet up to their school years. They are also more likely to accept – and even enjoy – vegetables for life. Sweet potato, zucchini (courgette) and broccoli provide essential nutrients while gently introducing your baby to diverse tastes.

2. Fruits

Once your baby has established a good variety of vegetables, fruits can be introduced to add natural sweetness to their diet and to help prevent constipation. Certain fruits, such as soft pear, can help babies stay regular when starting solids.

3. Proteins

Beef, lamb, chicken and white fish are all important sources of protein. I also encourage you to start solids with a mixture of iron-rich plant-and animal-based proteins to ensure your baby benefits from a variety of nutrients. This also promotes a sustainable and well-rounded approach to eating. Excellent choices for vegetarian proteins are legumes, eggs and tofu. In the Purées chapter (see page 71), you can find details on what to look for, how to prep and how to incorporate proteins into purées. See pages 31–2 for how to introduce egg and soy allergens.

4. Grains

In the past, white rice was commonly offered as a baby's first grain in the form of rice cereal (see opposite). However, all refined grains, such as white bread, white rice and sugary cereals, are stripped of their nutrients during processing, providing fewer nutrients and less fibre compared with wholegrains. They can also contribute to blood-sugar spikes, energy crashes and a preference for highly processed foods.

We now know it's far more beneficial to start with wholegrains, as they provide essential fibre, energy and nutrients to support healthy digestion and growth. So, when it's time to introduce grains, choose a variety of wholegrains, such as brown rice, oats, millet, quinoa, whole spelt, buckwheat, amaranth, kamut, teff and rye.

See page 83 for information on incorporating grains into purées.

5. Allergens

See pages 31–3 for information on the common allergens and how to introduce them, and pages 30 and 79 for how to add allergens to purées.

Small steps to big flavours

Once your baby is confidently enjoying a range of first foods, it's the perfect time to introduce gentle herbs and spices. This helps build a more adventurous and open palate, and lays the foundation for long-term healthy eating habits. Start with gentle herbs, such as cinnamon, basil or parsley – your baby's tastebuds are more sensitive than yours, and their tolerance for strong flavours is still developing. A small pinch in a purée or finger food your baby already knows and enjoys – think patties, pancakes or savoury muffins – is a good starting point. Gradually build up from there, keeping flavours subtle to avoid overwhelming tiny palates. This is a beautiful way to boost both flavour and nourishment while keeping mealtimes exciting and varied.

Here are some great herbs and spices to introduce, and ways to use them so they really shine.

Herb/spice	How to use
Basil (fresh or dried)	• Mix into vegetable purées (e.g. broccoli) • Add to pasta sauces and bakes • Add small amounts to fruit purées (e.g. mango, peach)
Cinnamon (fresh or ground)	• Add to porridges (e.g. oatmeal, brown rice, quinoa) • Mix into yoghurt • Sprinkle over roast pumpkin (e.g. squash) • Add to fruit purées (e.g. apple, pear, banana) • Mix into vegetable purées with a touch of unsalted butter
Cumin (ground)	• Sprinkle into vegetable purées (e.g. carrot, pumpkin/squash, sweet potato) • Mix into lentils, chickpeas or black beans • Use as a base spice in baby-friendly curries • Dust over roasted vegetables • Stir through cooked brown rice or quinoa
Garlic (powder or fresh – cooked only, never raw)	• Blend into protein-rich purées (e.g. fish, chicken, tofu, lamb) • Stir into pasta dishes, sauces and savoury muffins • Add to soups or stews • Blend roasted garlic into vegetable purées • Use alongside gentle herbs (e.g. basil or thyme)
Ginger (fresh or ground)	• Add a small amount to purées or stews • Stir fresh (grated) or ground into yoghurt with fruit • Add a slice to soups (remove before serving)
Mint (fresh or dried)	• Blend with vegetable purées (e.g. pea, zucchini/courgette, green bean) • Combine with fruit purées (e.g. mango, watermelon, apple) • Add to warm water or mild teas for older babies
Nutmeg (fresh or ground)	• Stir into vegetable purées (e.g. sweet potato, carrot, pumpkin/squash) • Mix into yoghurt • Use only a tiny pinch (it can be overpowering)
Thyme (fresh or dried)	• Add to soups or stews during cooking • Sprinkle over roasted vegetables • Mix into purées or stews with chicken or lamb • Add to mashed or roasted potatoes
Turmeric (fresh or ground)	• Include in mild stews or curries • Add to smoothies • Stir into vegetable purées • Add to creamy soups • Combine with coconut milk in purées or brown rice • Pair with gentle spices (e.g. cumin or cinnamon)

Healthy fats for baby's growing brain and body

Once solids are introduced, focus on a variety of healthy fats. They are essential for your baby's development, especially when it comes to brain growth, hormone production and a well-regulated nervous system. They also help to keep your little one feeling full and content between meals and to establish a love of real, unprocessed food right from the start. I always encourage parents to focus on nourishing fats from wholefood sources, such as those listed below.

- Avocado
- Nut and seed butters
- Butter (grass-fed unsalted)
- Ghee (grass-fed)
- Lard (grass-fed)
- Beef tallow (grass-fed)
- Avocado oil (cold-pressed, unrefined)
- Coconut oil (virgin unrefined) – monitor for rare coconut allergies
- Cod liver oil – use under professional guidance
- Extra virgin olive oil
- Flaxseed oil – use under professional guidance
- Hemp seed oil (cold-pressed)
- Macadamia oil (cold-pressed)
- Sesame oil (cold-pressed)

Aim for balance and variety, and avoid highly refined industrial seed or vegetable oils, which provide little nutritional value.

How much should my baby eat?

Every baby is different, and that includes how much they eat. Some babies will be content with just a few spoonfuls at the start, while others may be hungrier and eat a little more from the get-go. There's no strict 'right' amount. While I have given some guidelines on page 6, the best thing you can do is trust your baby's cues (see the table, below).

When offering a new allergenic food, be more mindful of quantity. Start small and build up gradually (see page 30).

Signs of hunger	Signs of fullness
Reaches or leans towards the food	Turns head away and/or closes mouth firmly
Opens mouth eagerly	Becomes distracted or disengaged
Gets excited when they see food coming	Pushes food or the spoon away

When your baby rejects food

It is absolutely normal for a baby to reject their first foods. Each baby is unique; some may readily embrace new tastes, while others may need repeated exposure (see opposite). It's important to continue offering a variety of foods, even if your baby rejects it at first. Please don't despair; it is common to experience slight setbacks along the way. Remember that the main goal of baby's first tastes is to familiarise them with new flavours and for them to practise their feeding skills.

Here are some ways to troubleshoot, depending on what the underlying issue is.

Issue	What to do
Reluctance to sit in highchair or feeding chair	Change up the environment. Try moving the highchair outdoors or into a new room.
Disinterest in food (under 6 months)	Pause solids for a few days as your baby may not be developmentally ready. Offer milk and try again soon.
Disinterest in food (over 6 months)	Encourage food play: give your baby spoons to play with and let them squish, smear and explore without pressure – even a lick counts.
Dislike of food	Take a break and reintroduce later. It may take up to 16 tries before a new flavour is accepted. Avoid sweetening their new food with fruit or altering it.
Swallowing difficulties	Let your baby suck on a spoon or practise with smooth textures. Seek medical advice if persistent, as it could signal oral motor issues.
Fussing in pram or highchair	Check posture, straps, highchair footrest and comfort. Try feeding at a different time of day when your baby is more well rested.
Turning away or clamping mouth shut	These are fullness cues. Don't push. Offer again later without pressure.
Spitting out food constantly	This is often a texture issue. Try adjusting consistency to be smoother, thicker or more mashed. In the early weeks, spitting and gagging are also common as babies learn to coordinate chewing and swallowing.

When I first offered sweet potato to my son, he gobbled it up. I felt such a sense of relief and joy. But I learned that every baby is different. When it was my daughter's turn, she was much less adventurous. It took two weeks of gentle trying before she started to enjoy her solids. I reminded myself to stay calm and trust the process, and eventually she became an amazing eater.

The power of repetition

Repetition is one of the most powerful tools you have when it comes to shaping your baby's food preferences. Research consistently shows it can take between six and 16 exposures before a baby accepts a new flavour. In fact, one study found that an initially disliked vegetable was eventually accepted after just eight exposures, with the average intake increasing from 40 g (1½ oz) to more than 180 g (6 oz) – a remarkable 300+ per cent increase. Constant exposure can help to enhance preferences; for some babies it can take as little as two exposures before they accept the new food, and for others it may be more.

So, if your little one turns their head away at first, don't worry. The consensus is that the best way to encourage a baby to try new food is to offer it repeatedly. Just like learning to crawl, walk, sleep through the night or drink from a cup, developing a broad and balanced palate takes time.

If your baby resists a food, it's okay to take a break and return to it later. Try preparing it in different ways – roasted, steamed or mashed – and offer it alongside a familiar favourite. Avoid sweetening vegetables with fruit or mixing in foods your baby already likes. While that might encourage a few spoonfuls in the short term, it doesn't allow them to truly learn the flavour. Repeated exposure on its own, without pressuring or disguising, is the most effective way to build acceptance.

This early learning window sets the tone for later eating habits. Research demonstrates that babies who develop a taste for vegetables early are more likely to maintain vegetable-rich diets throughout childhood, supporting healthy weight gain and reducing the risk of fussy eating.

Think of it like introducing your baby to a new person. At first, they may be hesitant, but with a few calm, consistent interactions, they begin to feel comfortable and familiar. It's the same with food. With time, patience and a little creativity, your baby can learn to love a wide variety of nourishing wholefoods, setting the stage for a lifetime of healthy eating.

Supporting baby's gut health

Even with optimal support, babies may experience digestive challenges as their systems mature. Here are the most common challenges and how you can manage them. If your baby is suffering from any of these conditions, speak with your GP or paediatrician.

Issue	What to do
Constipation	Increase appropriate fluid intake; focus on fibre-rich foods, such as puréed prunes, pear, and peach; and try a gentle tummy massage in a clockwise direction.
Diarrhoea	Maintain hydration with appropriate fluids; temporarily simplify the diet under healthcare guidance; and consider specific probiotic strains recommended by your GP or paediatrician.
Reflux/colic	Evaluate feeding techniques and positioning; discuss potential food sensitivities with your healthcare provider. Some probiotic strains may be recommended; seek medical advice before use.

The prepared parent's guide to allergenic foods

Experts agree there is a critical window between 4–12 months to introduce allergenic foods – ideally around 6 months, but not before 4 months. Introducing these foods early and regularly may reduce the risk of developing food allergies. From then onwards, provided your baby is developmentally ready and has shown no signs of intolerance to other foods, you can introduce all common allergenic foods (see tables on pages 31–3).

Your baby may be at higher risk of having a food allergy if they have chronic eczema, an existing food allergy or if there is a strong family history of allergies, asthma or anaphylaxis. Consult your healthcare provider before introducing these foods.

When introducing allergenic foods to your baby, timing and method are important for monitoring potential allergic reactions (see page 34).

- Choose a day when your baby is well, and a morning or early daytime meal so you can observe them for at least two hours afterwards.
- Don't introduce any other new foods on the day you introduce a new allergenic food. You can mix the food into something familiar, such as vegetable purée.
- Never smear food on your baby's skin, as this won't help identify allergies. You can, however, rub peanut butter on their inner lip.
- Start with a very small amount on day one – e.g. about ¼–½ teaspoon of well-cooked egg or smooth peanut paste mixed into soft food. Gradually increase the amount over several days if no reaction occurs. If your baby tolerates the food well, continue doubling the amount until you reach a normal serving size, then include it in their diet regularly (about twice weekly) to maintain tolerance.

The common allergens

The following table covers the most common food allergies in children, as well as my tips on how to best introduce these. I've listed them in the order I recommend introducing them, but this is not critical. Eggs, milk and peanuts are the three most common allergenic foods for babies.

Once your baby has successfully tolerated a common allergenic food, continue to offer it regularly – ideally twice a week or more to help maintain tolerance. This advice applies to all major food allergens introduced in the first year.

What about honey?

While honey isn't considered a common allergen, it's one food that should never be offered to babies under 12 months. This is because honey can sometimes contain clostridium botulinum spores, which can lead to infant botulism, a rare but serious illness that affects a baby's immature digestive systems. After your baby turns 1, their digestive system is more developed and able to safely process these spores. However, the American Academy of Pediatrics recommends avoiding all added sugars, including honey, until 2 years of age to support healthy growth and food preferences.

Allergen	Begin with	Quantity	Alternatives
Eggs	Well-cooked whole egg, either hard-boiled or scrambled (mixed with breastmilk, formula or familiar foods). **Note** An infant who already has an egg allergy could be at risk of developing a peanut allergy later on.	⅛ teaspoon on day 1, ¼ teaspoon on day 2, ½ teaspoon on day 3 and so on. After successful introduction, continue to offer eggs at least 2–3 times every week.	**For baking (per egg):** • 1 teaspoon commercial egg replacer + 2 tablespoons water • 1 teaspoon bicarbonate of soda (baking soda) + 1 tablespoon vinegar + 1 tablespoon water • 1½ tablespoons extra virgin olive oil + 1 teaspoon baking powder + 1½ tablespoons water • ¼ cup (60 ml) aquafaba (the viscous liquid from cooked legumes like canned chickpeas) + ½ teaspoon cream of tartar **For binding (per egg):** • ¼ cup (50 g) mashed potato or pumpkin (squash) • ½ cup (130 g) mashed banana or puréed apple • Flax egg: 1 tablespoon ground flaxseed + 45 ml (1½ fl oz) warm water • Chia egg: 1 tablespoon chia seed meal + ¼ cup (60 ml) water (let it stand for a few minutes) • ¼ cup (60 ml) aquafaba (the viscous liquid from cooked legumes like canned chickpeas)
Peanuts	Smooth natural peanut butter (not whole peanuts), free from added oils, salt, sugar and additives, suc BHA 320. Blend with boiled and cooled water, breastmilk or formula to create a smooth, baby-safe consistency. **Note** An infant who already has an egg or dairy allergy could be at risk of later developing a peanut allergy. Moderate to severe eczema (atopic dermatitis) is a risk factor for a peanut allergy. Babies with severe eczema or egg allergy should be evaluated by a healthcare provider before peanut introduction, as they may benefit from earlier introduction (4–6 months) under medical supervision.	Offer ¼ teaspoon smooth peanut butter thinned with boiled and cooled water, breastmilk or formula (optional) and added to a familiar food, such as vegetable purée. Offer during the day when your baby is well, and observe for at least 2 hours. Gradually increase the amount over several days. After successful introduction, aim to include peanuts in your baby's diet two to three times per week.	• Almond or cashew butter (if not allergic to tree nuts) • Seed butters (pumpkin seed, sunflower seed, tahini)

Allergen	Begin with	Quantity	Alternatives
Fish	Fully cooked fish that flakes easily. Start with white fish, such as flathead, cod, hake or whiting, as they are milder and easier to digest than other types of fish. Choose sustainably sourced, low-mercury options. Avoid high-mercury fish such as shark, swordfish, king mackerel and tilefish.	Begin with ½–1 teaspoon of well-cooked, flaked fish mixed into vegetable purée. Gradually increase as your baby becomes accustomed to the taste and texture. Always check carefully for bones, even in filleted fish. Once successfully introduced, aim to include fish in their diet one to two times weekly.	• Chicken or tofu **For fish stock:** • Use low-salt vegetable stock or broth or Bone broth (see page 223)
Wheat and gluten	Ancient grains (barley, spelt, rye and kamut), sourdough wholemeal bread or wholemeal bread. Introduce gluten-containing foods from around 6 months of age, while continuing to breastfeed if possible, as this may modestly reduce the risk of developing coeliac disease. If your baby has a first-degree relative with coeliac disease or you have concerns, consult your healthcare provider before introduction.	Offer small amounts of sourdough spelt bread as finger food. Remember to introduce one grain at a time. Include wheat and gluten products two to three times weekly once successfully introduced.	• Quinoa • Brown rice • Buckwheat • Millet
Tree nuts	Nut butters (almond or cashew) with no added sugar, salt or unnecessary additives. Follow the same protocol as introducing peanuts (see page 31). **Note** Tree nut allergies can occur even if peanut tolerant. Introduce each tree nut separately.	Start with a small amount dabbed on the inside lip. If there's no sign of an allergic reaction, offer ¼ teaspoon mixed into familiar foods, such as porridge or vegetable purées. Gradually increase if well tolerated. Include tree nut products two to three times weekly once successfully introduced.	• Seed butters (sunflower seed, pumpkin seed, tahini) • Ground seeds
Soy	Introduce through GMO-free silken tofu, choosing organic when possible. Avoid miso and soy sauce due to high salt content. **Note** About 30–50 per cent of babies diagnosed with cow's milk intolerance also react to soy. Always consult your healthcare provider before introducing soy as a dairy alternative. The good news is that most children outgrow both intolerances by their toddler years.	Start with 1 teaspoon mashed tofu blended into fruit or vegetable purée. Gradually increase if well tolerated. Soy yoghurt and soy milk should not be first-line weaning foods as they may contain added sugar and unnecessary additives. Once successfully introduced, include soy products two to three times weekly.	• Pepitas (pumpkin seeds) • Sunflower seeds • Homemade hummus without tahini (see page 225)

Allergen	Begin with	Quantity	Alternatives
Sesame	Tahini (ground sesame seed butter) and hummus.	Start with ½ teaspoon tahini mixed through steamed vegetables, spread over sourdough toast or blended into porridge. Gradually increase over several exposures. Once successfully introduced, include sesame products two to three times weekly.	• Pepitas (pumpkin seeds) • Sunflower seeds • Homemade hummus without tahini (see page 225)
Dairy	Natural unsweetened yoghurt, natural unsweetened Greek-style yoghurt, unsalted butter, ghee, low-salt cheese and cream. **Note** An infant who already has a dairy allergy could be at risk of later developing a peanut allergy.	Introduce by using yoghurt, cheese, butter or milk in cooking. While dairy products can be safely introduced from 6 months, I recommend waiting until 8 months to prioritise iron-rich foods first, as calcium can interfere with iron absorption and babies receive enough of it from milk. Start with small amounts (for example, ⅛ teaspoon yoghurt) mixed with familiar foods. If well tolerated, gradually increase the amount and include dairy products as a regular part of your baby's varied diet. **Note:** Cow's milk should not be offered as a main drink until after 12 months. It's low in iron and can displace more nutritious foods. However, using small amounts in cooking, or offering yoghurt and cheese is perfectly fine from 8 months.	Before 12 months, plant milks should not replace breastmilk/formula. After 12 months, choose calcium-fortified plant milks, but also include natural calcium sources, like leafy greens, tahini, almonds, calcium-set tofu and beans. A varied diet provides better nutrition than relying only on fortified products. **For milk:** • Quality almond or coconut milk **For yoghurt:** • Coconut yoghurt **For cream:** • Coconut cream **For butter:** • Coconut oil • Extra virgin olive oil **For cheese:** • Silken tofu • Coconut cream
Shellfish *Shellfish allergies are usually lifelong, unlike many other childhood allergies that resolve over time. They are more common in adults.*	Use only thoroughly cooked, low-mercury, sustainably sourced shellfish, such as prawns, crab meat (except king crab), clams and mussels. While shellfish can be introduced from 6 months, many families wait until 8–10 months when babies can better handle the texture. **Note** Children with dust mite allergies may be at increased risk of shellfish allergy.	Start with ½–1 teaspoon of finely minced, well-cooked shellfish mixed into familiar foods. Ensure no shell fragments remain. Gradually increase if well tolerated. Include shellfish two to three times weekly once successfully introduced.	These alternatives provide similar protein benefits without shellfish exposure: • White fish • Salmon • Chicken • Tofu • Well-cooked legumes

Allergies versus sensitivities

Many babies develop mild food sensitivities at some stage, but these differ from allergies. While allergies involve the immune system and can cause serious reactions (see right), intolerances are more about your child's digestive system having trouble processing certain foods or food chemicals. Sensitivities might cause a tummy upset or loose stools. If your baby experiences a food sensitivity, I recommend speaking with a dietitian or nutritionist.

Monitoring for allergic reactions

After introducing a new allergen, watch your baby closely for two hours for immediate reactions. If your child shows any of the following symptoms, stop offering the food and seek medical advice:

- hives;
- swelling of the lips, face or eyes;
- difficulty breathing; or
- becoming unsettled.

If you see minor redness around the mouth, this is not necessarily an allergic reaction. It is more likely to be a skin irritation, but always check with your GP or paediatrician to be on the safe side.

Call an ambulance immediately if your child has a severe reaction (anaphylaxis). Signs include:

- becoming pale and floppy;
- difficulty breathing; or
- swelling of the tongue and throat – look out for noisy breathing, a change in their voice or cry, wheezing or a persistent cough.

Continue observing for delayed reactions, such as vomiting, diarrhea or eczema flares for one or two days. If there are no reactions within 48 hours, the food has been successfully introduced. Remember to offer it two or three times per week to maintain tolerance.

Living (and eating) well with food allergies

Managing food allergies might feel overwhelming at first but, with the right approach, you can confidently provide safe, nutritious meals. The key is establishing a reliable routine for checking ingredients and finding trusted brands and products that work for your family.

Start with simple swaps of allergenic ingredients while keeping meals familiar and appealing to your little one. And remember, allergies don't need to equal fussy eating. See pages 38–9 for my tips on fostering unfussy eaters, no matter the dietary restrictions.

Here's my practical guide to keeping your food-allergic child safe and well nourished:

- Always read labels three times – at the store, when unpacking and before using.
- Create a list of 'safe' brands and products once you've verified them. This makes shopping much easier next time. However, ingredients may change over time, so it's best practice to always check each time a product is used.
- Avoid products with unclear ingredients or foreign language labels.
- Be extra careful with imported foods, as labelling rules vary.
- Watch for 'may contain' warnings. Treat these foods as though they contain the allergen.
- Prevent cross-contamination by using separate cutting boards and utensils. Treat these as if they contain the allergen unless otherwise advised by your healthcare provider.
- Educate all caregivers about your child's allergies.
- Always carry prescribed emergency medications (if applicable).
- Have an action plan written by your healthcare provider. Keep a copy in a visible place at home (like on the fridge), carry one with you, and make sure all caregivers and childcare providers have one too.

H_2O 101: Introducing water

While water is an important part of an adult's diet, babies have different hydration needs depending on their age and stage. For the first few months of life, breastmilk or formula provides all the fluid and hydration they require, so offering extra water is unnecessary – in some cases, it can even be harmful. Offering water to a baby under 6 months can fill their tiny stomach, reducing their appetite for milk.

As your baby begins solids, offering small amounts of water is not only about hydration. It can help to prevent constipation, and it's an opportunity for them to practise drinking from a cup, which helps develop oral motor skills and coordination. Learning to sip from an open cup or straw cup encourages proper tongue movement and strengthens the muscles needed for speech and feeding.

The table below outlines how and when to offer water.

Age	Quantity
Newborn to 6 months	No additional water
6–7 months	Small amounts of water with meals. Bottled water should contain less than 200 mg sodium and less than 250 mg sulfate per litre. All water should be boiled and cooled before use. Start by offering one or two small sips a couple of times a day (no more than ¼ cup/60 ml per day) in an open cup or straw cup. If your baby refuses, don't worry. They may simply not be thirsty. Gradually increase as your baby starts eating more solids and reduces milk feeds.
8–12 months	If you are reducing formula or breastfeeds, small amounts of water with meals can help support digestion and prevent constipation. All water should be boiled and cooled. Do not replace required milk feeds with water. Around 120–240 ml (3¾–8 fl oz) plain water per day is generally sufficient at this stage, depending on your baby's solid intake, climate and remaining milk feeds. Use a baby-friendly cup that encourages proper oral motor development. Look for one that is spill resistant, easy to grip, supports natural sipping or sucking motions and is made from non-toxic, BPA-free materials. Transition from an assisted open cup to an independent cup as coordination improves.

Monitoring hydration

If you have any concerns about your baby's water intake, please consult a medical professional immediately. Signs of dehydration include:

- fewer than half the number of their regular wet nappies within 24 hours;
- dark yellow urine;
- tearless crying;
- dry skin or chapped lips; and
- overall lethargy and lack of interest.

Step 3: Finger foods and family meals

6–12 months

See pages 67–9 for age-appropriate meal plans.

Introducing finger foods is an exciting milestone, but it can feel overwhelming. There's often pressure to 'get it right' from day one: to offer only real, whole, nutrient-dense foods, and to avoid all the pitfalls. For many parents, including myself when I started out, this pressure is compounded by the very real fear of choking (see pages 40–1) and serious allergic reactions (see pages 30–4), which can make it hard to relax and enjoy the moment. That fear is valid and it's something so many of us share – it does go away, I promise!

That's why I like to think of this stage as the perfect opportunity for a Real Food family reset (see pages 12–13). It's a chance to simplify, reconnect and take the pressure off.

One of the most powerful ingredients in nourishing your baby is family connection. This is about creating a positive, pressure-free environment and building small, sustainable habits that support a healthy relationship with food. These early experiences lay the foundation for raising confident, adventurous and unfussy eaters. In the early days, I prioritised family meals over bath, play and sleep schedules. This may not work for everyone, but it made a huge difference to my babies' early eating experiences.

From 6 months, babies can start exploring a variety of finger foods (small portions of food that can be eaten with their hands). Some parents choose to follow baby-led weaning (BLW). This is a method that encourages babies to exclusively feed themselves. This approach works best once your baby has good head and neck control and only from 6 months onwards. BLW encourages adventurous eating habits and allows you to prepare just one meal for the baby and family, making it practical and budget friendly for busy parents. However, self-feeding takes practice.

See pages 45–7 for on-the-go essentials to help make feeding your little one a breeze, wherever you are.

Raising unfussy eaters from the first bites

These are my top tips to help you navigate this next stage of your baby's real-food journey with confidence, calm and a whole lot of joy.

Serve balanced meals early

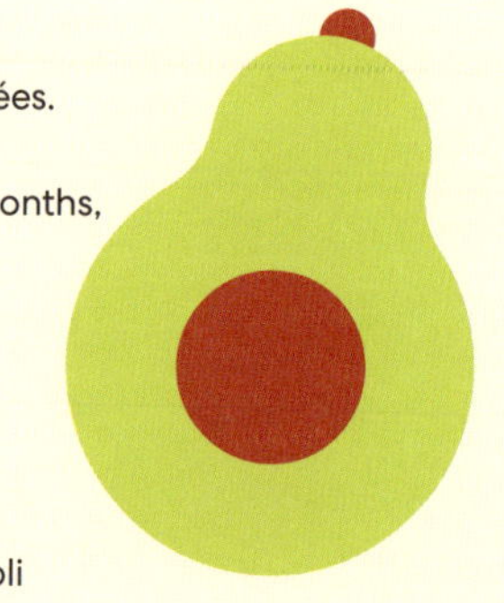

By this stage, many babies will have started exploring a variety of vegetable purées. If this isn't the case for your baby yet, it's still best to begin with softly steamed vegetables. Then you can move onto iron-rich foods, such as red meat. After 6 months, ensure meals consist of at least three of these components:

1. protein (see page 79);
2. slow-release carbohydrates;
3. healthy fats (see page 27); and
4. a wide range of colourful vegetables with meals.

For example, steamed carrots, avocado cubes and shredded chicken; or broccoli florets, lamb cutlet and mashed sweet potato with unsalted butter.

Babies benefit from having choices, just like adults enjoy a meal with multiple components. If they tire of one food, they'll have others to explore and fill up on.

Let babies get messy

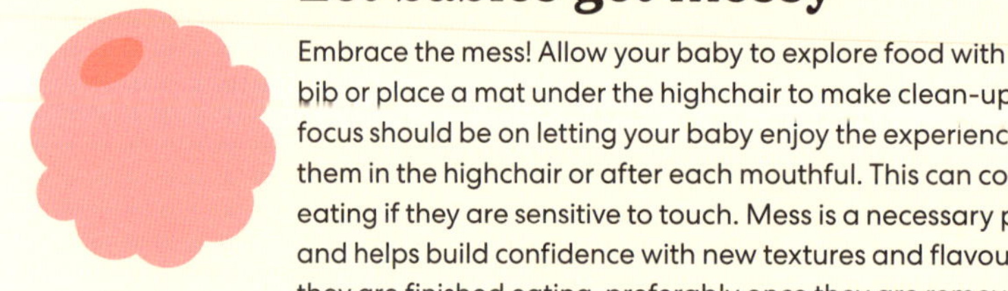

Embrace the mess! Allow your baby to explore food with their hands and face. Use a bib or place a mat under the highchair to make clean-up easier, but remember, the focus should be on letting your baby enjoy the experience. Avoid constantly wiping them in the highchair or after each mouthful. This can contribute to an aversion to eating if they are sensitive to touch. Mess is a necessary part of their sensory learning and helps build confidence with new textures and flavours. Wipe your baby when they are finished eating, preferably once they are removed from the highchair.

Encourage self-feeding

Allow your baby to choose what, how much and how quickly to eat. You can support their independence by offering foods they can hold, such as broccoli or cauliflower florets, which also make excellent dippers for purées.

Offer a selection of nutritious, age-appropriate, cooked finger foods directly onto the highchair tray or table. In the beginning, spoons and bowls aren't necessary, as your baby is learning to pick up food with their hands and bring it to their mouth. This tactile exploration is an important part of developing self-feeding confidence and preventing spoon rejection later on. Remember, there's no need to rush utensils – hands are their best tools and babies learn best through play, exploration and following your lead.

If you're using a mixed-feeding approach and offering purées by spoon, provide one or two spoons for your baby to hold, suck on or try to use themselves. You can gently guide their hands if they show interest. Over time, they'll begin to coordinate the movement and use a spoon more independently. Have a few on hand, as they'll likely end up on the floor!

Case study: Responsive feeding

One of my clients was struggling with her 9-month-old son, who wasn't gaining weight and was frequently waking up for milk. Despite visiting numerous doctors and specialists, including a gastroenterologist, she couldn't find a solution. When I visited them at home and observed a mealtime, I discovered that she was following a baby book's guidelines, offering minimal amounts and variety in one-course meals. While suitable for younger babies, the amount was inadequate for his age. I encouraged her to give him mashed avocado, pear, steamed veg and more servings of lamb purée. Her baby eagerly ate the nutritious options, indicating hunger. I devised a menu plan with recipes and guided her on responding to her baby's hunger and fullness cues. Two weeks later, her baby had made big improvements, gaining 600 g (1 lb 5 oz) and enjoying longer stretches of sleep. My client realised she had been too apprehensive to trust her baby's cues. Learning what those cues were was crucial to help ensure her little one was adequately fed.

Offer sensory variety

Introduce a range of textures, colours and flavours. For example:

soft steamed veggies (e.g. broccoli, cauliflower or sweet potato);

+

smooth purées or mashed foods (e.g. avocado or banana);

+

soft strips of grilled chicken or fish for protein; and

+

iron-rich purée (e.g. lamb or beef).

This variety helps your baby become more adventurous with food and reduces the likelihood of them rejecting new items later. It also stops them from expecting all food to feel and taste the same.

Create other sensory opportunities

Eating is a sensory experience. Allow your baby to smell, touch and explore food. Let them play with foods, such as cooked pasta or soft fruit slices, during mealtimes. Offer different textures, such as mashed potato alongside soft-cooked beans. Remember, while babies don't need spoons or bowls yet, it can be helpful to let them hold or play with a spoon during meals, even if they aren't using it to feed themselves yet.

Focus on family meals

Eating together as a family helps your baby learn by watching you. Sit down and eat the same or similar foods to model positive eating behaviours. Use this time to create a relaxed, social atmosphere. Avoid distractions, like screens, so your baby can focus on enjoying their food.

When my babies started solids, I prioritised family mealtimes, often giving them a bath first so we could wait for their dad to join us after work and sit down together for dinner. If a later meal doesn't suit your routine, you can simply put a small portion on your plate and eat alongside them earlier in the evening. Do what works best for you and your family.

My top finger foods

When starting solids, your baby won't yet have developed a pincer grip and they will only be able to grab foods with their whole fists. Therefore, the easiest finger foods for your baby are those that are chip-shaped or have a natural handle, such as cooked broccoli, cauliflower or sweet potato wedges. You can also use finger foods as dippers – your baby can dunk these into purées or you can continue to spoonfeed alongside finger foods. You'll be combining self-feeding with the nutrition of purées. These are my top picks:

- Avocado fingers
- Steamed or baked sweet potato wedges
- Steamed or baked pumpkin (squash) fingers
- Steamed broccoli or cauliflower (the stems act as a handle)
- Steamed zucchini (courgette)
- Banana fingers
- Soft pear wedges
- Mango pips and mango wedges
- Papaya or melon fingers
- Strips of grilled chicken or grilled fish
- Lamb cutlets
- Omelette strips (to be cautious, offer egg white first, then egg yolk)

Smart prep, safe meals: Managing choking risks

One of the most common concerns parents have when starting baby-led weaning (BLW) is choking. I was one of those parents. My solution was to use a mesh feeder; after the first week of using it, my confidence increased and we ditched the feeder. I experienced an episode of my baby gagging, which I interpreted as choking (see opposite to understand the difference). Thankfully, I had a close friend with me and she stepped in. My baby was never in danger, but as a first-time mum, despite my knowledge as a nutritionist, my fear got the better of me. So, if you are nervous about introducing finger foods, ensure you have a friend or family member with you for the first few introductions.

As a parent, it can feel overwhelming to let your baby take the lead in feeding themselves. Whether you choose traditional spoonfeeding or BLW, it's important to remember that the risk of choking is always present when introducing solids. The good news is that there are different strategies you can use to reduce this risk. These precautions also apply to babies who are spoonfed.

- Always test the food yourself before giving it to your baby to make sure: it is soft enough to mash with your tongue against the roof of your mouth; there are no small pieces or fibres that could break off when sucked or chewed (e.g. very soft, slow-cooked strips of meat); it won't form a crumb in their mouth; and it is at least as long as their fist, on at least one side of the food.
- Don't offer your baby any food that could be a choking hazard, including foods that are: **round** (e.g. whole grapes, cherry tomatoes, hot dogs) – always cut these lengthways, and avoid popcorn altogether; **hard** (e.g. large pieces of raw vegetables and fruits, whole nuts; and; **sticky** (e.g. large dollops of nut butter).

- Do not try to put finger foods into your baby's mouth – they must choose what, how much and how quickly to eat.
- Ensure baby is securely and properly seated in their highchair, sitting upright and not leaning back.
- Never leave them unattended while eating, and watch closely during the meal.
- Learn first aid so you know what to do if your baby does begin to choke.

It's important to understand the difference between choking and gagging when introducing solids. Gagging is a natural reflex that helps your baby learn how to chew and swallow. While it might look scary and cause you extreme anxiety when it's happening, it isn't harmful.

Stay calm if your baby gags. If you become anxious every time your baby is gagging, it could alarm them and cause them to feel anxious too, which may increase their risk of choking.

Choking	Gagging
• Inability to cry or cough • High-pitched sounds • Difficulty breathing • Blue skin, usually around the mouth • Look of fear	• Retching or vomiting • Coughing • Crying • Open mouth and cupped tongue • Red or purple face

Mealtime mess: The food-throwing phase

As a baby's oral motor skills begin to improve, food throwing tends to increase. Typically, food throwing begins around 8–12 months as babies gain better hand control and start exploring cause-and-effect relationships. At this stage, they may drop or throw food simply to see what happens, gauge your reaction or test their independence. The behaviour often peaks between 12–18 months. While it can be frustrating, food throwing is a normal developmental phase and part of learning self-regulation at the table. Here are some ways to manage food throwing:

- **Ensure proper seating** A stable highchair with a footrest supports their posture and reduces frustration, which can help your baby focus on eating.
- **Keep mealtimes short and predictable** Limit meals to around 20–30 minutes. Overlong mealtimes increase the chance of boredom and food throwing.
- **Reduce portions** Offer smaller amounts of food to minimise waste. You can always serve more if needed.
- **Offer an alternative** If throwing is about exploration, provide a sensory play activity outside of mealtimes.
- **Encourage self-feeding** Allowing independence with pre-loaded spoons or easy-to-grasp foods can reduce frustration and increase engagement.
- **Stay calm and consistent** Reacting with frustration can reinforce the behaviour. Instead, use a neutral tone and calmly say, 'Food stays on the plate.'
- **Use a catch mat** Placing a washable mat under the highchair makes clean-up easier.
- **End the meal when necessary** If your baby is full or playing instead of eating, calmly end the meal, rather than allowing food throwing to escalate.
- **Offer praise** Praise your baby when food stays on the tray by saying, 'Good job keeping your food on the plate!'

Step 4: Little foodies

12+ months

Congratulations! You've reached a significant milestone in your parenting journey. The first year of feeding has laid the groundwork for your child's relationship with food, which will continue to develop and flourish in the years ahead.

I remember feeling both proud and a little nostalgic as each of my children celebrated their first birthdays. That year passes in such a blur of firsts: first smiles, first tastes, first steps.

If I could share one piece of wisdom from my experience as both a nutritionist and as a mother, it's this: the wholefood approach you've embraced during this first year isn't something your child will outgrow, it's a foundation for life. The recipes throughout this book aren't just 'baby food' to be left behind. They're family food designed to nourish everyone at your table, with textures and portions that can be adjusted as your little one grows.

My daughter is now in her tween years and my son is a teenager, and I can see daily how those early food choices shape their choices now. They navigate food with confidence and balance. When they're out, they enjoy eating with their friends and are no different to your typical tween/teenager. However, at home they still genuinely appreciate wholesome meals and often request favourite recipes from their early years – the same recipes you'll find in this book.

This natural self-regulation didn't happen by accident. It came from those formative first years being grounded in whole, real foods. The meatballs, vegetable fritters and fruit-sweetened baked goods that delighted them as toddlers evolved naturally into the more complex dishes they enjoy today, but the nutritional foundation remains unchanged.

Everything you do will make a difference. Each carefully prepared meal, each positive food experience and each moment spent eating together as a family helps create patterns that will benefit your child throughout their life. This approach isn't just about nutrition. It's about nurturing a healthy, balanced relationship with food that will serve them well into adulthood.

Milk versus meals

If your baby is still relying heavily on milk at 12+ months, consider whether they need more solid food variety, protein and healthy fats to feel satisfied (see page 67). With the meal plans (see pages 64–9), you'll find advice on phasing out milk feeds in favour of solids. Some babies take longer to adjust, and that's okay. The key is to follow their cues while gently encouraging a shift towards food-based nutrition. It's important that milk is not replacing solid food in their diet. Continue breastfeeding for as long as you and your baby desire, but make sure a variety of solid foods are the main source of nutrition after 12 months (see case study, page 39).

What about cow's milk?

Introducing cow's milk into your baby's diet as a drink requires careful consideration. Cow's milk is low in iron and can make babies feel full, decreasing their interest in other essential iron-rich foods. High calcium intake from dairy products can also interfere with iron absorption. Therefore, it's important to offer cow's milk in moderation, and not before 12 months. My general guidance is to include it in meals, rather than rely on it as a drink, and always ensure a balanced diet. Include a variety of iron-rich foods as well as appropriate calcium-rich servings, which can come from a combination of dairy- and plant-based foods. Water is the best drink you can offer.

Navigating food at childcare

Navigating food at childcare can feel overwhelming, especially when you've worked so hard to establish healthy eating habits at home. As one of the first appointed chief nutrition officers in the childcare sector, and as a mum, I understand the anxiety that comes with entrusting your little one's nutrition to others. Let's turn that worry into empowerment with some practical steps.

Choosing a centre: Your nutrition checklist

To make sure your little one's nutrition and eating habits are maintained, look for the following things:

- O A menu designed by a nutritionist or dietitian
- O Meals, including sauces and marinades, prepared onsite with fresh ingredients and minimal packaged foods
- O Meals using wholegrains, such as brown rice, quinoa and oats, and not primarily white bread, multigrain bread, white pasta, white rice and refined wheat crackers
- O Veggies served three to three to five times during the day, alongside snacks and main meals, with a variety of colours
- O Extra virgin olive oil and unsalted butter used in cooking – not vegetable oils and margarine
- O Baby-weaning programs that are sugar free
- O Iron-rich red meat dishes that are homemade – think meatballs, bolognese, casseroles and curries, rather than store bought items, like processed meats (sausage rolls, sausages, ham etc)
- O Ideally, toddler meals that are sugar free, and preschool meal plans that are free from refined sugars
- O Written protocols, staff training and daily staff updates on allergy management. Clear labelling, separate prep areas and designated colour-coded utensils are also important
- O Planned backup/alternative meals that are stored properly, rather than last-minute substitutions not overseen by a nutritionist or dietitian

It can be difficult to talk to a potential childcare centre about these things, but remember: you're not being difficult, you're being diligent. Your child's nutrition matters. Keep conversations collaborative, not confrontational. Follow up regularly on agreed changes and ask to see policies in writing. You can also connect with other parents for support.

On-the-go essentials

Packing food for your little one's adventures can feel daunting, but you can master the art of portable meals. Let's break this down into practical, manageable strategies.

Temperature and timing

- Pack hot foods in the morning – they will stay warm for four to five hours in a thermos container.
- Cold foods need an ice pack if out more than two hours.
- Room-temperature foods are your friend!

Packing vegetables

- At home, steam slightly firmer than needed – they'll soften in the container.
- Pack vegetables in separate containers or use leak-proof dividers to keep vegetables separated and maintain texture.
- Cut into age-appropriate sizes.
- Can be served at room temperature.

Dining out

- Request simple preparations (steamed, baked or grilled).
- Ask for no added salt/sugar in preparations.
- Stick to familiar foods – avoid introducing new foods while out.
- Bring backup options just in case.
- Skip raw foods (under 12 months), such as salads and sushi, for safety.

Practical tips

- Always pack more than you think you'll need.
- In the early stages of starting solids, include familiar foods and one new option at a time.
- Stick to familiar foods if you're not sure about how they have been prepared or it's later in the day.
- Cut everything into age-appropriate sizes (pinky-finger width).
- Pack wipes and a clean bib.
- Consider mess factor for different situations.

Safety first

- Take the usual precautions to reduce the risk of choking: avoid common choking hazards (see pages 40–1), keep textures consistent with your baby's current stage, and always ensure mealtimes are supervised.
- Make sure baby is fully upright for eating – never feed in a moving vehicle.
- Use proper seating where possible (highchair or secure booster). If no highchair is available, lap feeding is fine as long as your baby is upright, calm and closely supervised.
- Avoid feeding in prams or car seats.
- Pack your own utensils and a clean feeding mat.
- Choose appropriate foods for your destination.

Equipment

6–12 months

- Small, leak-proof containers with secure lids
- Soft silicone spoons (gentle on gums, no sharp edges)
- Insulated food jar to keep purées warm
- Ice pack or gel pack for temperature safety
- Splat mat or mini feeding mat for mess control
- Bibs with food catchers (pack backups)
- Small cooler bag for expressed breastmilk or formula
- Pre-sterilised water bottles (for mixing formula safely)
- Portable change mat for impromptu feeding spots
- Open training cup or baby-sized cup with handles (ideal for introducing sips of water at meals)
- Soft silicone or straw training cup (as a backup if open cups aren't yet accepted)
- Soft cloth napkins or non-toxic wipes for cleaning hands and faces

12–18 months

- Suction bowls or plates to minimise tipping
- Toddler-friendly spoons and forks with easy-grip handles
- Straw cups with spill-proof lids
- Snack containers with simple open-close mechanisms
- Stainless steel bento-style boxes for finger foods
- Travel highchair or clip-on booster seat
- Silicone placemats with raised edges
- Insulated lunch bag with built-in ice-pack slot
- Food-safe allergy alert labels for childcare settings
- Soft cloth napkins or non-toxic wipes for cleaning hands and faces

18+ months

- Stainless steel bento-style boxes (four to six compartments for balanced meals)
- Mini thermos containers for warm, home-style meals
- Flip top–straw water bottles
- Small silicone tongs to encourage self-serving
- Leak-proof containers for sauces and dips
- Reusable snack and sandwich bags (BPA free)
- Travel booster seat with safety harness
- Fun-shaped food picks to encourage variety
- Stainless steel toddler cutlery, including knives for spreading, with blunt tips and easy-grip handles to encourage independence while staying safe
- Soft cloth napkins or non-toxic wipes for cleaning hands and faces

3–5 years

- Stainless steel bento-style boxes (four to six compartments for balanced meals)
- Mini thermos containers (different sizes) for soups, pastas or stews
- Easy-to-use water bottles
- Reusable food wraps for sandwiches or wraps
- Easy-open snack containers for growing independence
- Slim and small kid-friendly ice packs
- Full child-sized cutlery set with carry case
- Sandwich and veggie cutters in fun shapes

Winning on-the-go combinations

Quick trips (2–3 hours)

- Yoghurt blueberry pancakes 8+ months (see page 105) + steamed broccoli florets
- Cheesy veggie muffins 8+ months (see page 173) + steamed carrot batons + avocado cubes
- Arancini balls or patties + steamed green beans
- Pumpkin zucchini loaf, cut into fingers 8+ months (see page 180) + steamed cauliflower florets + thinly sliced apples

Main meals for daycare/long days

- One-pot chicken & tomato risotto 10+ months (see page 145) + steamed broccoli florets and zucchini fingers
- Creamy pumpkin mac'n'cheese 10+ months (see page 147) + steamed green beans and carrot sticks
- Iron-boosting beef & lentil patties 6+ months (see page 150) with potato mash + steamed cauliflower florets and pumpkin wedges
- Crunchy golden fish fingers 8+ months (see page 132) + steamed sweet potato and broccoli florets

Snacks

- Crunchy broccoli nuggets 8+ months (see page 170) + steamed carrot sticks
- Veggie-loaded scones 10+ months (see page 184) + steamed sweet potato
- Banana oat cookies 6+ months (see page 204) + steamed cauliflower florets
- Blueberry lemon muffins 10+ months (see page 193) + steamed broccoli florets

Travel/flights

- Easy veggie fritters 6+ months (see page 151) + banana fingers + homemade snack (such as a bliss ball or muesli bar, see from page 208)
- Berry oat brekkie muffins 8+ months (see page 93) + beef purée pouch + avocado cubes
- Cheesy butter crackers 10+ months, if texture is appropriate (see page 185) + Butternut hummus 6+ months (see page 224) + boiled eggs

Baby's first birthday: An added and refined sugar-free celebration guide

The reality is that babies and toddlers have no preconceived expectations about birthday celebrations. Their joy comes from the atmosphere, the attention and, yes, the delicious food that speaks to the taste preferences they've developed. When children have been nourished with whole, natural foods from the beginning, these are the foods that bring them comfort and pleasure.

When wholesome party food is presented colourfully and playfully, children are naturally drawn to it. Fruit kebabs threaded with strawberries, blueberries and chunks of watermelon become magic wands. Veggie platters arranged to form rainbow patterns with dips served in hollowed-out capsicums (peppers) become edible art. Children respond to colour, presentation and fun.

A sugar-free birthday cake: It's possible!

The birthday cake often becomes the focal point of concern for parents wanting to avoid added and refined sugars. Yet babies are delighted by the ritual of the cake, the singing, the attention and the special candle that they help blow out, as well as having their very own portion. This far outweighs how much they care about the sweetness. You'll find some cake ideas on pages 188 and 197.

Rethinking gift bags

One aspect of children's parties that often revolves around sugar is the take-home party bag. Early in my parenting journey, I decided that none of our celebrations would include bags full of sweets. Instead, I've found that children are delighted by small, useful items that extend the joy of the celebration. Here are some of my favourites:

- tiny pots with seeds and soil for growing herbs or flowers;
- small modelling clay sets with cookie cutters;
- bath bombs or bubble bath in small containers;
- reusable silicone straws in bright colours;
- mini board books (for babies and toddlers);
- homemade, natural playdough in reusable containers;
- wooden toys, such as spinning tops or small puzzles.

Tip If you do want to include something edible, consider homemade, like a small jar of gummies or a bliss ball or energy bar wrapped in baking paper and tied with string. These provide the special feeling of a birthday gift without compromising on wholefood values.

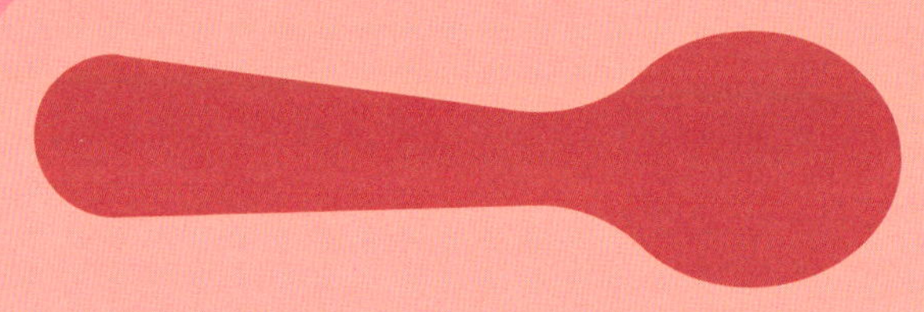

Your wholefood party food table

Veggie platters with dips

Never underestimate the appeal of a beautifully arranged vegetable platter. My secret is to cut vegetables into different shapes: cucumber rounds, capsicum (pepper) strips, carrot sticks and halved or quartered cherry tomatoes. Arrange them in patterns or pictures. A favourite at our parties was the 'veggie train', where each type of vegetable fills a different 'carriage', with hummus serving as the 'engine'. Pair with protein-rich dips, such as Beetroot hummus (see page 224), and healthy fats dips, such as avocado mash or yoghurt-based Tzatziki (see page 238) for a creamy calcium-rich option.

Fruit kebabs or fruit cake

Thread chunks of seasonal fruits onto child-safe skewers for an instant hit. I use small wooden appetiser sticks and alternate colours. Strawberries, banana slices, blueberries and melon chunks create a rainbow effect that children find irresistible. Use short, blunt appetiser sticks or remove fruit pieces from the stick before giving them to toddlers.

Mini pizzas

Make homemade chickpea pizza bases (see pages 165), the Pumpkin patch pizza (see page 163) or use small wholemeal Lebanese or pita bread as bases to create colourful mini pizzas. Top with homemade Tomato sauce (see page 239), grated vegetables and a sprinkling of cheese. For my daughter's rainbow-themed third birthday, we arranged pizzas in colour order on a long platter, using different coloured vegetables – red capsicum (pepper), carrot, corn, zucchini/courgette, eggplant (aubergine) – to create fun visuals that kept the kids asking for more.

Homemade gummies

These nutritious treats have the fun factor of conventional lollies but deliver gut-supporting gelatine and real fruit, instead of artificial colours and flavours (see page 212 for three flavour variations). Use different shaped silicone moulds and refrigerate until set. The children at my son's birthday party loved dinosaur gummies – proof that wholesome foods can be just as exciting as their conventional counterparts.

Bliss balls

These nutrient-dense treats satisfy the desire to hold and squish. Plus, they're naturally sweet. Use natural colourings, such as dragonfruit or raspberry powder, to create a colourful display. They can be arranged in patterns on a serving plate. For recipes, see pages 208, 209, 215, 218 and 219.

Homemade crackers and dips

One of my children's favourite party foods has always been crunchy and buttery homemade seed crackers (see page 185) paired with nutritious dips. When my son turned 2, we made star-shaped seeded crackers that became the conversation piece of the celebration. Adults couldn't believe they were homemade, while the children delighted in the crunchy texture and fun shapes.

Cupcakes

I've included a delicious chocolate cupcake recipe with date and cacao frosting, perfect for first birthday celebrations (see page 192). They are completely free from refined sugar, so little ones can enjoy them without the sugar rush. For my son's first birthday, I made these cupcakes and arranged them in the shape of a number one. He absolutely loved it – and, yes, he had more than just one!

Party food ***(clockwise from bottom left)***

- Pumpkin patch pizza (see page 163)
- Vanilla cake with coconut cream frosting (see page 188)
- Powerhouse choc bliss balls (see page 209)
- Chocolate cupcakes (see page 192)
- Birthday fruit cake (see page 197)
- Healthy chocolate balls (page 215)

Elevating hydration: Making water the star

I've always believed that staying hydrated shouldn't be an afterthought at children's parties. It should be one of the highlights. When I skipped the juice boxes and cordials at our celebrations, I worried children might miss these sweet options. Instead, what I discovered was that, with a little creativity, water and coconut water became the most sought-after refreshments at the party. Fruit-infused water dispensers with floating berries, cucumber slices and mint leaves not only hydrated everyone but became decorative elements that the children found fascinating. A 'mocktail' of diluted coconut water with a splash of fruit juice served in special cups made everyone feel included in the celebration, including the older children and siblings.

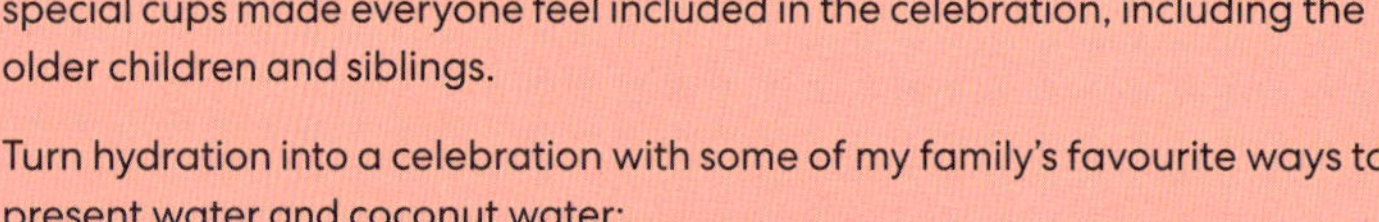

Turn hydration into a celebration with some of my family's favourite ways to present water and coconut water:

Rainbow water bar

Set up a station with several clear dispensers, each containing water infused with different coloured fruits and herbs. We use:

- strawberries and watermelon for red;
- oranges and mango for orange;
- lemons for yellow;
- cucumber and mint for green;
- blueberries for blue; and
- red grapes for purple.

Children love choosing their 'colour' and often return to try each variation. For babies under 12 months and toddlers still developing chewing skills, use a mesh strainer/infuser to keep fruit separate from the water.

Frozen treasure ice cubes

In the days leading up to the party, freeze small berries cut lengthways, tiny edible flowers or small pieces of fruit into ice cubes. Serve these in a clear jug of water or individual cups. My son was fascinated watching the 'treasures' slowly emerge as the ice melted. For younger children, create the visual effect using coloured ice cubes made from puréed fruits frozen in ice-cube trays. They will slowly tint the water as they melt without creating choking hazards.

Watermelon agua fresca

Blend watermelon, strain out the pulp and serve this naturally sweet water in small cups with a fresh mint-leaf garnish. The vibrant colour and subtle sweetness have made this a perennial favourite at my daughter Summer's birthday celebrations.

Coconut water

For children over 2, serve coconut water infused with different natural flavours, such as lime and mint, strawberry and basil or pineapple.

Cup decorating station

For older siblings, supply small reusable water cups and washable decorating materials as both an activity and a practical way to keep track of drinks. Children love personalising their cups, and knowing which cup is theirs makes them more likely to stay hydrated throughout the party.

Navigating social expectations

Perhaps the biggest challenge in creating wholefood celebrations isn't the food itself, it's managing the expectations and sometimes judgement of others. I've encountered raised eyebrows and well-meaning suggestions to 'just let them have cake this once' more times than I can count.

What I've learned is that confidence is key. When you present your wholefood spread with pride and enthusiasm, with a focus on what you're offering, rather than what you're avoiding, the reception is almost always positive. I never frame our celebrations in terms of restriction. Instead, I showcase the abundance of delicious, colourful foods, which happen to nourish growing bodies.

Those who push back often change their minds once they see how much fun the kids have eating what's there. My child's watermelon cake (see page 197) is gobbled up.

Remember that your choices as a parent reflect your values and the health priorities you hold for your family. By creating joyful, abundant wholefood celebrations from the start, you're establishing traditions that honour both pleasure and nourishment; a balance that will serve your children throughout their lives.

Flexibility as children grow

As my children have got older, our approach to celebrations has evolved. After 2, we introduced natural sweeteners, such as pure maple syrup and honey, in modest amounts for special occasions. By this point, their palates were well established, with a preference for wholesome foods. This allowed the natural party plates to remain just that: occasional special foods, rather than daily expectations.

The foundation we laid in those first two years has proven invaluable. From age 2, when my kids went to parties, they ate whatever was on offer and we knew it was food to be enjoyed at parties. Even now, when faced with the often-overwhelming sugar-laden options, they enjoy themselves but are always happy to come home to nutritious, real-food options. They were given an opportunity to enjoy a robust wholefood diet and now naturally self-regulate. That's balance.

This, in my opinion, is perhaps the greatest gift that I am sharing with you: the joy and benefits of a wholefood start. It doesn't mean our children never enjoy sugary processed foods but that they develop the ability to truly taste food, to recognise satiety and to enjoy celebrations without becoming overwhelmed by sugar.

Creating memories beyond the menu

While I've focused on food, remember that celebrations are about far more than just what we eat. The activities, decorations and, most importantly, the loving attention we shower on our children, create the true memories of these special days. That joy, love and connection is something that no cupcake can ever replace.

So, if a fully wholefood birthday party doesn't feel realistic for you this year, that's okay. My hope is that you'll feel inspired to incorporate even just a few of these delicious, wholesome ideas into your celebrations or even everyday moments. Whether it's a single wholefood snack or a fully refined sugar-free celebration, each choice plants the seeds of nourishing habits and lasting memories.

Step 5: The Unfussy Eaters Club

Whether you're just starting solids or navigating the preschool years, one of the most common concerns I hear from parents is, 'What if my child becomes a fussy eater?' The good news is that fussy eating isn't a fixed trait. For most children, it's a behaviour that can be gently reshaped with the right strategies, consistency and support.

This chapter brings together my top tips for raising unfussy eaters at every stage of development. While many of the strategies in this book are introduced in the early months, they are just as effective for toddlers, preschoolers and even older children. Pick one or two strategies to begin with. Celebrate the small wins. Know that each positive food interaction – no matter how tiny – is a step towards raising a confident, well-nourished eater.

You'll also find guidance here for children with food allergies and intolerances. With the right foundations and a wholefood-first approach, even children with dietary restrictions can develop a positive, adventurous relationship with food.

Above all, remember fussy eating doesn't define your child, and it doesn't define you as a parent. With patience, consistency and connection, it is absolutely possible to create mealtimes that feel calm, joyful and nourishing for the whole family.

When to seek help

While fussy eating is often a normal phase, there are times when it may signal something more. Underlying issues such as oral motor delays, sensory sensitivities, reflux, constipation, low muscle tone, or other digestive disturbances can all contribute to persistent feeding challenges. If your child consistently refuses entire food groups, gags or vomits frequently, avoids certain textures, or shows distress at mealtimes, I encourage you to seek support. Early assessment from a feeding therapist, paediatric dietitian, nutritionist, occupational therapist or speech pathologist can help identify the root cause and gently guide your child towards a more comfortable and enjoyable relationship with food.

As a practitioner and mum, I want to gently reassure you: if something feels off, please don't ignore it. The earlier we seek support, the easier it is to turn things around. I've worked with families in these situations and seen truly incredible transformations. Even if it turns out to be nothing, getting things checked offers peace of mind. And if there is something deeper going on, early intervention is a great gift you can give your child.

Top tips for avoiding fussy eating

Here's how to encourage positive mealtime behaviours at each stage, so the journey is smooth and enjoyable.

4–6 months

The way you introduce your baby to their first foods can play a crucial role in fostering a positive relationship with eating and minimising fussy eating later.

- **Create a positive feeding environment** Make eye-level connection; stay positive; keep mealtimes relaxed; and choose the right time.
- **Engage, encourage and participate** Mirror their actions; and offer a spoon to hold (have two or three on hand).
- **Start small and simple** Begin with tiny tastes and single flavours; and avoid sweetening with fruit.
- **Focus on proper techniques** Use a soft, flat spoon and a steady and level spoon technique; give time to swallow; and ensure proper positioning.
- **Encourage exploration and repetition** Let them get messy. Repetition is key.
- **Watch and respond to cues** Follow their lead.
- **Model healthy eating** Eat together and include baby in family mealtimes.

7–8 months

Your baby is transitioning from early tastes to more regular meals. It's a crucial window to expand their palate and lay the foundation for a varied, balanced diet, before natural food neophobia (fear of new foods) emerges around 18–24 months.

- **Continue vegetable variety** Offer a wide range of vegetables daily, rotating colours and preparation methods; don't give up after one rejection; and serve previously rejected vegetables alongside familiar favourites.
- **Progress textures gradually** Move from smooth purées and mashed foods to finger foods; and introduce mixed textures gently.
- **Support self-feeding** Offer age-appropriate finger foods; pre-load spoons and let baby guide them to their mouth; embrace the mess; and seat baby upright in a highchair with foot support.
- **Handle food preferences gently** Fluctuating preferences are normal at this age. Avoid creating entirely separate meals for the family; reintroduce rejected foods regularly; and remember, facial expressions of surprise or disgust don't always mean dislike.
- **Create positive mealtimes** Establish a consistent routine and designated eating space; limit meals to 20–30 minutes; minimise distractions; and model enjoyment by eating the same foods as you offer your baby.

At this age, food refusal is rarely a sign of true 'fussiness'. It's exploration, boundary testing and learning through experience. Stay calm, keep offering variety and trust the process. If your baby continues to reject food, it is best to discuss with your GP or paediatrician to eliminate underlying reasons.

9–12 months

This is when babies become more independent eaters, so it's a crucial phase for shaping long-term eating habits and avoiding fussy eating later on. Appetites can vary due to teething, growth spurts and distractions, making it essential to maintain a structured approach to mealtimes.

- **Handle temporary fussy phases with consistency** Continue offering a variety of foods without pressure; rotate food presentation (steamed/roasted/mashed); offer dips and sauces to make foods more appealing; eat the same foods alongside baby to normalise trying new flavours; and expect food throwing as cause-and-effect exploration.
- **Introduce more complex textures to expand their food repertoire** Combine soft and slightly firmer textures; offer naturally varied foods; encourage chewing and manipulating food to strengthen jaw muscles; support pincer grasp development with small pieces of food; and allow baby to use utensils even if most food is eaten with hands.
- **Support appetite fluctuations without pressure** Offer three meals and one to two snacks daily, adjusting portions based on hunger cues; avoid pressure or force-feeding; and ensure a calm eating space with minimal distractions. If a meal is refused, offer milk at the next scheduled feed, not immediately in place of a refused meal.

Beyond 12 months

As you move beyond the first year, you'll face new challenges. Toddlers can suddenly become selective about what they'll eat. Preschoolers might be influenced by what they see other children eating. School-age children will encounter a world of processed foods marketed directly to them.

Keep this book close at hand in your kitchen. The recipes and guidance here will serve you well beyond the baby years. As your child grows, you'll find yourself returning to these pages, not just for nutrition advice but for meal ideas that the whole family can enjoy together. Adjust seasonings, increase portions and allow textures to become more complex, while maintaining a real-food foundation with real, whole ingredients.

The second 1000 days

While the first 1000 days (up to 2 years) are essential, the second 1000 days (until age 5) are equally important. This is when your child's gut microbiome matures, their brain continues to grow rapidly and their food preferences become deeply rooted.

If you're reading this and your child is already 2, 3, 4 or 5 and struggling with picky eating, take heart: it's never too late to reset, and small changes can make a big difference. Many parents come to this point feeling frustrated, guilty or unsure how to undo habits that have formed. Don't worry, positive change is absolutely possible.

Here's how to gently shift your child's palate back towards wholefoods and mealtime peace:

1. Start with a reset week

Begin by gradually clearing out ultra-processed snack foods and replacing them with more nourishing options. Focus on offering regular meals and snacks made from whole, simple ingredients, such as veggies, fruit, proteins, wholegrains and healthy fats. Start with one home-cooked family meal per day. Choose a dish that's easy, satisfying and shared. Look for opportunities to swap in less processed snacks or homemade alternatives where possible. Small changes over time can make a big difference.

2. Focus on simple swaps, one or two at a time

Use your new knowledge of label reading (see page 14) to start upgrading your pantry. Choose one or two packaged foods each week to swap for cleaner, lower-sugar or additive-free options. These small changes, made consistently, can have a big impact on your child's long-term food preferences and health.

3. Make wholefoods visible again

Keep cut veggies and colourful fruit on the counter. Offer water in a special cup or bottle. Reduce visual access to ultra-processed foods at home.

4. Rebuild your food culture

Establish a 'real food is normal' mindset by modelling it yourself. Cook together when you can. Let your child help with small tasks or plate their own food. Keep meals screen free and focus on connection.

5. Add variety within a safe routine

Create a predictable structure around meals and snacks. At each meal, offer at least one familiar 'safe food' and one previously rejected or new food without pressure.

6. Reintroduce previously rejected foods

Offer them in new ways: roasted carrot instead of steamed, grated zucchini (courgette) in muffins, broccoli 'trees' with a colourful dip. Novelty and presentation can help reignite curiosity.

7. Eat together as often as possible

Even if it's just a snack or a small portion of what they are eating, your presence matters. Children mirror what they see, and they feel more comfortable trying new foods when you're alongside them.

8. Embrace the division of responsibility

Your job is to provide nutritious meals at regular times. Your child's job is to decide whether and how much to eat. Recognising this reduces mealtime battles and builds long-term trust.

9. Be consistent, not rigid

Change takes time. Stay the course, remain calm and celebrate small wins. One bite of a new food is a success worth noticing.

10. Offer small choices to build autonomy

As your child approaches age 4 or 5, giving them some input into food decisions helps reduce resistance and fosters independence. Offer two healthy options and let them choose: 'Would you like a lamb pasta bake or spaghetti with lentil sauce tonight?' You're still guiding the choices but they feel empowered, and that builds confidence and cooperation at mealtimes.

Tip Some resistance is normal, but stay consistent. With time, small changes can shift the whole family's food culture.

What progress can look like

Progress with fussy eating doesn't happen overnight, and it rarely looks like a clean plate. Instead, these subtle but powerful signs can indicate that your reset is working:

- Your child allows a new food to stay on their plate, even if they don't eat it yet.
- They touch, smell or explore a previously rejected food.
- They tolerate a new food being on the table or served to someone else.
- They take a bite of a new or previously rejected food, even if they spit it out.
- They start asking questions or showing curiosity about ingredients or cooking.
- They come to the table more willingly, even if they still eat selectively.
- They begin helping with meal prep, grocery shopping or setting the table.
- Mealtimes become calmer and more connected.
- They drink more water or show a shift away from processed snacks.
- They ask for something you made from scratch, even just once!

Every one of these moments is a sign your child is becoming more open, confident and comfortable around food. Celebrate the small wins, as they build the foundation for a lifetime of positive eating.

Kids with allergies can be unfussy eaters too

Having a baby or toddler with food allergies can make mealtimes difficult, but it doesn't have to create a fear of food. A lot of my clients come to see me maybe one or two years after their children are diagnosed. By this time, their child's 'safe' foods have dwindled down to only a short list of eight to ten items. One reason for this is an element of fear and trepidation around new foods, and those that are seen as potentially dangerous, which is understandable. We need to ensure that no matter how we as parents are feeling, we aim to stay positive and help our children enjoy a relaxed relationship with food regardless of their allergies or intolerances. Here are my go-to tips to help you:

- **Stay positive** Focus on enjoying what your child can eat, rather than what they can't. Avoid dramatic, fear-based language when talking about allergens. Instead of 'this food is dangerous', say 'we avoid this because it doesn't make your body feel good'.
- **Don't limit exposure to safe foods** This means including your child in shopping, meal planning and cooking, and encouraging them to pick up safe ingredients. Introduce safe foods in different ways (raw/cooked/puréed) to ensure variety, and let your child try safe recipes from different cultures.
- **Teach your child to advocate for themselves** Help them develop confidence in explaining their allergies to others, teaching them simple phrases like, 'I'm allergic to peanuts, so I can't eat this' and 'can you let me know if this has dairy in it?'
- **Empower other family members** Educate other family members about allergies by discussing them calmly, providing factual information and putting pictures of the foods your allergic child can't have in the kitchen for younger family members. Ensure all caregivers are up to date with their first-aid training, so you can reassure everyone they are in safe hands. Remember not to overreact if another family member makes a mistake.
- **Model positive food behaviours** Speak positively about food in front of your child and show curiosity and enthusiasm for trying new, safe foods.
- **Use child-friendly resources** As your child grows, start to read books or watch videos about other toddlers or young children managing their food allergies.

For babies and children with allergies, always work with your allergy specialist, paediatric dietitian or nutritionist to ensure your child's diet is nutritionally balanced and that safe foods are introduced appropriately.

The golden rules

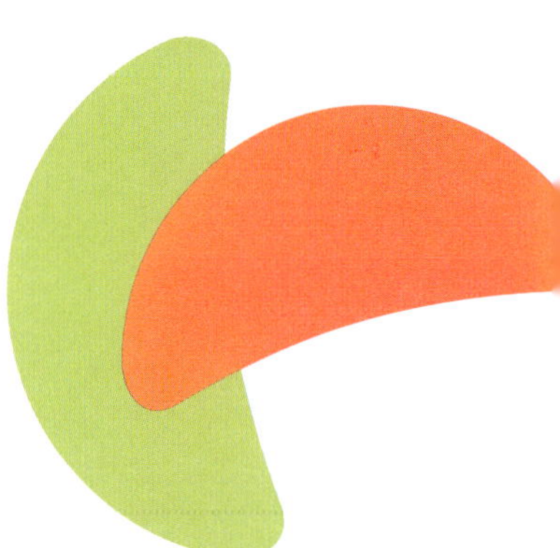

Through all stages and ages, return to these principles:

- Trust your child's appetite – it will vary naturally with growth and activity.
- Continue offering a variety of whole foods without pressure.
- Keep mealtimes positive and free from battles.
- Involve your little one in food preparation as soon as they show interest.
- Maintain family meals as a cornerstone of your daily routine.
- Remember that your role is to provide nutritious options. Their role is to decide how much to eat.
- Have confidence in your food choices.

While these principles work for most children in most situations, trust your parental intuition. If you're concerned about your child's growth, eating patterns or overall health, don't hesitate to consult your paediatrician, a registered dietitian, qualified nutritionist or feeding specialist. Some children may need extra support or modified approaches.

The Unfussy Eaters Club guide to essential nutrients

When your child pushes away a plate of veggies or insists on eating only 'white foods', it's easy to feel discouraged and concerned about nutritional gaps. I understand how disheartening it can be when it feels like nothing is working. But the good news is, with a little creativity and a lot of patience, it is possible to nourish even the fussiest of eaters.

This guide is here to support you. It breaks down the essential nutrients growing bodies need and shares practical, achievable strategies to help you get them into your child's diet without turning every meal into a battle. You'll discover ways to weave nutrients into the foods your child already loves, along with family-friendly meals that make eating well feel effortless.

Remember, it's not about perfection. It's about creating gentle, consistent exposure to whole, nutritious foods in ways your child feels safe and curious to explore. Start with where they're at now and build from there. Whether it's blending leafy greens into smoothies, baking iron-rich veggies into muffins or offering new textures they'll actually try, these ideas have been tried and tested by families just like yours.

Nutrient	Fussy eater tips	Family meal and snack ideas
Calcium	• Make colourful yoghurt ice blocks (great for sore gums) • Create cheese faces on wholegrain toast • Blend leafy greens into favourite smoothies • Make Powerhouse choc bliss balls (see page 209)	• Natural yoghurt with fresh fruit • Overnight pudding (see page 108) • Easy hidden-chickpea pizza (see page 165) • Nourishing herby fish bites (see page 172)
Folate	• Add finely chopped spinach to meatballs • Create green smoothies with hidden leafy greens (see page 221) • Make bean and avocado dips	• Summer's green pancakes (see page 115) • Green goodness bites (see page 183) • Sweet potato & broccoli slice (see page 181) • Powerhouse choc bliss balls (see page 209)
Iodine	• Make crispy seaweed chips • Create ocean-themed meals • Use fun-shaped egg moulds • Make colourful dairy smoothies (see pages 90, 220 and 221)	• Salmon & quinoa patties (see page 153) • Mediterranean fish pot (see page 131) • Cheesy savoury blondies (see page 175) • Strawberry yoghurt marshmallows (see page 214)
Iron	• Blend spinach into fruit smoothies (see page 221) • Make mini meat patties in fun shapes • Add puréed lentils to pasta sauce • Create delicious bliss balls with apricots and seeds (see page 208)	• Tummy-warming bean shakshuka (see page 100) • Iron-rich lamb & veggie balls (see page 120) • Easy lentil & sweet potato pot (see page 125) • Classic bolognese (see page 126)
Vitamin B12	• Make mini meat kebabs • Create egg art • Use cookie cutters to cut out cheese slices • Make yoghurt-based fruit dips	• Rainbow veggie frittata (see page 148) • Hearty beef stew (see page 119) • Baked millet & flathead pilaf (see page 133) • Strawberry yoghurt marshmallows (see page 214) • Sweet potato & apricot scrolls (see page 194)
Vitamin B6	• Make bliss balls with nut butter and oats • Create potato faces with vegetable features • Offer homemade dips with interesting shapes for dipping	• Banana & cinnamon pancakes (see page 88) • Orange & thyme chicken drumsticks (see page 128) • Sweet potato & apricot scrolls (see page 194) • Chickpea & pumpkin bites (see page 176)
Vitamin C	• Make fruit faces with citrus slices • Freeze berries for a fun snack texture • Hide capsicum (pepper) in tomato-based sauces • Create colourful 'dippy plates' with vegetables rich in vitamin C	• Berry chia jam (see page 228) • Gut-friendly green smoothie (see page 221) • Veggie-loaded pasta sauce (see page 134) • Fresh fruit
Vitamin D *Hard to get from food alone. A combination of outdoor time and fortified products may be needed.*	• Make egg faces • Create fish finger sushi rolls • Design outdoor picnic adventures • Use cookie cutters for egg sandwiches	• Crunchy golden fish fingers (see page 132) • Cheesy chia omelette (see page 112) • Cheesy tuna & veggie lasagne (see page 136) • Picnic lunches in the sunshine (make sure to be sun safe)
Zinc	• Make crispy chickpea chips • Create seed-coated chicken strips • Blend nuts/seeds into smoothies • Make fun dips with legumes	• Protein-packed chicken nuggets (see page 160) • Lamb & vegetable koftas (see page 159) • Coconut fish curry (see page 143) • Lentil & veggie cottage pie (see page 140)

PART TWO

The food

Meal plans for starting solids and baby-led weaning

Transitioning your child to solids can be quite the journey, so these meal plans are designed to help you along the way. They are my general recommendations. As always, follow your healthcare provider's specific advice and trust your baby to determine how much they need to eat or how much milk they need to drink. Don't forget to continue offering breastmilk or formula between meals to ensure adequate nutrition. And remember, appetite fluctuations are normal.

Cooking for the whole family

It doesn't have to be hard to cook one meal for the whole family. To adapt the dishes for the rest of the family, it's as simple as portioning out baby's meal, then for older kids and adults:

- increase portion sizes;
- serve with complementary side dishes; and
- add salt and seasonings (optional).

4–5 months

At this stage, solid food is about practice and gentle exposure to flavour and texture. It's not about meeting your baby's nutritional needs. Your baby's milk feeds are still their main source of nourishment. Offer solids 30–60 minutes after a milk feed once a day to begin with. Work up to three meals per day, and let your baby guide how much they eat. Here are some guidelines:

- Start with a smooth, thin purée consistency.
- Offer vegetables first. No added fruit, rice cereal or sweeteners.
- Introduce one new food every two days to gently ease your baby into solids and monitor for tolerance. If no adverse reactions or concerns arise (see page 34), you can begin offering a new food daily in week two.
- Use a soft-tipped baby spoon or allow your baby to suck from the spoon.
- Batch-cook single vegetable purées. This will help save time as they can be used in mixed vegetable combos later on.
- Don't use salt or seasonings yet.

Tip Cauliflower and broccoli can cause gas in some babies due to their naturally high fibre and sulphur content. Start with a small amount and observe your baby's response. Some babies tolerate them well, while others may need a little more time. Don't worry if your baby seems a bit gassy – it's often temporary as their digestive system adapts.

Week one (one meal)

Repeat each new food for two consecutive days. This eases your baby into solid textures while building confidence in digestion and allowing you to observe for potential reactions.

	Mon	Tue	Wed	Thu	Fri	Sat	Sun
Breakfast	Milk feed 1	Milk feed 1	Milk feed 1	Milk feed 1	Milk feed 1	Milk feed 1	Milk feed 1
Mid-morning	Milk feed 2	Milk feed 2	Milk feed 2	Milk feed 2	Milk feed 2	Milk feed 2	Milk feed 2
Lunch	Milk feed 3 + sweet potato	Milk feed 3 + sweet potato	Milk feed 3 + avocado	Milk feed 3 + avocado	Milk feed 3 + pumpkin (squash)	Milk feed 3 + pumpkin (squash)	Milk feed 3 + zucchini (courgette)
Mid-afternoon	Milk feed 4	Milk feed 4	Milk feed 4	Milk feed 4	Milk feed 4	Milk feed 4	Milk feed 4
Dinner	Milk feed 5	Milk feed 5	Milk feed 5	Milk feed 5	Milk feed 5	Milk feed 5	Milk feed 5
Evening	Milk feed 6	Milk feed 6	Milk feed 6	Milk feed 6	Milk feed 6	Milk feed 6	Milk feed 6

Week two (two meals)

Introduce one new food each day, assuming your baby has no adverse reactions at breakfast. Mix previously tolerated foods at lunch. There's no need to repeat solo foods unless revisiting for preference or tolerance.

	Mon	Tue	Wed	Thu	Fri	Sat	Sun
Breakfast	Milk feed 1 + yellow squash	Milk feed 1 + carrot	Milk feed 1 + green beans	Milk feed 1 + broccoli	Milk feed 1 + parsnip	Milk feed 1 + butternut (squash)	Milk feed 1 + cauliflower
Mid-morning	Milk feed 2	Milk feed 2	Milk feed 2	Milk feed 2	Milk feed 2	Milk feed 2	Milk feed 2
Lunch	Milk feed 3 + zucchini (courgette) + sweet potato	Milk feed 3 + yellow squash + avocado	Milk feed 3 + carrot + zucchini (courgette)	Milk feed 3 + green beans + sweet potato	Milk feed 3 + pumpkin (squash) + zucchini (courgette)	Milk feed 3 + parsnip + avocado	Milk feed 3 + butternut (squash) + yellow squash
Mid-afternoon	Milk feed 4	Milk feed 4	Milk feed 4	Milk feed 4	Milk feed 4	Milk feed 4	Milk feed 4
Dinner	Milk feed 5	Milk feed 5	Milk feed 5	Milk feed 5	Milk feed 5	Milk feed 5	Milk feed 5
Evening	Milk feed 6	Milk feed 6	Milk feed 6	Milk feed 6	Milk feed 6	Milk feed 6	Milk feed 6

Week three (three meals + veggies & fruit)

This meal plan is designed for babies who are ready for a more structured solids routine. Typically, if you have started solids at 4 or 5 months, your baby is ready for this menu from around 5 months, when they are showing enthusiasm for food, managing soft textures well and have already been exposed to a wide range of vegetables.

At this stage, you may begin offering three meals per day, alongside breastmilk or formula, with small portions of fruit and gentle veggie combinations (see table below) while slowly increasing variety. Milk should remain your baby's main source of nutrition at this stage.

You don't need to follow this plan rigidly. Use it as a flexible guide to inspire balanced combinations, colour variety and gentle introduction of new flavours and foods. Keep in mind to:

- offer new food at breakfast or lunch;
- avoid sweetening vegetable purées with fruit;
- let your baby's development guide progression, rather than sticking to strict timelines;
- build on veggie acceptance and use organic or local ingredients when in season;
- always follow your baby's cues and adjust quantities, textures and pace to suit their development; and
- offer milk before meals, as milk is still your baby's primary source of nutrition.

	Mon	Tue	Wed	Thu	Fri	Sat	Sun
Breakfast	Milk feed 1 + banana & avocado	Milk feed 1 + zucchini (courgette) & pumpkin (squash)	Milk feed 1 + apricot & pear compote	Milk feed 1 + butternut (squash) & peas	Milk feed 1 + papaya	Milk feed 1 + avocado & sweet potato	Milk feed 1 + apple & pear
Mid-morning	Milk feed 2	Milk feed 2	Milk feed 2	Milk feed 2	Milk feed 2	Milk feed 2	Milk feed 2
Lunch	Milk feed 3 + sweet potato, beetroot & green beans	Milk feed 3 + fennel & peas	Milk feed 3 + pumpkin (squash), cauliflower & zucchini (courgette)	Milk feed 3 + broccoli, sweet potato & carrot	Milk feed 3 + pumpkin (squash), green beans & baby spinach	Milk feed 3 + butternut (squash), beetroot & yellow squash	Milk feed 3 + potato, cauliflower & fennel
Mid-afternoon	Milk feed 4	Milk feed 4	Milk feed 4	Milk feed 4	Milk feed 4	Milk feed 4	Milk feed 4
Dinner	Milk feed 5 + yellow squash & parsnip	Milk feed 5 + carrot, swede & parsnip	Milk feed 5 + peas, potato & yellow squash	Milk feed 5 + green beans, zucchini (courgette) & avocado	Milk feed 5 + carrot, yellow squash & potato	Milk feed 5 + parsnip, zucchini (courgette) & pumpkin (squash)	Milk feed 5 + sweet potato, avocado & green beans
Evening	Milk feed 6	Milk feed 6	Milk feed 6	Milk feed 6	Milk feed 6	Milk feed 6	Milk feed 6

6–8 months

From 6 months, breastmilk and formula no longer provide your baby with the amounts of iron, zinc and vitamin B12 they need to thrive. These essential nutrients need to be introduced through solid foods. If you are starting solids at 6 months, you can follow a fast-tracked version of the week one to three meal plans (see pages 65–6). This is because your baby is a bit older, has a more mature digestive system and likely has stronger oral-motor skills, so they can usually move through the early stages more quickly. Instead of repeating each food for two days (as we do in week one), you can introduce one new food per day, starting with vegetables and progressing to well-tolerated combinations. By week two, you'll likely be able to offer two meals a day, and by week three, your baby can be established on three meals per day. This should include a variety of vegetables and iron-rich foods, such as meat, lentils and eggs. Offer finger food or a combination of finger food and purées. You can still use the baby-led weaning meal plans, just at a slightly quicker pace and:

- offer one new food each day, rather than every two days, in the beginning. Build up to a number of new foods daily if there are no adverse reactions;
- introduce iron-rich foods earlier, like red meat, chicken, legumes, eggs (see page 25) by week three;
- gradually increase to two meals per day by the end of week two and three meals by the end of week three, following your baby's cues. Progress onto the finger food meal plan (see page 68), adapting veggies into age-appropriate finger food shapes rather than purées;
- offer all veggies listed in the 4–5 months meal plans but steam in appropriate finger food shapes, rather than puréeing;
- introduce allergenic foods one at a time. Watch for adverse reactions (see page 34); and
- offer water with meals in small amounts to support hydration and practise cup skills.

Follow your baby's cues and don't worry if they eat only small amounts at first. The goal is exploration.

Finger food

By now your baby is becoming a curious, confident eater and is ready to explore real-food meals that go beyond purées. This stage is about building structure – three balanced meals per day made with nutrient-rich wholefoods that support brain development, immunity and growth. Iron, zinc, healthy fats and protein are particularly important.

Whether you're following spoonfeeding, baby-led weaning or a flexible mix of both, this plan is designed to support your baby's transition to family-style meals. Offer solids before milk when possible (waiting 30–45 minutes allows your baby time to digest their meal and ensures they still drink sufficient milk), follow your baby's hunger and fullness cues, and allow time for messy, sensory-rich exploration. There's no need to pressure your baby to eat a certain amount. Every bite is progress and the aim is to practise the necessary skills to eat more complex foods in the coming months.

Solid meals should complement but not replace your baby's milk feeds at this age. Milk will still provide most of their nutrition during this transition period. The goal is to gradually shift the balance, so that by 8–9 months, solids are starting to meet more of your baby's nutritional needs, particularly for iron, zinc and other key nutrients. Breastfed babies may still feed around six to eight times in 24 hours, although this will naturally begin to reduce as solids increase. Formula-fed babies typically have four to six feeds per day (roughly 600 ml/21 fl oz per day) – follow your baby's cues and the guidance on the tin.

To gradually drop a milk feed, offer solids before milk, gradually reduce the milk quantity for the feed you want to drop, replace the dropped feed with a nutritious snack or meal, and offer water with meals to support hydration.

Signs your baby is ready to drop a feed

- Showing more interest in solids and eating larger portions.
- Drinking less milk or refusing it.
- Naturally spacing out feeds on their own.
- Sleeping well without a night feed.

	Mon	Tue	Wed	Thu	Fri	Sat	Sun
Breakfast	Oat porridge (cinnamon pear; page 99) + avocado cubes + milk feed 1	Anytime egg muffin (page 103) + melon fingers + milk feed 1	Sweet potato & cinnamon pancakes (page 104) + banana fingers + milk feed 1	Oat porridge (banana blueberry; page 99) + avocado cubes + milk feed 1	Summer's green pancakes (page 115) + papaya cubes + milk feed 1	Toast, Hummus (page 224) & mashed avo + milk feed 1	Wholesome banana muffin (page 196) + avocado cubes + milk feed 1
Mid-morning	Milk feed 2	Milk feed 2	Milk feed 2	Milk feed 2	Milk feed 2	Milk feed 2	Milk feed 2
Lunch	Falafel balls with Beetroot hummus (pages 162 and 224) + steamed vegetables	Orange & thyme chicken drumsticks (page 128) + steamed vegetables	Creamy pumpkin & coconut soup (page 157) + Veggie-loaded scone (page 184)	Rainbow veggie frittata (page 148) + steamed vegetables	Easy lentil & sweet potato pot (page 125) + steamed vegetables	Nourishing herby fish bites (page 172) + steamed vegetables	Iron-rich lamb & veggie meatballs (page 120) + roasted vegetables
Mid-afternoon	Milk feed 3	Milk feed 3	Milk feed 3	Milk feed 3	Milk feed 3	Milk feed 3	Milk feed 3
Dinner	Hearty beef stew (page 119) + steamed vegetables	Salmon & quinoa patties (page 153) + steamed vegetables	Lamb cutlets (page 154) + potato wedges + steamed vegetables	Chicken & zucchini meatballs in roasted capsicum sauce (page 121) + steamed vegetables	Iron-boosting beef & lentil patties (page 150) + steamed vegetables	Coconut fish curry (page 143) + steamed vegetables	Butter chicken (page 139) + steamed vegetables
Evening	Milk feed 4	Milk feed 4	Milk feed 4	Milk feed 4	Milk feed 4	Milk feed 4	Milk feed 4

This sample meal plan shows only daytime feeds, and does not include possible early-morning or late-evening milk feeds. Every baby is different, so follow their feeding cues if breastfeeding, or the preparation and feeding instructions on the tin if formula feeding.

8–12 months

Your baby is likely enjoying three meals a day and showing interest in feeding themselves. Now, it's all about building confidence with real food and progressing from soft finger foods to more varied textures as they develop. Most babies this age can handle soft lumps and small pieces. This flexible meal plan will help you:

- move towards family-style meals with appropriate modifications;
- offer a balance of iron, protein, healthy fats and fibre;
- support self-feeding, spoon practice and open-cup use (introduce an open cup with a small amount of water at mealtimes);
- introduce healthy, tummy-filling snacks that will start to replace the mid-afternoon milk feeds (see below); and
- save time by focusing on multitasking meals, serving dinner for lunch the next day.

	Mon	Tue	Wed	Thu	Fri	Sat	Sun
Breakfast	Cheesy chia omelette (page 112) + milk feed 1	Gut-friendly green smoothie (page 221) + milk feed 1	Beetroot & buckwheat crepes (page 106) + milk feed 1	Overnight pudding (apple pie; page 109) + milk feed 1	One-ingredient buckwheat bread, Hummus (pages 226 and 224) & mashed avo + milk feed 1	Berry oat brekkie muffin (page 93) + milk feed 1	Tummy-warming bean shakshuka (page 100) + milk feed 1
Mid-morning	Natural yoghurt + steamed vegetables + fresh fruit	Chamomile veggie rusk (page 235) + steamed vegetables + fresh fruit	Steamed vegetables + fresh fruit + avocado slices	Natural yoghurt + steamed vegetables + fresh fruit	Banana fingers with Tahini & date spread (page 231) + steamed vegetables	Natural yoghurt + steamed vegetables + fresh fruit	One-ingredient buckwheat bread (toasted), Tahini & date spread (pages 226 and 231) + steamed vegetables + fresh fruit
Lunch	Classic bolognese (page 126) + steamed vegetables	Crunchy golden fish fingers (page 132) + roasted vegetables	Easy hidden-chickpea pizza (page 165) + steamed vegetables	Sneaky veggie chicken noodle soup (page 166) + steamed vegetables	Lamb & vegetable koftas (page 159) + roasted vegetables	Hearty minestrone soup (page 156) + steamed vegetables	One-pot chicken & tomato risotto (page 145) + steamed vegetables
Mid-afternoon	Carrot & beetroot date ball (page 219) + steamed vegetables + Hummus (page 224) + milk feed 2	Oat & quinoa wrap & Beetroot hummus (pages 232 and 224) + steamed vegetables + fresh fruit + milk feed 2	Banana, choc & cinnamon smoothie (page 220) + steamed vegetables + milk feed 2	Pumpkin pie bliss ball (page 218) + steamed vegetables + milk feed 2	Cheesy butter crackers with Hummus (pages 185 and 224) + steamed vegetables + fresh fruit + milk feed 2	Veggie-loaded scone (page 184) + steamed vegetables + fresh fruit + milk feed 2	Blueberry lemon muffin (page 193) + steamed vegetables + milk feed 2
Dinner	Crunchy golden fish fingers (page 132) + roasted vegetables	Easy hidden-chickpea pizza (page 165) + steamed vegetables	Sneaky veggie chicken noodle soup (page 166) + steamed vegetables	Lamb & vegetable koftas (page 159) + roasted vegetables	Hearty minestrone soup (page 156) + steamed vegetables	One-pot chicken & tomato risotto (page 145) + steamed vegetables	Cheesy tuna & veggie lasagne (page 136) + steamed vegetables
Evening	Milk feed 3	Milk feed 3	Milk feed 3	Milk feed 3	Milk feed 3	Milk feed 3	Milk feed 3

Purées

This chapter is designed to make it easy to follow my approach to introducing purées: offer vegetable purées first, followed by fruit options, then – after 6 months of age – prioritise iron-rich proteins, grains and allergens.

Each section covers how to prep ingredients for puréeing, plus my favourite combos. Remember to start by introducing one new food at a time and use real, whole foods.

Once your ingredients are ready for puréeing, simply blend until smooth in a blender or food processor. You can steam your veggies together; if they require different cooking times (e.g. sweet potato and green beans), simply remove the ones that are done and leave the others to steam a little longer. Test the temperature of the purée on the inside of your wrist before serving. It should be warm (body temperature), not hot.

From 6 months, I strongly recommend moving towards finger foods and mashed foods to reduce the risk of fussy eating, promote the development of appropriate oral motor skills and encourage family meals.

Adding liquids

Add boiled and cooled filtered water if necessary. I recommend avoiding adding formula or breastmilk as these contain natural sugars, so babies get used to enjoying these types of foods sweetened. However, if your baby is resistant to any of these foods after numerous tries, you can add breastmilk or formula for the first few. It may help them try the new food being offered. Once accepted, swap back to cooled, boiled water or simply leave out.

Storing purées

Discard any leftover purée that has touched your baby's mouth. Otherwise, store leftovers in an airtight container in the fridge for up to 2–3 days, or in small portions in the freezer for up to 3 months – but remember, some fruits and vegetables don't keep well once puréed. Avocado, banana, pear, melon and stone fruit (such as peach and nectarine) tend to oxidise, turn brown or watery and lose their flavour quickly, so they are best eaten immediately or stored for no more than a day in the fridge. The same goes for veggies with high water content, including zucchini (courgette), cucumber and tomato; they can separate and become slimy when stored. A few drops of lemon juice (for babies over 6 months) can help slow browning, or try combining these with longer-lasting options, such as apple or carrot, for better results. Meat and grain purées can be kept in the fridge for 24–48 hours, if stored correctly.

Reheating purées

Be sure to thoroughly and evenly reheat purées. Ones that contain animal products must be heated until steaming hot to kill any potential bacteria. Allow to cool to a safe serving temperature before offering to your baby.

Vegetable purées

The goal when preparing vegetables for puréeing is to cook them until they are very soft. The best ways to do this are:

- **Steaming** This is best for preserving nutrients (be sure not to overcook!), and it's my preferred method. Place vegetables in a steamer basket over a saucepan of boiling water and cover. Steam over medium heat for the recommended time (see page 74).
- **Boiling** This is fast and simple, though nutrients can leach into the cooking water. Boiling is ideal for hard root vegetables but less suited to leafy greens unless the cooking liquid is retained in the purée.
- **Roasting** Spread veggies in a single layer on a baking tray, with the exception of beetroot (which can be wrapped in baking paper). Roast at 200°C (400°F). This takes longer than steaming or boiling but creates lovely caramelised flavours. This makes the vegetables sweeter and more appealing as babies develop their taste preferences. The downside is that babies can then prefer these sweeter versions to steamed.

On the following page, you'll find a quick-reference table for preparing some of the best vegetables for purées.

There's no need to wait for food to cool down before puréeing. It just needs to be cooled before being served to baby or refrigerated or frozen.

Vegetables to introduce from around 6 months, or with care in earlier weeks due to possible sensitivity or gas production (see below), include cabbage, radish, raw onion, garlic, celery, tomato, mushroom and eggplant (aubergine). Spinach and beetroot can usually be introduced earlier if your baby is ready and tolerating other vegetables well. Start with small amounts, mix with other vegetables and monitor for reactions.

Tip Vegetable purées may be gas-producing, which is another good reason to offer them early in the day. To release gas after eating, do bicycle legs, massage your baby's tummy gently in a clockwise direction, keep them upright for 15–20 minutes and gently burp them. This is particularly effective for vegetables that may produce more gas, such as cauliflower and broccoli. Most of all, pay attention to your baby's cues. If they show signs of discomfort, try offering smaller portions. Combining gas-producing veggies with gentler options, such as zucchini (courgette) and root vegetables, can also ease the transition.

Vegetable	Steam (medium heat)	Boil (medium heat)	Roast (200°C/400°F)
Asparagus, woody stems removed and lower half peeled	10–15 minutes		
Beetroot, whole			45–50 minutes, then cool and peel
Broccoli, chopped (florets only, peeled stem from 6 months)	12–15 minutes		
Carrot, peeled and chopped	15–20 minutes		15 minutes covered, then 10–15 minutes uncovered
Cauliflower (florets only, peeled stem from 6 months)	12–15 minutes (whole)		
Green beans	15 minutes	8–10 minutes	
Green peas	10–12 minutes	8–10 minutes	
Leek (white part only), sliced	10–15 minutes		20–25 minutes
Parsnip, peeled and chopped	12–15 minutes		25–30 minutes
Potato, peeled and chopped (never offer potato that is green or has sprouted)	15–20 minutes	15–20 minutes	30–35 minutes
Pumpkin (squash), seeds removed, peeled and chopped	15–20 minutes		25–30 minutes
Silverbeet (leaves only)	5–7 minutes		
Spinach	5–7 minutes		
Sweet potato, peeled and chopped	15–20 minutes	15–20 minutes	30–35 minutes (whole)
Yellow squash, trimmed, peeled and sliced	8–10 minutes		
Zucchini (courgette), peeled and chopped initially	10–12 minutes		20–25 minutes

My top vegetable purée combos

4–6+ months

All of the ingredients in these combos need to be cooked as per the instructions in the table (opposite).

Broccoli & carrot

2 cups (240 g) broccoli florets (fresh or frozen)

1 large (150 g/5½ oz) carrot

Broccoli & pumpkin

2 cups (240 g) broccoli florets (fresh or frozen)

1½ cups (300 g) pumpkin (squash)

Butternut & sweet potato

1 cup (200 g) butternut pumpkin (squash)

1 cup (140 g) sweet potato

Carrot, yellow squash & parsnip

1 large (150 g/5½ oz) carrot

150 g (5½ oz) yellow squash

1 large (140 g/5 oz) parsnip

Carrot, zucchini & pumpkin

1 large (150 g/5½ oz) carrot

1 large (160 g/5½ oz) zucchini (courgette)

1½ cups (300 g) pumpkin (squash)

Cauliflower & green beans

2½ cups (200 g) cauliflower florets (fresh or frozen)

1 cup (100 g) green beans (fresh or frozen)

Pea, cauliflower & parsnip

1 cup (120 g) green peas (fresh or frozen)

1½ cups (120 g) cauliflower florets (fresh or frozen)

1 large (140 g/5 oz) parsnip

Potato, green beans & broccoli

1 large (250 g/9 oz) potato

1½ cups (150 g) green beans (fresh or frozen)

1½ cups (180 g) broccoli florets (fresh or frozen)

Pumpkin, cauliflower & zucchini

1½ cups (300 g) pumpkin (squash)

1½ cups (120 g) cauliflower florets (fresh or frozen, optional)

1 large (260 g/9¼ oz) zucchini (courgette)

Sweet potato & zucchini

1 cup (140 g) sweet potato

1 small (130 g/4½ oz) zucchini (courgette)

Sweet potato, carrot & green beans

1 small (130 g/4½ oz) sweet potato

1 large (150 g/5½ oz) carrot (optional)

1½ cups (150 g) green beans (fresh or frozen)

Yellow squash & parsnip

175 g (6 oz) yellow squash

1 large (140 g/5 oz) parsnip

Tip Avoid sweetening vegetable purées with fruit; it may mask the natural flavour of the vegetables, making it harder for your baby to develop a genuine liking for them. If your baby rejects them, try again another day. It can take up to 16 exposures before a new flavour is accepted.

Fruit purées

In the table below, you'll find the basics of preparing and cooking fruits commonly used in purées. Make sure to blitz until very soft. Soft fruits, such as avocado, banana, berries, mango, rockmelon, watermelon, papaya and kiwi, can be puréed without cooking, though there are some things to remember:

- If your baby is less than 6 months, only offer avocado and banana in their uncooked state.
- For babies under 7 months, steam berries and peel all fruit, such as apple and pear, before puréeing. Fibre in the skin can cause digestive irritation.
- Always use ripe fruit.
- Wash all raw fruit with the skin on, even if you will be peeling them.
- Use a fine-mesh sieve to remove the seeds from mashed berries and watermelon. You can strain other puréed fruits too, if desired.

Fruit	Steam (medium heat)	Boil (medium heat)	Roast (200°C/400°F)
Apple, peeled, cored, cut into small chunks	8–10 minutes		15–20 minutes
Berries, stems removed	3–5 minutes		
Dried fruit (sulphur free, unsweetened), quartered if large		For every ½ cup (85 g) dried fruit, cover with about 1 cup (250 ml) water and boil for 15–20 minutes (for softer fruits, such as prune and apple) or 45–50 minutes (for firmer fruits, such as apricot and date), or until soft and plump. Add more water during cooking if needed	
Pear, peeled and cored, cut into small chunks	8–10 minutes		15–20 minutes
Stone fruit (apricot, nectarine, peach, plum), peeled, seeds removed, cut into small chunks	5–8 minutes		

My top fruit purée combos

4–6+ months

The ingredients in these combos need to be cooked, apart from avocado and banana, which can be left raw before puréeing. See cooking instructions in the table (opposite).

Apple & blackberry

2 medium (360 g/12¾ oz) apples

1 cup (160 g) blackberries (fresh or frozen)

Apple & pear

2 medium (360 g/12¾ oz) apples

2 medium (200 g/7 oz) pears

Apricot & pear

4 medium (400 g/14 oz) pears

1⅓ cups (230 g) sulphur-free dried apricots

½ teaspoon ground cinnamon

Seeds scraped from 1 vanilla pod or 1 teaspoon vanilla extract or powder

Avocado & pumpkin

1 cup (200 g) pumpkin (squash)

½ large (100 g/3½ oz) avocado

A little banana, for extra creaminess

Avocado & sweet potato

1 cup (200 g) sweet potato

½ large (100 g/3½ oz) avocado

Banana & avocado

1 large (160 g) banana

½ large (100 g/3½ oz) avocado

Banana & blueberry

1 large (160 g/5½ oz) banana

¾ cup (120 g) blueberries (fresh or frozen)

Blueberry & apple

2 medium (360 g/12¾ oz) apples

1 cup (160 g) blueberries (fresh or frozen)

Mango & peach

1 (250g/9 oz) mango

2 medium (200g/7 oz) peaches

Papaya & banana

½ medium (125g/4½ oz) papaya

1 large (160 g/5½ oz) banana

Peach & apricot

2 medium (200g/7 oz) peaches

¾ cup (125 g) sulphur-free dried apricots

Pear & raspberry

2 large (300 g/10½ oz) pears

1 cup (160 g) raspberries (fresh or frozen)

Pear & kiwi *(from 6 months)*

2 large (300 g/10½ oz) ripe pears

2 (200g/7 oz) kiwis

Tip Don't forget, you can do much more with fruit purées than just serve them alone. Swirl into porridge or yoghurt, or spread on toast for older babies and toddlers. Their naturally sweet flavour makes them a great alternative to sugary jams, while the fibre-rich ingredients help to keep your baby's digestion on track.

Introducing proteins, grains and allergens

From 6 months, you can begin adding proteins, grains and common allergens to purées. Remember to introduce one new food at a time and to start with small amounts of new proteins and allergens (1–2 teaspoons; see page 30 for more on introducing allergens).

Proteins

Tip Only offer chicken liver once or twice per week, in small amounts (1 teaspoon puréed per serve) due to its high vitamin A content.

Nut butters are also a great source of protein. Use smooth nut butter with no added sugar, vegetable oil or salt. Ensure it is runny enough to blend well. If needed, you can warm the nut butter slightly to make it easier to mix.

Ensure proteins are thoroughly cooked and have appropriate texture (very smooth or very soft and moist). Always choose:

- pasture-raised or organic chicken (dark meat is richer in essential nutrients);
- fresh, low-mercury, wild-caught, sustainably sourced fish;
- grass-fed lamb and beef;
- pasture-raised or organic eggs; and
- organic or non-GMO tofu with no additives.

Plant-based options

For families following a vegetarian or flexitarian approach, there are excellent wholefood sources of plant-based protein suitable for babies from 6 months. These include:

- iron-rich legumes such as red lentils, split mung beans and black beans – always cooked until very soft and puréed or mashed;
- tofu – choose organic, non-GMO tofu with no additives. Silken or soft tofu is easiest to digest and can be blended into purées or mixed with veggies;
- iron-rich grains, such as amaranth, quinoa, teff and millet – serve well-cooked and blended for best texture and digestibility;
- ground seeds and nut butters – tahini (hulled for younger babies), almond butter and ground chia, hemp or flaxseeds provide healthy fats and protein. Always choose unsweetened, smooth versions with no added salt or additives; and
- dark leafy greens such as spinach or silverbeet can add iron when combined with vitamin C-rich fruits or vegetables to support absorption.

Start with small amounts and rotate sources to offer variety and balanced nutrition. Pair plant-based iron sources with foods high in vitamin C to support better iron uptake.

Protein	Steam/poach/boil (medium heat)	Fry/roast (medium heat/180°C/350°F or as specified)
Chicken (boneless, skinless breast or thigh), cut into small cubes or strips	Steam or poach for 12–15 minutes, or until fully cooked (no pink remains)	Roast (drizzled with extra virgin olive oil + herbs of choice) at 200°C (400°F) for 18–20 minutes, or until fully cooked (no pink remains in centre)
Chicken liver, rinsed, connective tissue or membranes removed, cut into small pieces	Steam for 6–8 minutes, or until fully cooked (no pink remains)	Fry (with 1 teaspoon extra virgin olive oil) for 3–4 minutes each side, or until completely browned, breaking up clumps with a wooden spoon
Egg	Hard boil or poach for 10–12 minutes, then cool and peel	
Lamb, fat trimmed, cut into cubes		Roast for 25–30 minutes, or until fully cooked and tender
Lentils, brown or red (dried)	Boil ½ cup (95 g) lentils in a saucepan with 1½ cups (375 ml) water or Bone broth (see page 223) over high heat, then reduce to low and simmer, covered, for 20–25 minutes, or until tender but still holding their shape	
Lentils, brown (canned), drained and rinsed	Steam for 5 minutes	
Minced (ground) beef		Fry (with a little extra virgin olive oil) for 10 minutes, or until completely browned, breaking up clumps with a wooden spoon
Salmon (skinless and boneless – check thoroughly), cut into small pieces	Steam or poach for 6–8 minutes, or until fully cooked (opaque and flakes easily)	Roast (drizzled with extra virgin olive oil) for 10–12 minutes, or until fully cooked (opaque and flakes easily)
Firm or soft tofu	Steam for 5 minutes (or serve at room temperature)	Firm tofu only: roast (drizzled with extra virgin olive oil) for 20–25 minutes, or until lightly golden on the outside but soft
Turkey (boneless and skinless), cut into small cubes or strips	Steam for 15–20 minutes, or until fully cooked (no pink remains)	Roast (drizzled with extra virgin olive oil) at 200°C (400°F) for 18–20 minutes, or until fully cooked (no pink remains)
White fish (skinless and boneless – check thoroughly), cut into small pieces	Steam for 5–8 minutes, or until fully cooked (opaque and flakes easily)	Roast (drizzled with extra virgin olive oil + herbs of choice) for 10–12 minutes, or until fully cooked (opaque and flakes easily)

Note For the purée combinations on the following pages, the icons indicate where the purées DO include the allergen.

My top protein purée combos

4–6+ months

All proteins, legumes and grains must be thoroughly cooked before serving. Steam, boil, roast or fry as indicated; for boiling/steaming, water or Bone broth (see page 223) may be used. For roasting/frying, extra virgin olive oil is recommended. See cooking instructions in the tables opposite and on pages 74 and 76.

Almond butter, pear & zucchini

1 large (150 g/5½ oz) pear

½ cup (75 g) zucchini (courgette)

1–2 teaspoons almond butter (add when puréeing)

Asparagus, leek, spinach & beef

100 g (3½ oz) minced (ground) beef

½ cup (100 g) asparagus

¼ cup (20 g) leek

½ cup (15 g) baby spinach

½ cup (125 ml) low-salt beef stock or Bone broth (see page 223)

Baked salmon, pumpkin & zucchini

100 g (3½ oz) boneless, skinless salmon fillet

½ cup (100 g) pumpkin (squash)

½ cup (75 g) zucchini (courgette)

Banana & peanut butter

1 large (160 g/5½ oz) ripe banana

1–2 teaspoons smooth peanut butter

Beef, carrot, peas & cauliflower

100 g (3½ oz) minced (ground) beef

½ cup (70 g) carrot

⅓ cup (40 g) green peas (fresh or frozen)

¼ cup (60 g) cauliflower florets (fresh or frozen)

Bone broth, rice & veggies

½ cup (100 g) mixed green beans, zucchini (courgette) and carrot (fresh or frozen)

⅓ cup (40 g) brown rice flakes cooked in 1 cup (250 ml) Bone broth (see page 223)

Brown lentils, pumpkin & spinach

1 cup (200 g) pumpkin (squash)

1 cup (180 g) canned brown lentils (or ½ cup/100 g dried brown lentils)

½ cup (15 g) baby spinach

Butternut & egg

1 cup (200 g) butternut pumpkin (squash)

1 boiled egg

Chicken, carrot, broccoli & cumin

1 cup (150 g/5½ oz breast or 165 g/5¾ oz thigh) skinless chicken

1 large (150 g/5½ oz) carrot

½ cup (60 g) broccoli florets (fresh or frozen)

⅓ teaspoon ground cumin

Chicken, sweet potato & broccoli

100 g (3½ oz) boneless, skinless chicken breast

1 medium (180 g/6 oz) sweet potato

½ cup (60 g) broccoli florets (fresh or frozen)

Flathead, pumpkin & zucchini

½ cup (60 g) boneless, skinless flathead fillet (or other white fish fillet)

1 medium (200 g/7 oz) zucchini (courgette)

1 cup (200 g) pumpkin (squash)

Lamb, pumpkin & peas

100 g (3½ oz) lamb

1 cup (200 g) pumpkin (squash)

¼ cup (30 g) green peas (fresh or frozen)

Red lentil, sweet potato & green beans

½ cup (95 g) dried red lentils

1 medium (180 g/6 oz) sweet potato

¾ cup (75 g) green beans (fresh or frozen)

Scrambled egg, spinach & potato

1 egg, scrambled with 1 teaspoon extra virgin olive oil (optional)

½ cup (15 g) baby spinach

1 medium (170 g/5¾ oz) potato

Silken tofu, carrot, broccoli & cauliflower

½ cup (125 g) silken tofu

½ cup (70 g) carrot

¼ cup (30 g) broccoli florets (fresh or frozen)

¾ cup (60 g) cauliflower florets (fresh or frozen)

Turkey, sweet potato & spinach

100 g (3½ oz) boneless, skinless turkey breast

1 medium (180 g/6 oz) sweet potato

½ cup (15 g) baby spinach

White fish, carrot, parsnip & broccoli

100 g (3½ oz) boneless, skinless cod or haddock fillet (or other white fish fillet)

½ cup (70 g) carrot

½ cup (70 g) parsnip

¼ cup (30 g) broccoli florets (fresh or frozen)

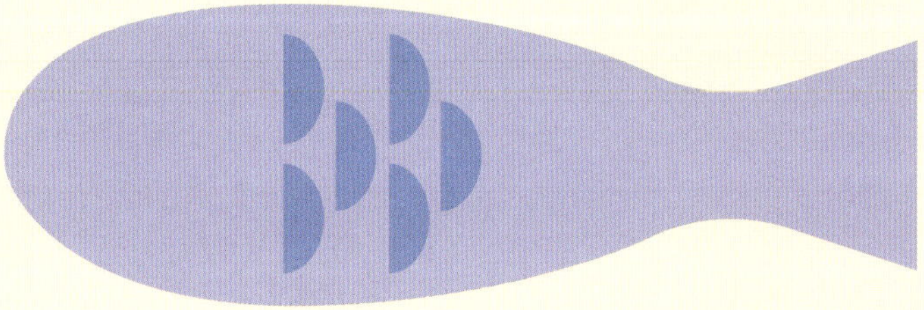

Grains

When it comes to preparing grains, there are a few things to remember:

- Rinse grains thoroughly in a strainer under cold running water (with the exception of oats).
- Cook all grains until very soft (for easy digestion).
- You can soak most grains to reduce cooking time and increase digestibility.
- You can cook grains in homemade no-salt vegetable broth for added flavour.
- The combinations (on the following pages) use pre-cooked grains. Cook the grains separately, then combine with the listed vegetables and fruits.

Grain	Boil (medium heat)
Amaranth	For every ½ cup (90 g), boil in 1½ cups (375 ml) water for 20–25 minutes, or until soft and water is absorbed About 35 g (1¼ oz) uncooked amaranth makes ½ cup (90 g) cooked
Brown rice	For every 1 cup (210 g), boil in 3 cups (750 ml) water for about 45 minutes, or until soft and creamy About 40 g (1½ oz) uncooked brown rice makes ½ cup (90 g) cooked
Buckwheat	For every ½ cup (95 g), boil in 1½ cups (375 ml) water for 10–15 minutes, or until soft About 30 g (1 oz) uncooked buckwheat makes ½ cup (100 g) cooked
Millet	For every ½ cup (100 g), boil in 1½ cups (375 ml) water for 15–20 minutes, until soft and water is absorbed About 35 g (1¼ oz) uncooked millet makes ½ cup (85 g) cooked
Quinoa	For every ½ cup (95 g), boil in 1½ cups (375 ml) water for 15 minutes, or until water is absorbed. Stand, covered, for 5 minutes, then fluff with a fork before serving or puréeing About 25 g (1 oz) uncooked quinoa makes ½ cup (90 g) cooked
Rolled oats	For every ½ cup (55 g), boil in 1 cup (250 ml) water for 5–7 minutes, or until creamy and soft. For younger babies, add an extra ½ cup (125 ml) water and cook for an additional 2–3 minutes for a softer texture About 45 g (1½ oz) uncooked rolled oats makes ½ cup (120 g) cooked

My top veg/fruit and grain purée combos

Amaranth & berries

½ cup (90 g) cooked amaranth

½ cup (80 g) mixed berries

Amaranth, green bean & potato

½ cup (50 g) green beans (fresh or frozen)

½ cup (75 g) potato

½ cup (90 g) cooked amaranth

2 small (20 g) silverbeet leaves

Banana, buckwheat, cinnamon & turmeric

½ cup (100 g) cooked buckwheat

1 medium (110 g/3¾ oz) banana

1 teaspoon ground cinnamon

½ teaspoon ground turmeric

Beetroot, apple, tahini & brown rice

½ cup (80 g) grated beetroot

½ cup (90 g) cooked brown rice

1 medium (180 g/6 oz) apple, steamed

1 tablespoon tahini

½ teaspoon ground cardamom

Tip The amounts given for the grains in these recipes are for cooked grains. See the table on page 83 for the uncooked equivalents.

Cook grains in homemade vegetable stock/broth (with no salt) for more flavour. Grains are great puréed with fruit. Just cook the grains in water, rather than stock or broth, then purée with the fruit.

Beetroot, apple, blackberry, mint & quinoa

1 large (125 g/4½ oz) beetroot

1 medium (180 g/6 oz) apple

½ cup (80 g) blackberries

1 tablespoon mint leaves

½ cup (90 g) cooked quinoa

Brown rice, banana & nutmeg

½ cup (90 g) cooked brown rice

1 medium (110 g/3¾ oz) banana

Pinch of ground nutmeg

Brown rice, pumpkin & sage

½ cup (90 g) cooked brown rice

¾ cup (150 g) pumpkin (squash)

½ teaspoon dried sage

Buckwheat, cauliflower & peas

½ cup cooked (100 g) buckwheat

¾ cup (60 g) cauliflower florets

½ cup (60 g) green peas (fresh or frozen)

Buckwheat, peach & cardamom

½ cup (100 g) cooked buckwheat

1 medium (100 g) peach

¼ teaspoon ground cardamom

Millet, carrot & parsnip

½ cup (85 g) cooked millet

½ cup (70 g) carrot

½ cup (65 g) parsnip

Oats, apple & cinnamon

1 cup (110 g) cooked rolled oats

1 medium (180g/6 oz) apple

¼ teaspoon cinnamon (optional)

Oats, spinach & zucchini

⅓ cup (35 g) cooked rolled oats

½ cup (15 g) baby spinach

½ cup (75 g) zucchini (courgette)

Quinoa, broccoli & sweet potato

½ cup (90 g) cooked quinoa

½ cup (60 g) broccoli florets (fresh or frozen)

½ cup (140 g) sweet potato

1 teaspoon pure vanilla extract or powder

Quinoa, pear & vanilla

½ cup (90 g) cooked quinoa

1 medium (150 g) pear

½ teaspoon pure vanilla extract or powder

My top veg, protein and grain purée combos

Amaranth, turkey, broccoli & avocado

½ cup (90 g) cooked amaranth

100 g (3½ oz) boneless, skinless turkey breast

½ cup (60 g) broccoli florets

½ small (50 g/1¾ oz) avocado

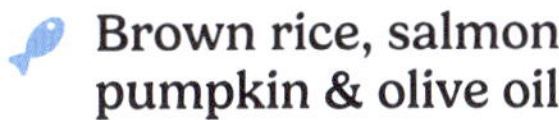

Brown rice, salmon, pumpkin & olive oil

½ cup (90 g) cooked brown rice

100 g (3½ oz) boneless, skinless salmon fillet

½ cup (100 g) pumpkin (squash)

Brown rice, tofu, sweet potato & tahini

½ cup (90 g) cooked brown rice

½ cup (125 g) firm tofu

½ medium (90 g) sweet potato,

1 teaspoon tahini

Buckwheat, white fish & zucchini

½ cup (100 g) cooked buckwheat

100 g (3½ oz) boneless, skinless cod or haddock fillet (or other white fish fillet)

½ cup (75 g) zucchini (courgette)

Millet, nut butter, cauliflower & pumpkin

½ cup (85 g) cooked millet

1 teaspoon smooth nut butter

¾ cup (60 g) cauliflower florets

½ cup (100 g) pumpkin (squash)

Millet, red lentils, carrot & coconut oil

½ cup (85 g) cooked millet

150 g (5½ oz) cooked red lentils

½ cup (70 g) carrot

1 teaspoon coconut oil (add after puréeing for flavour)

Oats, egg yolk, spinach & avocado

½ cup (120 g) cooked rolled oats

1 egg yolk

½ cup (15 g) baby spinach

½ small (50 g) avocado

Quinoa, chicken, avocado & sweet potato

½ cup (90 g) cooked quinoa

100 g (3½ oz) boneless, skinless chicken breast

½ small (50 g/1¾ oz) avocado

½ small (75 g/2½ oz) sweet potato

Quinoa, lamb, peas & olive oil

½ cup (90 g) cooked quinoa

100 g (3½ oz) lamb

¼ cup (30 g) green peas (fresh or frozen)

Oats, chicken liver, carrot & avocado

½ cup (120 g) cooked rolled oats

1 teaspoon chicken liver

½ cup (70 g) carrot

½ small (50 g/1¾ oz) avocado

Tip A simple porridge made of millet and buckwheat is also a great combo. Use equal amounts of each.

Breakfast

6+ months

Makes 12

Prep 10 mins (+ cooling)

Cook 12 mins

 Vegan

 Dairy free

 Egg free

 Fish free

 Peanut free

 Sesame free

Soy free

 Tree nut free

Banana & cinnamon pancakes

These fluffy egg-free banana pancakes are a perfect first pancake for little ones, made with simple, nourishing ingredients to support growing bodies. Naturally sweet thanks to ripe bananas and packed with fibre from oats and pumpkin seed meal, they provide a steady source of energy for busy little explorers. A splash of coconut milk keeps them deliciously soft, while cinnamon adds a hint of warmth and flavour. Whether served as bite-sized pieces for self-feeding or mashed for early eaters, these pancakes are a wholesome and satisfying start to the day.

½ cup (55 g) rolled oats

¼ cup (35 g) pumpkin seed meal

¼ teaspoon ground cinnamon

2 small (160 g/5½ oz) bananas, sliced

⅓ cup (80 ml) coconut milk

1 tablespoon coconut oil, for frying

Serving suggestions

Mashed banana or avocado

Boiled and cooled water

Sliced fresh berries

Natural unsweetened coconut yoghurt

Place the oats, pumpkin seed meal and cinnamon in a high-speed blender and pulse for 10 seconds, or until the oats have broken down into a consistency that resembles quick oats.

Add the banana and coconut milk, and blend until smooth.

Heat the oil in a large frying pan over medium heat. In batches, spoon heaped tablespoons of the batter into the pan and cook for 2 minutes each side, or until golden brown. Allow to cool.

Offer the pancakes in soft, manageable strips when baby is starting solids. You can mash them with banana, avocado or boiled and cooled water to make it easier to manage.

For babies 8+ months, offer small bite-sized pieces to encourage self-feeding, topped with sliced fresh berries and yoghurt.

Make it ...

Gluten free Swap oats for brown rice, quinoa flakes or certified gluten-free oats.

Boosted Add 2 teaspoons chia seeds or flaxseeds.

Pantry friendly Swap pumpkin seed meal for almond meal or flour of choice.

Family friendly (2+) Serve drizzled with pure maple syrup or raw honey (optional) and topped with fresh berries and dairy-free yoghurt; for a thicker, fluffier consistency, add ½ teaspoon baking powder and ¼ teaspoon bicarbonate of soda (baking soda) to batter.

School friendly Perfect lunch-box filler for recess.

Leftovers Store in an airtight container in the fridge for up to 2 days or freeze for up to 3 months.

6+ months

Serves 2

Prep 10 mins

Easy berry bliss smoothie

- Vegan
- Dairy free
- Egg free
- Fish free
- Gluten free
- Sesame free
- Soy free
- Tree nut free (unless using cashews)

I love sharing smoothies with my kids. As soon as they were old enough, I began making a big jug to enjoy together. With small tweaks for myself, it was always an easy win for everyone, and I froze any leftovers in popsicle moulds – great for teething relief. This creamy smoothie is a delicious, gut-friendly option. Packed with fibre-rich pears, known for their gentle constipation-relieving properties, and antioxidant-rich berries, this is both nourishing and naturally sweet. Coconut milk creates a smooth, velvety texture. With no banana, it's a great alternative for babies who may struggle with tummy issues.

1½ cups (375 ml) coconut milk

2 cups (320 g) frozen mixed berries

1 medium (100 g/3½ oz) ripe pear, cored and chopped

¼ cup (40 g) pepitas (pumpkin seeds) or cashews, soaked for 15 minutes and drained

1 teaspoon fresh lemon juice (optional but recommended)

Optional extras

½ cup (15 g) baby spinach

2–3 (30–45 g/1–1½ oz) pitted soft medjool dates (soaked and drained, if needed)

½ teaspoon pure vanilla extract or powder, or scraped seeds from ½ vanilla pod

Place all the ingredients, including the optional extras (if using), in a high-speed blender and blend until smooth and creamy.

Serve immediately in small open cups or cups with a straw. If the mixture is too thick for a straw, thin it out with some water or extra coconut milk. Offer your baby ¼ cup (60 ml) to begin with and slowly increase to around ½ cup (125 ml) by 12 months. (This is only a guide; your baby may drink more or less.)

Make it ...

Creamy Swap mixed berries for banana.

Sweeter Add more medjool dates.

Seasonal Swap pear for banana or mango.

Family friendly (2+) Freeze smoothie into popsicle moulds.

Leftovers Store, covered, in the fridge for up to 2 days or freeze in popsicle moulds for up to 3 months.

9+ months

Makes 20 slices

Prep 15 mins (+ cooling)

Cook 55 mins

Brain-boosting banana bread

 Vegetarian

 Fish free

 Peanut free

 Sesame free

 Soy free

 Tree nut free

This banana bread holds a special place in our home: it's how my babies first discovered banana bread, and it's been a family favourite ever since! Soft, naturally sweet and packed with nourishing ingredients, it's an awesome way to introduce wholesome flavours to little ones aged 9–12 months. Unlike store-bought versions, which can contain more than 4 teaspoons of sugar per slice and unnecessary preservatives, this recipe is free from refined sugars and full of goodness. Made with wholemeal spelt flour (or easily adapted to be gluten free), it's rich in gentle fibre to support tiny tummies, while flaxseeds provide essential omega-3s for brain and eye development.

1½ large (260 g/9¼ oz) ripe bananas

3 large pasture-raised or organic eggs

½ cup (125 ml) milk of choice

6 (90 g/3¼ oz) pitted soft medjool dates

½ cup (125 ml) melted coconut oil

1½ cups (225 g) wholemeal spelt flour

2 tablespoons flaxseed meal

1 teaspoon pure vanilla extract or powder, or scraped seeds from 1 vanilla pod

1 teaspoon ground cinnamon

1 teaspoon baking powder

½ teaspoon bicarbonate of soda (baking soda)

Serving suggestions

Natural unsweetened yoghurt

Mashed banana

Berry chia jam (see page 228)

Leftovers Store in an airtight container in the fridge for up to a week or freeze for up to 3 months.

Preheat the oven to 180°C (350°F) and line the base and sides of a loaf tin with baking paper.

Place the bananas, eggs, milk, dates and oil in a food processor. Process until smooth, scraping down the side once or twice to help blend evenly. Add the remaining ingredients. Process until well combined and smooth.

Pour the batter into the prepared tin and bake for about 55 minutes, or until a cake tester or skewer inserted comes out clean.

Allow to cool in the tin for a few minutes, then turn out onto a wire rack and allow to cool further before cutting into slices.

Slice the banana bread into thin, soft strips or small bite-sized pieces to encourage self-feeding. Mash the banana bread with a little yoghurt, banana or berry chia jam for a softer texture.

Make it …

Gluten free Swap flour for brown rice flour, buckwheat flour, millet flour or a gluten-free flour blend.

Dairy free Use coconut, soy or oat milk and coconut yoghurt.

Egg free Swap egg for a store-bought egg replacer, or a flax egg (1 egg = 1 tablespoon ground flaxseed + 45 ml/1½ fl oz warm water) or a chia egg (1 egg = 1 tablespoon chia seed meal + ¼ cup/60 ml water).

Boosted Add extra seeds, such as hemp, sunflower or chia.

Pantry friendly Swap flaxseeds for chia, hemp or sunflower seeds or pepitas (pumpkin seeds); use wholemeal flour.

Family friendly (2+) To sweeten, add ¼ cup (40 g) coconut sugar to batter or swap dates for ⅓ cup (65 g) coconut sugar. Reduce sugar over time; add approx. ½ cup (85 g) dark chocolate chips to batter.

School friendly Perfect for recess.

8+ months

Makes 36

Prep 15 mins (+ cooling)

Cook 15 mins

Berry oat brekkie muffins

Vegetarian

Fish free

Sesame free

Soy free

Naturally sweetened with medjool dates, packed with juicy berries and bursting with fibre and healthy fats, these fluffy muffins provide slow-releasing energy to keep adventurous babies fuelled and satisfied. The combination of almond and oat flours creates a light, nourishing texture that's easy for tiny hands to grasp and chew. I love making a batch on Sunday and having them ready to go for breakfast, lunch boxes or after-school snacks. It's the kind of recipe that makes weekday mornings feel calmer.

- 1½ cups (180 g) almond flour
- 1 cup (100 g) oat flour
- 1 teaspoon baking powder
- ½ teaspoon bicarbonate of soda (baking soda)
- 2 pasture-raised or organic eggs
- ½ cup (125 ml) milk of choice
- ⅓ cup (80 ml) melted coconut oil
- 6 (90 g/3¼ oz) pitted soft medjool dates or ⅓ cup (90 g) Date & cinnamon paste (see page 227)
- 1 teaspoon pure vanilla extract or powder
- 1 cup (160 g) mixed fresh berries

Preheat the oven to 180°C (350°F) and line a mini muffin tray with paper cups. (Alternatively, use a silicone muffin tray.)

Place the almond flour, oat flour, baking powder, bicarb, eggs, milk, oil, dates or date paste and vanilla in a food processor or high-speed blender. Process until well combined and smooth, scraping down the side once or twice to help blend evenly. Gently fold in the berries.

Spoon the batter into the prepared muffin tray and bake for 12–15 minutes, or until a cake tester or skewer inserted comes out clean. Allow to cool before serving.

Serve mashed, in small bite-sized pieces or whole for baby-led weaning.

Leftovers Store in an airtight container in the fridge for up to a week or freeze for up to 3 months.

Make it ...

Dairy free Swap milk for coconut, oat or soy milk.

Gluten free Swap oat flour for brown rice flour, buckwheat flour, millet flour or a gluten-free flour blend.

Egg free Swap egg for a store-bought egg replacer, or a flax egg (1 egg = 1 tablespoon ground flaxseed + 45 ml/1½ fl oz warm water) or a chia egg (1 egg = 1 tablespoon chia seed meal + ¼ cup/60 ml water).

Seasonal Swap berries for bananas; if using paste, swap for Apricot & pear or Apple & fig (see page 233).

Fussy-eater proof Blend berries into batter or omit.

Pantry friendly Swap almond and oat flours for 280 g (10 oz) spelt flour or wheat flour.

Family friendly (2+) Use a standard-sized muffin tray; add ¼ cup (30 g) dark chocolate chips to batter and top with more chocolate chips or top with choc date frosting; to sweeten, add ¼–⅓ cup (60–80 ml) pure maple syrup to batter.

Omega-3 toast fingers

6+ months

Serves 4

Prep 5 mins

Cook 5 mins

Dairy free

Egg free

Peanut free

Sesame free

Soy free

Tree nut free

My son would always eat his sardines and mashed avocado. My friends were often in disbelief, but he truly loved them. Babies accept sardines; it's us as parents who tend to turn our noses up at the idea. I encourage you to start with sardines before trying tuna. I've used this methodology with all my clients. On toast fingers with avocado, sardines are a nutrient-dense, omega-3-rich snack. Sardines provide an excellent source of healthy fats, calcium and vitamin D to support bone and brain development, while avocado adds creaminess and essential nutrients.
This simple yet powerful combo is an ideal first finger food.

1 medium avocado (approx. 150 g/5½ oz), peeled and sliced

100–120 g (3½– 4¼ oz) jar sardines in springwater, drained

2 slices wholegrain sourdough bread, toasted

Place the avocado and sardines in a bowl and mash together thoroughly until smooth, ensuring any small bones are crushed (they are fine to remain in the mixture).

Spread a thin layer of the mixture onto the toasted bread. Serve immediately for optimal freshness and taste.

Cut the toast into finger-sized pieces for easy handling.

Make it ...

Gluten free Swap sourdough for gluten-free bread.

Milder Mix sardines with extra avocado or a spoonful of steamed and mashed sweet potato.

Pantry friendly Swap sardines for canned mackerel, tuna or salmon (ensure it's in springwater or extra virgin olive oil).

Fussy-eater proof Spread mashed mixture in a sandwich and add grated low-salt cheese (if dairy free isn't necessary) to mask texture while still offering nutritional benefits.

Family friendly (2+) Sprinkle finely chopped flat-leaf parsley leaves and/or a squeeze of lemon for extra flavour.

Leftovers Avoid storing leftovers, as the avocado may brown and the sardines can develop a strong odour.

Toast for tiny hands

To ensure toast is safe for your baby and minimises choking risk, follow these tips.

- **Avoid over-toasting** Extremely crunchy or dry toast can become a choking hazard, as it may break into hard pieces.
- **Choose quality bread** Opt for wholegrain or sourdough bread with no additives, avoiding bread with large seeds or tough grains.
- **Add moisture** A soft spread, such as mashed avocado, Hummus (see page 224) or yoghurt, can help soften the toast, making it easier to chew and swallow.

Aged 6–8 months (starting solids)

- **Lightly toasted** Toast the bread just enough to firm up slightly without making it crispy or hard. The bread should be soft but sturdy enough to hold toppings.
- **Cut into finger-sized strips** Cut the toast into long, thin pieces (about the size of your index finger) to make it easier for your baby to grasp and self-feed.
- **Avoid crusty ends** Sourdough crusts can be tough for early eaters, so remove the crusts to reduce the risk of gagging.

Aged 8–12 months (more confident eaters)

- **Moderately toasted** Toast the bread slightly longer, ensuring it's still soft enough to chew but firm enough not to become gummy.
- **Cut into small pieces** Babies may prefer smaller, bite-sized squares to encourage self-feeding.

10 baby-friendly toast-finger toppings

- **Scrambled eggs** Soft and fluffy, spread on toast for a protein boost.
- **Tzatziki** A mild cucumber and yoghurt dip made for spreading (see page 238).
- **Mild guacamole** Avocado and lime with a sprinkle of coriander (cilantro).
- **Mashed lentils** Rich in iron and ideal for spooning onto toast.
- **Mashed pumpkin and salmon** A creamy, calcium-rich topping that also pairs well with herbs (see page 26).
- **Tahini & date spread** Spread thinly for added healthy fats and protein (see page 231).
- **Mashed chickpeas and steamed carrot with a drizzle of olive oil** A protein-packed savoury option.
- **Beetroot hummus** Vibrant, slightly sweet and packed with nutrients (see page 224).
- **Peanut butter and banana** Adds protein and potassium, so it's a winning combo.
- **Ricotta and pear mash** Mild ricotta or soft goat's cheese mashed with soft, ripe pear creates a creamy, slightly sweet spread that's rich in calcium and gentle on little tummies.

S
T
T
O
A

10+ months

Serves 3

Prep 15 mins

Cook 10 mins

Pumpkin pie French toast

- Vegetarian
- Dairy free
- Fish free
- Peanut free
- Sesame free
- Soy free
- Tree nut free

This pumpkin French toast is a warm, comforting breakfast packed with nourishing ingredients. The natural sweetness of ripe banana and pumpkin gives this dish a deliciously soft texture, while cinnamon adds a gentle warmth to every bite. Soaked in a wholesome egg and milk mixture, the bread turns beautifully golden and crisp on the outside while staying soft inside. Serve as finger food or top with berries and banana for an energy-fuelled family brekkie.

2 pasture-raised or organic eggs

½ cup (125 ml) coconut milk

1 large (160 g/5½ oz) ripe banana, mashed

½ cup (115 g) steamed or roasted pumpkin (squash)

½–1 tablespoon white chia seeds, to taste

1 teaspoon pure vanilla extract or powder

½ teaspoon ground cinnamon

Coconut oil, for frying

6 slices wholemeal, sourdough or gluten-free toast

Serving suggestions

Natural unsweetened coconut yoghurt

Mashed berries (fresh or frozen)

Mashed or sliced banana

Place the eggs, milk, banana, pumpkin, chia seeds, vanilla and cinnamon in a high-speed blender and blend until smooth. Transfer the mixture to a bowl. (Alternatively, you can mash it all together by hand.)

Heat the oil in a frying pan over medium heat. Dip a bread slice in the egg mixture, thoroughly coating both sides. Allow any excess mixture to drain back into the bowl, then place two or three slices in the pan (depending on the size of your pan). Fry for 2–3 minutes each side, or until golden brown. Repeat with the remaining bread slices.

You can also add coconut yoghurt, soft mashed berries or thin banana slices on top for added sweetness and texture.

For babies 6–9 months, cut the French toast into soft, finger-sized strips that are easy to hold and chew, or mash with banana.

Make it ...

Gluten free Use gluten-free bread.

Hearty Pair it with scrambled eggs or nut butter for added protein.

Seasonal Swap pumpkin for sweet potato.

Pantry friendly Swap chia seeds for flaxseeds.

Family friendly (2+) Serve drizzled with pure maple syrup or raw honey, a sprinkle of ground cinnamon, a handful of fresh berries and a dollop of unsweetened Greek-style, natural or coconut yoghurt for a balanced and satisfying breakfast.

Leftovers Store in an airtight container in the fridge for up to 4 days or freeze for up to 3 months.

6+ months

Serves 2–4

Prep 5 mins

Cook 7 mins

Oat porridge three ways

- Vegetarian
- Egg free
- Fish free
- Peanut free
- Sesame free
- Soy free
- Tree nut free

This nourishing porridge trio offers a comforting breakfast packed with wholesome ingredients and delicious variations for the whole family. Whether you choose the savoury pumpkin, creamy banana blueberry or warming cinnamon pear option, these bowls are a whole new world of textures and flavours for your baby. Oats provide slow-release energy, support digestion and offer essential nutrients, such as B vitamins, iron, protein and magnesium, which all help growing little ones. Add the optional toppings for babies 8 months and over.

Porridge base

1 cup (110 g) rolled or quick oats

2 cups (500 ml) coconut milk of choice, plus extra if needed

1 teaspoon pure vanilla extract or powder (omit for savoury pumpkin version)

1 teaspoon ground cinnamon (omit for savoury pumpkin version)

Combine the porridge base ingredients in a saucepan. Add the ingredients for your chosen flavour variation.

Bring to a gentle simmer over low heat and cook, stirring frequently, for 5–7 minutes, or until thick and creamy. Add extra milk or some boiled water for a runnier consistency if needed.

Mash or purée the porridge for a smoother consistency.

For babies 8+ months, offer the porridge in a thick texture for finger feeding or preload a spoon for self-feeding and add any of the optional toppings.

Make it ...

Dairy free Use plant-based milk, such as coconut, almond or oat, and use natural unsweetened coconut yoghurt as optional topping; for pumpkin version, use extra virgin olive oil instead of butter and swap cheese for nutritional yeast flakes or omit.

Gluten free Swap oats for brown rice or quinoa flakes, or certified gluten-free oats.

Batch cooked Make a big batch for the family – it lasts for 4 days in the fridge and can be heated up for a quick and easy breakfast.

Family friendly (2+) Add a variety of fun toppings to boost flavour and texture, like grated low-salt cheese for a savoury twist, a sprinkle of chia seeds for added fibre, 1 tablespoon almond butter for healthy fats, or a dollop of natural unsweetened yoghurt for extra calcium and richness.

Leftovers Store in an airtight container in the fridge for 4 days or freeze for up to 3 months.

1. Savoury pumpkin

½ cup (100 g) mashed steamed or roasted pumpkin (squash)

½ teaspoon flaxseed meal

¼ teaspoon ground nutmeg

Drizzle of olive oil or small knob of unsalted butter (optional)

Optional topping (8+ months)

1 tablespoon grated low-salt cheese (for extra creaminess)

2. Banana blueberry

1 medium (110 g/3 ¾ oz) ripe banana, mashed

½ cup (80 g) blueberries (fresh or frozen)

Optional toppings (8+ months)

Sliced banana

Sprinkle of chia seeds

Small dollop of natural unsweetened yoghurt (for extra creaminess)

3. Cinnamon pear

½ cup (100 g) grated, finely diced or puréed pear

½ teaspoon ground cinnamon

Optional toppings (8+ months)

Pear slices

Sprinkle of crushed pepitas (pumpkin seeds) or crushed sunflower seeds (for texture)

Small dollop of natural unsweetened yoghurt (for extra creaminess)

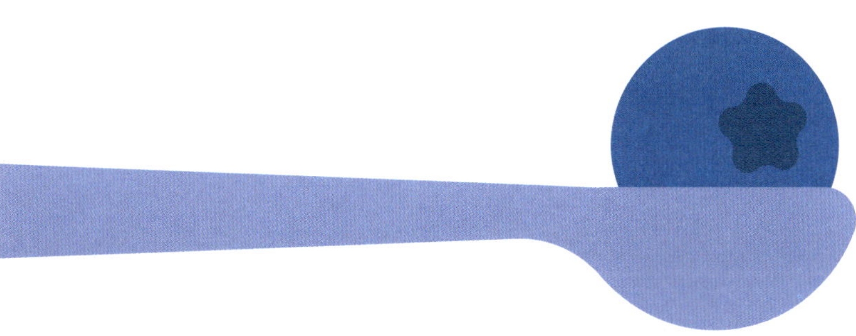

8+ months

Serves 6

Prep 5 mins

Cook 25 mins

Tummy-warming bean shakshuka

 Vegetarian

 Dairy free

 Fish free

 Gluten free

 Peanut free

 Sesame free

 Soy free

 Tree nut free

Show your little one how delicious eggs can be by baking them in a tomato and bean sauce. Packed with protein, along with iron-rich spinach and vitamin C from capsicum (pepper) and tomato, this dish is a nutrient-dense powerhouse for your baby and everyone else at the table. It's also an excellent way to boost everyone's veggie intake at breakfast.

½ medium (75 g/2½ oz) brown onion, chopped

½ (120 g/4¼ oz) red capsicum (pepper), seeds removed and chopped

1–2 garlic cloves, to taste

1 tablespoon extra virgin olive oil

1 teaspoon sweet paprika

1 teaspoon ground cumin

400 g (14 oz) can cannellini beans, drained and rinsed

1½ cups (375 ml) tomato passata (puréed tomatoes)

1–2 tablespoons Date & cinnamon paste (see page 227) or unsweetened 100 per cent pear purée (homemade or store-bought)

½–1 cup (15–30 g) baby spinach, finely chopped (depending on how fussy your little eater is, optional)

6 pasture-raised or organic eggs

Preheat the oven to 180°C (350°F).

Place the onion, capsicum and garlic in a food processor and process until finely crushed or puréed, scraping down the side once or twice to help blend evenly.

In a large ovenproof frying pan or skillet, heat the oil and cook the mixture for 3–5 minutes, or until softened.

Add the spices, beans, passata and date paste or pear purée and simmer for 10 minutes.

Stir in the spinach (if using) until wilted, then gently crack the eggs over the sauce. Do not stir.

Transfer the pan to the oven. Bake for 10–15 minutes, or until cooked through.

It's best to ensure the eggs are cooked through and to offer strips of egg alongside mashed shakshuka sauce with toast soldiers for dipping.

Make it ...

Seasonal Swap spinach for greens of choice.

Creamy Add a dollop of natural unsweetened yoghurt and avocado slices for a fresh/creamy contrast.

Pantry friendly Swap cannellini for canned/cooked legumes or beans of choice.

Fussy-eater proof Mash beans before serving; purée sauce after spinach wilts; omit spinach.

Family friendly (2+) Sprinkle goat's cheese on top (if dairy free isn't necessary) or serve with warm Soft naan (see page 230), wholegrain toast (if gluten free isn't necessary) or over a bed of quinoa or couscous for a filling meal.

Leftovers Store in an airtight container in the fridge for up to 3 days.

Anytime egg muffins

8+ months

Makes 12 mini muffins

Prep 15 mins (+ cooling)

Cook 20 mins

Vegetarian

Fish free

Gluten free

Peanut free

Sesame free

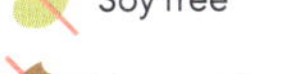
Soy free

Tree nut free

A batch of these in the fridge or freezer has been a lifesaver for me many times. You know that frantic moment when you needed to be out the door five minutes ago, baby is on your hip wanting some attention and the bag is not packed? That was always the moment I'd pull out a couple of these muffins, hastily pop them in a container and run out the door. Packed with protein from eggs and ricotta, along with the gentle flavours of pumpkin and broccoli, they have the nutrients your child needs to thrive. And all the convenience you need as a parent.

- Butter or coconut oil, for greasing
- 1 tablespoon finely chopped onion
- ½ cup (115 g) steamed or roasted pumpkin (squash), cooled
- ¼ cup (50 g) steamed broccoli, cooled
- 2 large pasture-raised or organic eggs
- ½ cup (125 g) smooth ricotta
- 1 tablespoon fresh mixed herbs

Serving suggestion

- Soft fruit slices, such as avocado or banana

Preheat the oven to 180°C (350°F) and grease 12 holes of a mini muffin tray with some butter or coconut oil.

Place the onion, pumpkin and broccoli in a food processor and process until finely chopped or puréed, scraping down the side once or twice to help chop evenly.

In a medium bowl, combine the eggs, ricotta and herbs. Add the vegetable mixture and stir until well combined.

Divide the batter evenly among the prepared muffin pans. Bake for 15–20 minutes, or until cooked through. Allow to cool before serving.

Serve the muffins whole or in halves, depending on your baby's confidence with finger foods. Pair with soft fruit slices for a balanced and nourishing meal.

Make it ...

Dairy free Swap ricotta for coconut cream and use coconut oil for greasing.

Cheesy Top with grated low-salt cheese before baking.

Seasonal Swap pumpkin and broccoli for steamed or roasted vegetables of choice.

Family friendly (2+) Serve as a grab-and-go breakfast or finger food platter addition; pair with a side of leafy greens or a dollop of natural unsweetened yoghurt and fresh herbs for a delicious and balanced meal.

School friendly Perfect lunch-box filler for recess.

Leftovers Store in an airtight container in the fridge for up to 3 days or freeze for up to 3 months.

6+ months

Makes 12

Prep 10 mins

Cook 10 mins

Sweet potato & cinnamon pancakes

Vegetarian

Dairy free

Fish free

Gluten free

Peanut free

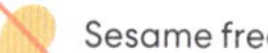
Sesame free

Soy free

Soft, naturally sweet and packed with nourishing ingredients, these are a great first pancake for babies from 6 months onwards. The sweet potato, banana and almond meal means they're full of fibre, healthy fats and essential nutrients to support little tummies. The eggs provide protein for growing bodies, while cinnamon adds a gentle warmth and flavour. The soft texture and easy-to-hold shape make self-feeding easy, whether served plain, with a smear of nut butter or topped with fresh fruit for older children. It's a simple, delicious way to start the day!

4 pasture-raised or organic eggs

1 small (80 g/2¾ oz) ripe banana

1½ cups (300 g) steamed or roasted sweet potato

3 tablespoons almond meal

½ –1 teaspoon ground cinnamon, to taste

Coconut oil, for frying

Place all the ingredients, except the oil, in a food processor and process until smooth, scraping down the side once or twice to help blend evenly.

Brush a large frying pan with oil and heat over medium heat. In batches, spoon about 2 tablespoonfuls of batter into the pan and cook for 2–3 minutes on each side.

Serve mashed or as finger food.

Make it ...

Nut free Swap almond meal for coconut flour, buckwheat flour or wholemeal spelt flour (if gluten free isn't necessary).

Seasonal Swap sweet potato for pumpkin.

Different For babies 8+ months, swap sweet potato for ricotta or natural unsweetened or coconut yoghurt.

Family friendly (2+) Top with natural unsweetened or coconut yoghurt, sliced banana and a drizzle of raw honey or pure maple syrup (optional).

Leftovers Store in an airtight container in the fridge for up to 3 days or freeze for up to 3 months.

8+ months

Makes 16

Prep 10 mins (+ cooling)

Cook 15 mins

Yoghurt blueberry pancakes

Soft, fluffy and naturally sweetened with medjool dates and juicy blueberries, serve up these berry pancakes as breakfast or a snack from 8 months onwards. The Greek-style yoghurt adds a boost of protein and calcium to support growing bones, while wholemeal spelt flour provides gentle fibre for digestion. Have a fussy eater in your house? Blend the batter, blueberries and all, before cooking.

- Vegetarian
- Fish free
- Peanut free
- Sesame free
- Soy free
- Tree nut free

1 large pasture-raised or organic egg

½ cup (130 g) natural unsweetened Greek-style yoghurt

½ cup (125 ml) milk of choice

3 (45 g/1½ oz) pitted soft medjool dates

1 tablespoon melted coconut oil, plus extra for greasing

1 teaspoon pure vanilla extract or powder

1 cup (150 g) wholemeal spelt flour

1 teaspoon baking powder

Pinch of ground cinnamon

½ cup (80 g) blueberries (fresh or frozen)

Serving suggestions

Berry chia jam (see page 228)

Banana, cut into fingers and halved

Crushed blueberries (fresh or frozen)

Place the egg, yoghurt, milk, dates, oil and vanilla in a food processor and process until smooth, scraping down the side once or twice to help blend evenly.

In a large bowl, sift together the flour, baking powder and cinnamon. Slowly add the wet mixture, stirring gently, until combined. Be careful not to over-mix – it's okay if the batter is a bit lumpy.

Gently fold in the blueberries, being careful not to crush them.

Heat a frying pan over medium heat and lightly grease with extra oil. Scoop about ¼ cupfuls of batter onto the pan to form pancakes. Cook for 2–3 minutes each side, or until golden brown and cooked through. Stack the pancakes on a plate to cool. Repeat with the remaining batter, regreasing the pan between batches.

Serve mashed or as finger food, spread with berry chia jam or with banana or crushed blueberries on the side, if you like.

Make it ...

Dairy free Swap yoghurt for natural unsweetened coconut yoghurt.

Gluten free Swap flour for buckwheat flour or a gluten-free flour of choice.

Egg free Swap egg for a large ripe mashed banana.

Seasonal Swap blueberries for berries of choice.

Boosted Add 1–2 teaspoons flaxseed meal or chia seeds to batter.

Fussy-eater proof Omit blueberries; blend batter in a blender until smooth.

Family friendly (2+) To sweeten, add 1–2 teaspoons of raw honey or pure maple syrup to batter; top pancakes with yoghurt, berries and/or a drizzle of maple syrup or honey.

Leftovers Store in an airtight container in the fridge for up to 4 days or freeze for up to 3 months.

8+ months

Makes 8

Prep 5 mins

Cook 15 mins

Beetroot & buckwheat crepes

 Vegetarian

 Dairy free

Fish free

 Gluten free

 Peanut free

 Sesame free

 Soy free

These vibrant, pretty-in-pink crepes are a nutritious and versatile addition to your family's mealtime. There are lots of nourishing ingredients and no refined sugar - a delicious way to support growing appetites while keeping mealtimes fun and colourful. Nothing store-bought here! Naturally gluten free and packed with fibre, protein and essential nutrients, the crepes are a gentle way to introduce earthy beetroot and wholesome buckwheat. And there are plenty of ways to serve them: in plain strips, rolled with a savoury filling or topped with fruit for a naturally sweet option. Note: Some optional fillings contain allergens, such as dairy, wheat or fish, so adjust according to your child's dietary needs.

1 cup (120 g) buckwheat flour

1½ cups (375 ml) almond milk

2 pasture-raised or organic eggs

1 teaspoon coconut oil, plus extra for frying

¼ cup, tightly packed (60 g) grated beetroot

1–2 (15–30 g/½–1 oz) pitted soft medjool dates (optional, for sweet crepes)

Optional savoury fillings

Mashed avocado and goat's cheese

Scrambled eggs and avocado

Hummus (see page 224) and steamed, mashed veggies

Ricotta and steamed pumpkin (squash)

Omega-3 toast fingers (see page 94)

Optional sweet fillings

Nut or seed butter and mashed berries or banana

Berry chia jam (see page 228) and ricotta

Mashed banana and ground cinnamon

Chopped fresh fruit and natural unsweetened yoghurt or coconut cream

Place all the ingredients in a food processor or high-speed blender and process until smooth and creamy, scraping down the side once or twice to help blend evenly.

Brush a small frying pan with a little extra coconut oil. Place over medium heat. Pour ½ cup (125 ml) of batter into the pan and swirl to cover the base.

Cook for 2–3 minutes, or until light golden. Flip over and cook for another minute. Transfer to a plate, covering to keep warm. Repeat with the remaining the batter, regreasing the pan as needed.

Spread an optional filling over the crepes (if using) and serve torn into strips for easy grasping or cut them into bite-sized pieces for self-feeding.

Opt for a mild filling, like mashed avocado or hummus and steamed and mashed pumpkin. If serving as a sweet option, spread with berry chia jam or mashed banana with a sprinkle of cinnamon.

For babies 10+ months, fill the crepes with your preferred savoury or sweet options, roll up and slice into halves or quarters and serve as finger food or you can mash.

Make it ...

Nut free Swap milk for nut-free milk of choice.

Seasonal Swap beetroot for carrot or parsnip.

Different Swap flour for brown rice flour, wholemeal spelt flour or oat flour.

Pantry friendly Swap coconut oil for unsalted butter or ghee and almond milk for milk of choice.

Family friendly (2+) Serve with a salad, roasted veggies or a yoghurt dip for a balanced meal; for extra flavour, add fresh herbs, a squeeze of lemon or a drizzle of raw honey.

Leftovers Store (unfilled) in the fridge for up to 4 days or freeze for up to 3 months.

8+ months

Serves 4

Prep 10 mins (+ 4 hrs chilling)

Overnight puddings three ways

Vegan

Dairy free

Egg free

Fish free

Peanut free

Sesame free

Soy free

We love starting our mornings with this quick and easy overnight chia and oat pudding. It's a versatile, nutrient-rich breakfast or snack. It has a base rich in fibre and healthy fats, and the three delicious flavour variations – strawberry coconut, sticky date and apple pie – provide a variety of textures and tastes to keep things interesting. Packed with natural sweetness and nourishing ingredients, it's great for babies, toddlers and children.

Pudding base

1 cup (110 g) rolled or quick oats

¼ cup (40 g) chia seeds

1¾ cups (435 ml) coconut milk

½ teaspoon pure vanilla extract or powder

½ teaspoon ground cinnamon

Combine the pudding base ingredients in a medium bowl. Stir well to mix everything together. Cover the bowl and refrigerate for at least 4 hours or overnight to allow the oats to soften and chia seeds to soak up the liquid.

Add your chosen flavour variation ingredients to the pudding mixture and stir through.

Serve the pudding mashed or blended for a smoother texture. Spoonfeed or allow your baby to explore by self-feeding with a pre-loaded spoon. The strawberry coconut variation is especially gentle for early eaters.

Make it ...

Gluten free Swap oats for brown rice or quinoa flakes or certified gluten-free oats.

Pantry friendly Swap dates or paste for Apricot & pear or Apple & fig paste (see page 233).

Family friendly (2+) Swap coconut milk for milk of choice; serve chilled with a sprinkle of extra chopped fruit, nuts or seeds for added crunch; layer pudding with yoghurt and fruit for a fun parfait-style breakfast or snack; for a warm, comforting option, briefly warm the apple pie variation before serving.

Leftovers Store in an airtight container in the fridge for up to 4 days or freeze for up to 3 months.

1. Strawberry coconut

⅓ cup (55 g) strawberries (fresh or frozen), chopped or puréed

1 tablespoon coconut cream or natural unsweetened coconut yoghurt

1–2 tablespoons Date & cinnamon paste (optional for extra sweetness, see page 227)

2. Apple pie

1 small (130 g/4½ oz) apple, peeled, cored and grated or puréed

1 tablespoon sulphur-free sultanas

1 tablespoon finely chopped or ground walnuts or almonds (optional)

Pinch of ground cinnamon

3. Sticky date

1 medium (110 g/3¾ oz) ripe banana, mashed

2 (30 g/1 oz) pitted soft medjool dates, thinly sliced and mixed with ½ teaspoon ground cinnamon or 2 tablespoons Date & cinnamon paste (see page 227)

8+ months

Serves 6–8

Prep 15 mins (+ cooling)

Cook 30 mins

Coconut berry crumble with cinnamon yoghurt

 Vegetarian

 Egg free

 Fish free

 Peanut free

 Sesame free

 Soy free

 Tree nut free

Berry filling

600 g (1 lb 5 oz) mixed berries (fresh or frozen)

1 teaspoon pure vanilla extract or powder

1 tablespoon chia seeds

Crumble topping

¼ cup (40 g) wholemeal spelt flour

⅓ cup (35 g) pepitas (pumpkin seeds)

½ cup (55 g) rolled or quick oats

½ cup (40 g) desiccated coconut

3 (45 g/1½ oz) pitted soft medjool dates

1 teaspoon ground cinnamon

¼ cup (60 ml) melted coconut oil

1 teaspoon pure vanilla extract or powder

Cinnamon yoghurt

2 cups (520 g) natural unsweetened Greek-style yoghurt

1 teaspoon ground cinnamon

This was one of the very first warm desserts I made when my babies started solids and, to this day, it's still a family favourite. The natural sweetness of the berries, the soft crumble topping and the hint of cinnamon make it both nourishing and comforting. I loved watching my little ones explore the soft textures and vibrant colours with wide-eyed curiosity. Now, we often enjoy it together as a weekend breakfast or cosy afternoon treat. We always have a swirl of creamy cinnamon yoghurt on the side.

Preheat the oven to 180°C (350°F).

Place the berry filling ingredients in a medium saucepan and cook over medium–low heat for 5 minutes, or until the berries have softened. Transfer the mixture to a 23 cm (9 in) round baking dish and set aside.

Place the crumble topping ingredients in a food processor and process until a crumble consistency is reached, scraping down the side once or twice to help blend evenly.

Cover the berry filling with the crumble topping. Bake for 20–25 minutes, or until golden brown.

Meanwhile, mix the yoghurt and cinnamon in a small bowl.

Allow the crumble to cool, then offer small spoonfuls or serve soft chunks of crumble with a side of the cinnamon yoghurt for dipping to encourage self-feeding.

Make it ...

Dairy free Swap yoghurt for natural unsweetened coconut yoghurt.

Gluten free Swap oats for brown rice or quinoa flakes, or certified gluten-free oats, and flour with gluten-free flour of choice.

Crunchy For older children and adults, sprinkle with chopped nuts or seeds.

Seasonal Swap berries for seasonal fruit of choice.

Fussy-eater proof Deconstruct this meal by serving crumble, berry filling and cinnamon yoghurt separately.

Family friendly (2+) Serve warm with a generous dollop of cinnamon yoghurt on top for a comforting dessert or breakfast; to sweeten, add 2 tablespoons pure maple syrup to filling; enjoy on its own or pair with a scoop of vanilla ice cream for a special treat.

Leftovers Store in an airtight container in the fridge for up to 4 days or freeze for up to 3 months.

8+ months

Serves 2

Prep 5 mins

Cook 5 mins

Cheesy chia omelette

Vegetarian

Fish free

Gluten free

Peanut free

Sesame free

Soy free

Tree nut free

This quick and easy omelette is a great way to incorporate eggs, an important first food for babies. Eggs are rich in essential nutrients such as choline, which supports brain development, while chia seeds provide a boost of healthy fats, fibre and plant-based omega-3s. This soft and fluffy omelette suits little ones learning to self-feed, while being just as satisfying for older children and adults. Make it your go-to for busy mornings or family lunches.

2 pasture-raised or organic eggs

2 tablespoons milk of choice

1 teaspoon chia seeds

Pinch of freshly ground black pepper (optional)

1 teaspoon extra virgin olive oil, ghee or butter

¼ cup, loosely packed (35 g) grated mozzarella

Serving suggestions

Gluten-free toast fingers or sourdough toast fingers (if gluten free isn't necessary)

Sautéed mushrooms

Tomato sauce (see page 239)

Steamed veggies

Avocado

Crack the eggs into a bowl and whisk them well. Stir in the milk and chia seeds. They'll help make the omelette extra fluffy and add a bit of crunch! Season with pepper (if using).

Heat the oil, ghee or butter in a non-stick pan over medium heat. Pour in the egg mixture, swirling the pan to cover the base evenly. As it starts to set, sprinkle over the mozzarella. Cook for 2–3 minutes, then fold the omelette in half and let the cheese melt inside.

Serve the omelette with sourdough toast fingers, sautéed mushrooms and tomato sauce.

For babies 6–7 months, cut the omelette into soft, finger-sized strips for baby-led weaning or mash it into a smooth texture for spoonfeeding. Pair with toast fingers, steamed veggies or avocado for a balanced meal.

Make it ...

Dairy free Omit mozzarella or swap for nutritional yeast flakes and use coconut milk.

Egg free Swap eggs for crumbled tofu.

Boosted Serve with mashed leftover roast or steamed vegetables.

Different Swap mozzarella for goat's cheese.

Family friendly (2+) Serve with roasted tomatoes and/or sautéed spinach for a nourishing breakfast or light lunch; sprinkle with extra herbs to enhance flavour.

Leftovers Store in an airtight container in the fridge for up to 2 days.

6+ months

Makes 10–15

Prep 5 mins (+ cooling)

Cook 10 mins

Summer's green pancakes

Vegetarian

Dairy free

Fish free

Peanut free

Sesame free

Soy free

Tree nut free

These are my daughter Summer's favourite pancakes. They offer a fun and gentle way to incorporate leafy greens in your little one's diet. Packed with iron-rich spinach to support healthy development and naturally sweetened with banana, they're soft, fluffy and easy for little hands to grab and explore. Whether your baby is starting solids or moving on to finger foods, these pancakes are a delicious mix of nutrients and flavour. Plus, they're versatile enough to grow with your child, making them a staple you'll come back to again and again. Batch cook these vibrant pancakes and freeze, so you have a quick, nutrient-packed option ready whenever you need it!

1 cup (30 g) baby spinach

2 large pasture-raised or organic eggs

¾ cup (95 g) oat flour

¼ cup (60 ml) coconut milk

1 small (80 g/2¾ oz) ripe banana

½ teaspoon baking powder

½ teaspoon bicarbonate of soda (baking soda)

Pinch of ground cinnamon

1 teaspoon extra virgin olive oil or coconut oil, for cooking

Serving suggestions

Tahini or nut butter (if sesame or tree nut free isn't necessary)

Sliced fresh berries

Natural unsweetened coconut yoghurt

Steam or boil the spinach until softened, then finely chop.

Place the spinach, eggs, flour, milk, banana, baking powder, bicarb and cinnamon in a high-speed blender and blend until smooth and creamy.

Heat a non-stick frying pan over medium–low heat and lightly coat with the oil. Drop spoonfuls of the batter into the pan, flattening each slightly into small rounds. Cook for 2–3 minutes each side, or until golden brown and firm enough for the baby to pick up.

Allow pancakes to cool slightly before serving.

Serve mashed or cut into small pieces and serve as finger food, ideal for little hands to grab and explore.

For children 2+, serve as mini snack-sized pancakes with a smear of tahini or nut butter and berries, or stack them up and dollop with coconut yoghurt for a fun breakfast twist.

Make it ...

Gluten free Swap flour for chickpea, buckwheat, millet or gluten-free flour blend.

Savoury Top with mashed avocado and/or grated low-salt cheese.

Seasonal Swap spinach for kale, silverbeet or greens of choice.

Boosted Add 1 teaspoon chia seeds to batter.

Family friendly (2+) Sprinkle with chopped seeds or nuts for extra crunch; to sweeten, add a drizzle of pure maple syrup.

Leftovers Store in an airtight container in the fridge for up to 4 days or freeze for up to 3 months.

Mains

6+ months

Serves 8

Prep 15 mins

Cook 2 hrs 15 mins

Hearty beef stew

 Dairy free

 Egg free

Fish free

 Gluten free

 Peanut free

 Sesame free

 Soy free

 Tree nut free

There's something so heartwarming about sharing a slow-cooked meal with my little ones, especially when it's passed down to me from my mum. This is a real favourite in our home – one of those comforting meals that brings everyone to the table and fills hungry bellies with goodness. Made with tender beef, sweet parsnip and soft carrot, it's rich in iron, protein and essential nutrients to support your children's growth and development. The soft, melt-in-the-mouth texture is ideal for curious little eaters – whether you're spoonfeeding or letting your baby explore finger foods.

1 kg (2 lb 4 oz) grass-fed beef rump steak, chopped

2½ tablespoons extra virgin olive oil

1 small (100 g/3½ oz) brown onion, finely diced

2 (80 g/2¾ oz) celery stalks, finely diced

2 large (320 g/11¼ oz) carrots, peeled and finely diced

1 large (160 g/5½ oz) parsnip, peeled and finely diced

2 tablespoons arrowroot

3 cups (750 ml) low-salt beef or vegetable stock or Bone broth (see page 223)

4 thyme sprigs

Serving suggestions

Soft-cooked brown rice, millet or quinoa

Potato mash

Preheat the oven to 180°C (350°F).

Rub the beef with 1½ tablespoons oil. Heat a large frying pan over medium heat, then sear the beef on both sides until browned. Transfer to a medium casserole dish.

In the same pan, add the remaining 1 tablespoon of oil, then the onion. Sauté for 2 minutes, or until softened. Add the celery, carrot and parsnip and cook for another 2 minutes.

Sprinkle with the arrowroot and stir until everything is coated.

Gradually pour in the stock or broth, then add the thyme and bring to the boil. Let it simmer for 2–3 minutes before transferring it to the casserole dish. Cover with foil. Bake for 1½–2 hours, or until the meat is tender.

Serve mashed, with rice or potato mash.

For babies 9+ months, offer small, tender chunks of beef and vegetables, cut into bite-sized pieces, and serve with rice, millet, quinoa or mashed potato.

Tip You can also cook this in a pressure cooker. Instead of transferring the beef to a casserole dish, transfer to the pressure cooker. Add the vegetable mixture and cook for 30 minutes–1 hour.

Make it ...

Seasonal Swap carrot and parsnip for root vegetables of choice, such as pumpkin, sweet potato, potato, swede or turnip.

Boosted Add 2–3 cups (60–90 g) baby spinach in the last 5 minutes of cooking.

Fussy-eater proof Purée vegetables until smooth before adding to casserole dish; serve beef and vegetables separately.

Family friendly (2+) Add 1–2 teaspoons tamari or soy sauce.

Leftovers Store in an airtight container in the fridge for up to 3 days or freeze for up to 3 months.

6+ months

Makes 16–20

Prep 15 mins

Cook 35 mins

Iron-rich lamb & veggie balls

 Dairy free

 Fish free

 Gluten free

 Peanut free

 Sesame free

 Soy free

 Tree nut free

Watch those little hands grab and squish soft, juicy meatballs. They are learning how to self-feed while being introduced to iron-rich lamb – and having fun doing it! Around 6 months and beyond is a critical iron-boosting window for babies, so make these meatballs and stock the freezer. Easy to prep ahead, they work beautifully as part of a main meal, in lunch boxes or even served cold on the go. Packed with finely grated veggies for extra fibre, flavour and goodness, I've designed these to be naturally tender. Yes, there'll be mess, but there'll also be joy as they learn to feed themselves.

1 small (100 g/3½ oz) brown onion, quartered

2 garlic cloves

2 medium (260 g/9¼ oz) carrots, peeled and roughly chopped

1 medium (160 g/5½ oz) zucchini (courgette), peeled and roughly chopped

1 pasture-raised or organic egg

500 g (1 lb 2 oz) grass-fed minced (ground) lamb

¼ cup (35 g) Gluten-free crumb mix or Rice 'breadcrumbs' (see page 243)

2 tablespoons arrowroot

1 tablespoon finely chopped flat-leaf parsley leaves

1 teaspoon dried Italian herbs

Serving suggestions

Sweet potato mash

Sweet potato wedges

Steamed veggies

Preheat the oven to 180°C (350°F) and line a large baking tray with baking paper.

Place the onion, garlic, carrot, zucchini and egg in a food processor. Process until crushed, scraping down the side once or twice to help chop evenly.

Place the lamb in a large bowl and add the vegetable mixture and remaining ingredients. Mix until well combined.

Roll the mixture into small balls, approx. ¼ cup per meatball, then place on the prepared tray. Bake for 30–35 minutes, or until golden brown and cooked through.

Serve the meatballs mashed or in soft chunks alongside mashed sweet potato and steamed vegetables.

For babies 9+ months, serve whole or cut into bite-sized pieces alongside soft sweet potato wedges and steamed veggies.

Make it ...

Egg free Swap egg for a store-bought egg replacer, or a flax egg (1 egg = 1 tablespoon ground flaxseed + 45 ml/1½ fl oz warm water) or a chia egg (1 egg = 1 tablespoon chia seed meal + ¼ cup/60 ml water).

Seasonal Swap vegetables for seasonal vegetables of choice.

Different Swap mince for beef mince.

Faster Press mixture into a lined baking dish and bake as a meatloaf.

Pantry friendly Swap arrowroot for tapioca flour or any flour of choice.

Fussy-eater proof Make sure vegetables are puréed and not detectable.

Family friendly (2+) Serve in a wrap or with potato mash or wedges and Tomato sauce (see page 239).

Leftovers Store in an airtight container in the fridge for up to 3 days or freeze for up to 3 months.

6+ months

Makes 16

Prep 15 mins (+ cooling)

Cook 55 mins

 Dairy free

 Fish free

 Gluten free

 Peanut free

 Sesame free

 Soy free

 Tree nut free

Chicken & zucchini meatballs in roasted capsicum sauce

Shh ... the bigger kids will never know there's hidden veg rolled into these chicken meatballs! And the little kids will love the naturally sweet, smoky roasted capsicum sauce they're baked in. I love that these suit everyone at the table – no separate meals needed! For bigger appetites, add sweet potato wedges and top with extra sauce.

1 medium (100 g/3½ oz) carrot, peeled and roughly chopped

1 small (130 g/4½ oz) zucchini (courgette), roughly chopped

1 small (130 g/4½ oz) apple, cored and roughly chopped

½ medium (75 g/2½ oz) brown onion, roughly chopped

1 garlic clove

⅓ cup (10 g) baby spinach

2 tablespoons flat-leaf parsley leaves

1 pasture-raised or organic egg

½ cup (75 g) Gluten-free crumb mix or Rice 'breadcrumbs' (see page 243), plus extra if needed

600 g (1 lb 5 oz) pasture-raised or organic minced (ground) chicken

Roasted capsicum sauce

2 medium (500 g/1 lb 2 oz) red capsicums (peppers), seeds removed and cut into chunks

1 small (100 g/3½ oz) brown onion, cut into wedges

3 garlic cloves, unpeeled

2 teaspoons dried oregano

2 tablespoons extra virgin olive oil

400 g (14 oz) tomato passata (puréed tomatoes)

Serving suggestions

Potato mash

Steamed veggies

Preheat the oven to 220°C (425°F) and line a large baking tray with baking paper.

To make the capsicum sauce, place the capsicum, onion and garlic on the prepared tray. Sprinkle with oregano, drizzle with oil and toss to coat. Bake for 20–25 minutes, or until golden brown and well roasted.

Cool slightly, then squeeze the garlic out of the skins into a high-speed blender or food processor. Add the capsicum, onion and passata and blend until smooth. Pour the sauce into a large casserole dish or deep baking tray.

Reduce the oven temperature to 200°C (400°F).

Place the carrot, zucchini, apple, onion, garlic, spinach and parsley in the clean blender or processor and process until smooth, scraping down the side once or twice to help blend evenly.

In a large bowl, combine the vegetable mixture with the remaining ingredients, adding extra crumbs if the mixture needs to be firmer.

Roll the mixture into small balls, approx. ¼ cup per ball, and place in the sauce in the dish. Bake for 25–30 minutes, or until the meatballs are cooked through.

Serve mashed or as finger food with mashed potato and steamed veggies.

Make it ...

Egg free Swap egg for a store-bought egg replacer, or a flax egg (1 egg = 1 tablespoon ground flaxseed + 45 ml/1½ fl oz warm water) or a chia egg (1 egg = 1 tablespoon chia seed meal + ¼ cup/60 ml water).

Seasonal Swap carrot and zucchini for vegetables of choice, such as pumpkin (squash), parsnip, sweet potato, swede or turnip; swap apple for pear or another vegetable.

Pantry friendly Swap crumb mix or rice 'breadcrumbs' for pumpkin seed meal.

Fussy-eater proof Sprinkle with low-salt cheese or additive-free breadcrumbs to help acceptance; deconstruct meal by serving meatballs, sauce, mash and steamed veggies separately.

Family friendly (2+) Add 1 tablespoon low-salt tamari and 1–2 teaspoons balsamic vinegar to capsicum sauce before blending; serve with roast sweet potato wedges and sprinkle with grated parmesan.

Leftovers Store in an airtight container in the fridge for up to 3 days or freeze for up to 3 months.

6+ months

Serves 8

Prep 15 mins

Cook 40 mins

 Vegetarian

 Dairy free

 Egg free

 Fish free

 Gluten free

 Peanut free

 Sesame free

 Soy free

 Tree nut free

Easy lentil & sweet potato pot

Fill tummies with this budget-friendly, vegetarian stew. I love that it requires just a few simple steps before I let it bubble away on the stove for 30 minutes – just enough time to get the kids bathed and in their PJs before dinnertime. Growing up, my babies always devoured this. I 'blame' the creamy coconut base! Pair that with gentle spices and the natural sweetness of sweet potato, and the tiny tastebuds in your house will be hooked too!

1 small (50 g/1¾ oz) brown onion, roughly chopped

2 garlic cloves

2 cm (¾ in) knob of ginger

1 (40 g/1½ oz) celery stalk, roughly chopped

1 small (80 g/2¾ oz) carrot, roughly chopped

1 tablespoon extra virgin olive oil

½ teaspoon ground coriander

½ teaspoon ground cumin

½ teaspoon ground turmeric

500 g (1 lb 2 oz) sweet potato, peeled and chopped

2 × 400 g (14 oz) cans or 800 g (1 lb 12 oz) cooked brown lentils, drained and rinsed

400 ml (14 fl oz) can coconut milk

2 cups (500 ml) low-salt vegetable stock or homemade broth (salt free for babies)

Freshly ground black pepper, to taste (optional)

Serving suggestions

Mashed avocado

Natural unsweetened yoghurt (if dairy free isn't necessary)

Place the onion, garlic, ginger, celery and carrot in a food processor and process until finely crushed, scraping down the side once or twice to help blend evenly.

Heat the oil in a large saucepan over medium heat. Add the onion mixture and sauté for 2–3 minutes. Add the spices and cook for another minute, stirring continuously.

Add the sweet potato, lentils, coconut milk and stock or broth and bring to the boil. Reduce the heat to low and simmer for 30 minutes.

Season with pepper (if using).

Mash or purée the mixture to desired consistency, ensuring any large sweet potato chunks are softened for easy chewing. Serve with a side of mashed avocado or a spoonful of yoghurt for added creaminess.

Make it ...

Vegan Swap yoghurt for natural unsweetened coconut yoghurt.

Seasonal Swap vegetables for vegetables of choice.

Pantry friendly Swap lentils for cooked legumes of choice.

Fussy-eater proof Make sure onion mixture is processed until very smooth.

Family friendly (2+) Serve over brown rice, quinoa or couscous or with warm Soft naan (see page 230) or steamed veggies for a heartier meal; add a sprinkle of coriander (cilantro) leaves, a dollop of natural unsweetened coconut yoghurt or a squeeze of fresh lime for a flavour boost.

School friendly Delicious in wraps or pack warm in a thermos for lunch.

Leftovers Store in an airtight container in the fridge for up to 3 days or freeze for up to 3 months.

Classic bolognese

8+ months

Serves 5

Prep 15 mins

Cook 40 mins

Dairy free

Egg free

Fish free

Peanut free

Sesame free

Soy free

Tree nut free

This iron-rich bolognese has been a go-to in my kitchen ever since I started introducing my babies to family meals. Made with grass-fed beef, iron-rich spinach and plenty of soft-cooked veggies, it's a great way to explore new textures while supporting healthy growth and development. The slow-simmered flavours create a naturally rich and delicious sauce that pairs beautifully with soft pasta, making it easy for babies to enjoy. This is a family favourite and often goes to school with my daughter in a thermos the next day.

- 1 tablespoon extra virgin olive oil
- 1 small (100 g/3½ oz) brown onion, finely chopped
- 2 garlic cloves, crushed
- 1 (40 g/1½ oz) celery stalk, finely chopped
- 500 g (1 lb 2 oz) grass-fed minced (ground) beef
- 1 large (150 g/5½ oz) carrot, peeled and grated
- 1 medium (160 g/5½ oz) zucchini (courgette), peeled and grated
- 400 g (14 oz) tomato passata (puréed tomatoes)
- 2 tablespoons no-added-salt tomato paste (concentrated purée)
- 1 cup (250 ml) low-salt beef stock or Bone broth (see page 223)
- 1 cup (30 g) baby spinach, finely chopped
- ¼ cup (15 g) basil leaves, finely chopped
- 2 teaspoons dried oregano
- 300 g (10½ oz) dried wholemeal spaghetti or pasta of choice

In a large saucepan, heat the oil over medium heat, then sauté the onion, garlic and celery for 2–3 minutes, or until softened.

Add the beef and cook for 3–4 minutes, or until browned.

Add the carrot, zucchini, passata, tomato paste and stock or broth and bring to the boil. Reduce heat to low and simmer for 25 minutes, or until the liquid has reduced.

Add the spinach, basil and oregano and cook for another 5 minutes, or until the vegetables have softened.

Meanwhile, cook the pasta in a large saucepan of boiling water according to package instructions. Drain.

To serve, cut the pasta into short, manageable pieces or mash slightly for younger babies, then spoon over the bolognese.

Make it ...

Gluten free Swap pasta for gluten-free pasta of choice.

Seasonal Swap carrot and zucchini for seasonal vegetables of choice, such as pumpkin (squash), swede or parsnip.

Fussy-eater proof Thinly slice and purée all vegetables in a food processor before combining with beef and tomato sauce.

Family friendly (2+) Serve with grated parmesan or low-salt cheese of choice and dried chilli flakes for a kick.

Leftovers Store in an airtight container in the fridge for up to 3 days or freeze for up to 3 months.

8+ months

Serves 6

Prep 15 mins

Cook 15 mins

Plant-powered bolognese

 Vegan

 Dairy free

Egg free

 Fish free

 Gluten free

 Peanut free

 Sesame free

 Soy free

 Tree nut free

Bolognese but vegan, this is my hearty, plant-based twist on the classic. Just blitz the veg, then sauté with lentils and tomatoes, and you're done in 30 minutes! It's packed with nourishing ingredients for little ones from 8 months up to the adults, and no-one will miss the meat, I promise! Using plant-based protein adds variety, even if your kids love meat. Lentils are rich in iron, contain beneficial fibre and actually count as a veggie serve. Plus, you can adjust the texture to suit every age.

1 small (100 g/3½ oz) brown onion, roughly chopped

1 (40 g/1½ oz) celery stalk, roughly chopped

2 garlic cloves garlic

1 medium (160 g/5½ oz) carrot, roughly chopped

1 medium (180 g) zucchini (courgette), chopped

1 tablespoon extra virgin olive oil

¼ cup (65 g) no-added-salt tomato paste (concentrated purée)

400 g (14 oz) can brown lentils, drained and rinsed

400 g (14 oz) tomato passata (puréed tomatoes)

1 cup (250 ml) low-salt vegetable stock or homemade broth (salt free for babies) or water

1 teaspoon dried oregano

350 g (12 oz) dried gluten-free penne pasta

Serving suggestions

⅓ cup (35 g) finely grated low-salt cheese (such as gouda, Swiss or mozzarella, optional, if vegan and dairy free aren't necessary)

Chopped basil leaves

Place the onion, celery, garlic, carrot and zucchini in a food processor and process until puréed and smooth, scraping down the side once or twice to help blend evenly.

Heat the oil in a large saucepan over medium heat. Add the vegetable mixture and sauté for 4–5 minutes.

Add the tomato paste, lentils, passata, stock or broth or water and oregano. Cover and simmer for 5 minutes, or until the vegetables have softened.

Using a stick blender, purée the sauce until desired consistency is reached (optional).

Meanwhile, cook the pasta in a large saucepan of boiling water according to package instructions. Drain.

Place the sauce over the pasta and stir through. Depending on your baby's stage, serve the pasta mashed or as finger food, sprinkled with cheese and basil.

Make it ...

Seasonal Swap vegetables for seasonal vegetables of choice.

Pantry friendly Swap lentils for kidney, or navy beans or chickpeas; swap pasta for wholemeal pasta (if gluten free isn't necessary).

Family friendly (2+) Add chilli flakes if desired.

Leftovers Store in an airtight container in the fridge for up to 3 days or freeze for up to 3 months.

6+ months

Serves 4

Prep 15 mins (+ cooling)

Cook 45 mins

 Dairy free

 Egg free

 Fish free

 Gluten free

 Peanut free

 Sesame free

 Soy free

 Tree nut free

Orange & thyme chicken drumsticks

Yum, yum, chicken drummies! This recipe was inspired by my bestie. We would make a big batch, share the load and freeze leftovers in small portions – it really helped when feeding our babies on busy days. I find the meat on drumsticks is always so succulent, especially when it's bubbled away in this easy one-pot dish. I've added fresh orange juice, butternut pumpkin (squash) and dried apricots to give this stew a subtle sweetness. It's one big bowl of protein, zinc and immune-supporting nutrients!

- 1 tablespoon extra virgin olive oil
- ½ (90 g/3¼ oz) leek, white part only, thinly sliced
- 1 garlic clove, crushed
- 1 teaspoon finely chopped fresh ginger
- 4 (300 g/10½ oz) pasture-raised or organic chicken drumsticks (or thighs)
- 1 cup (200 g) diced butternut pumpkin (squash)
- ½ cup (80 g) fresh corn kernels
- 2 sulphur-free dried apricots, thinly sliced
- 2 thyme sprigs
- Juice of 1 (160 g/5½ oz) orange
- 1 cup (250 ml) low-salt chicken stock or homemade broth (salt free for babies)

Heat the oil in a large saucepan or deep frying pan over medium heat. Add the leek, garlic and ginger and sauté for about 3 minutes, or until softened and fragrant.

Add the chicken and cook for 5 minutes each side, or until browned evenly.

Stir in the pumpkin, corn, apricots, thyme, orange juice and stock or broth, then bring to the boil. Reduce the heat to low and let it simmer gently for 30 minutes, or until the meat is cooked through and tender, and the veggies are soft.

Once cooled slightly, remove the chicken from the bone and either mash the mixture or cut the chicken into finger food–sized pieces and mash the vegetables separately as needed.

Make it ...

Seasonal Swap butternut for pumpkin of choice or sweet potato; swap corn for diced capsicum (pepper).

Leftovers Store in an airtight container in the fridge for up to 3 days or freeze for up to 3 months.

8+ months

Serves 4–6

Prep 15 mins

Cook 30 mins

Dairy free

 Egg free

 Gluten free

 Peanut free

 Sesame free

 Soy free

 Tree nut free

Mediterranean fish pot

The flexibility of this fish dish is what keeps me coming back to make this for my family. It has grown with my kids. When they were little, I mashed the fish and veg together, then as they started self-feeding, I'd serve the flaked fish separately to the vegetables with a side of brown rice. Now, we've upgraded to a little chilli, capers, a squeeze of lemon juice and some crusty bread to mop it up. And the leftovers for lunch the next day are even better, as the flavours deepen. Give it a go and make it fit for your family.

- 1½ tablespoons extra virgin olive oil
- 1 small (50 g/1¾ oz) brown onion, finely chopped
- 2 garlic cloves, crushed
- 1 large (150 g/5½ oz) carrot, peeled and finely diced
- 400 g (14 oz) tomato passata (puréed tomatoes)
- 1 tablespoon no-added-salt tomato paste (concentrated purée)
- 1½ cups (375 ml) low-salt vegetable stock or homemade broth (salt free for babies)
- ½ teaspoon dried oregano
- Pinch of freshly ground black pepper (optional)
- 600 g (1 lb 5 oz) low-mercury, sustainably sourced skinless, boneless white fish fillets (such as flathead), cut into small pieces
- 1 tablespoon finely chopped flat-leaf parsley leaves

Serving suggestions

- Soft-cooked brown rice or quinoa
- Sweet potato mash
- Steamed vegetables

Heat the oil in a large saucepan over medium heat and sauté the onion and garlic for 3–4 minutes, or until softened. Add the carrot, passata, tomato paste, stock or broth, oregano and pepper (if using) and bring to the boil. Reduce the heat to low and cook for 20 minutes, or until the vegetables have softened and the sauce has thickened.

Add the fish and cook for another 5 minutes.

Mash the fish and vegetables into a soft, textured consistency and mix with rice for easier eating. For babies practising baby-led weaning, serve the fish in soft, manageable flakes alongside small spoonfuls of rice, quinoa or mashed sweet potato and steamed vegetables for self-feeding.

Make it ...

Vegan Swap fish for a mix of tofu and canned/cooked chickpeas.

Hearty Serve with crusty sourdough bread or steamed buckwheat or wholemeal couscous.

Seasonal Swap carrot for vegetables of choice.

Fussy-eater proof Serve deconstructed, offering fish without sauce, and with rice/quinoa/mash on the side.

Family friendly (2+) Add a pinch of chilli flakes or smoked paprika; stir in a handful of olives or capers and finish with a squeeze of lemon juice and a sprinkle of extra parsley for freshness.

Leftovers Store in an airtight container in the fridge for up to 3 days or freeze for up to 3 months.

8+ months

Serves 8

Prep 15 mins

Cook 15 mins

Crunchy golden fish fingers

Dairy free

Gluten free

Peanut free

Sesame free

Soy free

Tree nut free

Did you know that some supermarket fish fingers contain as little as 40 per cent fish? The rest is made up of processed ingredients. This recipe is the perfect alternative: crunchy, full of flavour and made without nasty ingredients. These are lightly coated in a crispy rice crumb with a boost of cauliflower. Plus, there's essential omega-3s for brain development. Quick to make, they are a wholesome lunch or dinner for babies and toddlers.

680 g (1 lb 8 oz) low-mercury, sustainably sourced skinless, boneless white fish fillets

½ cup (60 g) arrowroot

1½ cups (215 g) Gluten-free crumb mix or Rice 'breadcrumbs' (see page 243)

¼ cup (60 ml) coconut milk

2 pasture-raised or organic eggs

½ cup (130 g) cauliflower purée (optional)

Extra virgin olive oil, for frying

Serving suggestions

Steamed veggies

Sweet potato mash

Cut the fish into finger-sized pieces. Place the arrowroot in a medium bowl. In a separate bowl, place the crumbs.

In a shallow bowl, use a fork to whisk together the milk, eggs and cauliflower purée (if using).

One at a time, dip each fish piece into the arrowroot, then the milk mixture and finally into the crumbs. Press down firmly to ensure each piece has a thick crumb coating.

Coat a large frying pan with 1–2 tablespoons of oil and heat over medium heat. In batches, pan-fry the fish for 3–4 minutes each side, or until golden brown. Drain on a paper towel-lined plate. (Alternatively, you can bake the fish for 15–20 minutes in an 180°C/350°F oven.)

Serve mashed or flaked into small, soft pieces. For self-feeding, offer in finger portions with a side of steamed veggies or mashed sweet potato.

Make it ...

Seasonal Swap cauliflower for zucchini (courgette) or broccoli.

Faster Cut prep time by crumbing whole fish fillets and fry, then cut into strips; bake in an 180°C (350°F) oven for 25–30 minutes (they won't be as crispy).

Pantry friendly Swap crumb mix or rice 'breadcrumbs' for Wholemeal sourdough breadcrumbs (see page 242) and arrowroot for wholemeal spelt flour (if gluten free isn't necessary); swap milk for soy, almond or rice milk.

Family friendly (2+) Serve with sweet potato wedges, steamed veggies and Tomato sauce (see page 239).

Leftovers Store in an airtight container in the fridge for up to 3 days or freeze for up to 3 months.

8+ months

Serves 4–6

Prep 15 mins

Cook 35 mins

Baked millet & flathead pilaf

 Dairy free

 Egg free

 Gluten free

 Peanut free

 Sesame free

 Soy free

 Tree nut free

Millet is a gentle, gluten-free grain that's full of iron and essential minerals; you'll find it at the supermarket. It's simple to cook, and when paired with flathead, plenty of veg and warming spices, it's the makings of a hearty *and* healthy meal. Don't be afraid to add turmeric and paprika to baby's dinner. These vibrant spices not only enhance the flavour but also add powerful anti-inflammatory benefits. This is my go-to for freezing in preparation of busy weeknights.

2 tablespoons extra virgin olive oil

1 small (100 g/3½ oz) brown onion, finely chopped

1 garlic clove, crushed

1 large (150 g/5½ oz) carrot, peeled and finely chopped or grated

2 cups (240 g) small broccoli florets

½ teaspoon ground turmeric

½ teaspoon sweet paprika

1 cup (200 g) millet, rinsed

2½ cups (625 ml) low-salt vegetable stock or homemade broth (salt free for babies), plus extra if needed

Freshly ground black pepper, to taste (optional)

400 g (14 oz) low-mercury, sustainably sourced skinless, boneless flathead fillets (or other low-mercury white fish fillets), cut into small pieces

Serving suggestions

Juice of ½ (90 g/3¼ oz) lemon

Finely chopped flat-leaf parsley leaves

Preheat the oven to 180°C (350°F).

Heat the oil in a large ovenproof frying pan over medium heat. Add the onion and garlic and sauté until softened. Stir in the carrot, broccoli and spices and cook for 2 minutes.

Add the millet and stir to coat. Cook, stirring occasionally, for 3 minutes.

Pour in the stock or broth, season with pepper (if using) and bring to a simmer. Cover with a lid and transfer to the oven. Bake for 20 minutes.

Remove the lid and arrange the fish pieces evenly over the millet mixture. Add extra stock or broth if it looks a bit dry. Return to the oven, uncovered. Bake for another 10–15 minutes, or until the fish is tender and flakes easily.

Serve mashed or in soft, small spoonfuls for easy chewing. For babies practising baby-led weaning, cut the fish into soft, manageable strips and offer with the pilaf. Add a squeeze of lemon juice and parsley to enhance flavour while keeping it mild for young palates.

Make it ...

Hearty Add canned/cooked chickpeas or peas before baking for extra texture.

Seasonal Swap carrot and broccoli for vegetables of choice.

Boosted Add baby spinach in last 10 minutes of cooking.

Different Swap flathead for salmon or a different white fish.

Pantry friendly Swap millet for brown rice.

Family friendly (2+) Top with grated low-salt cheese before baking for a golden crust; serve with steamed green beans, roasted sweet potato or cucumber sticks.

Leftovers Store in an airtight container in the fridge for up to 3 days or freeze for up to 3 months. Enjoy reheated in wraps with Tzatziki dip (see page 238) or yoghurt.

Veggie-loaded pasta sauce

8+ months

Serves 8

Prep 15 mins

Cook 30 mins

 Vegan

 Dairy free

 Egg free

 Fish free

 Gluten free

 Peanut free

 Sesame free

 Soy free

Tree nut free

This is an excellent staple to have on standby in the freezer. I've often relied on it when I have had a packed day and have no idea what to cook. Served over pasta or grains, with chicken or tofu, or even as a pizza sauce, this is the easiest way to add extra veggies to your children's diet. Packed with fibre, vitamins and antioxidants, leave it chunky or blend it smooth to adapt for all ages and stages. My son chooses this pasta sauce over bolognese any day.

1 tablespoon extra virgin olive oil

1 small (100 g/3½ oz) brown onion, finely chopped

2 garlic cloves, crushed

1 (40 g/1½ oz) celery stalk, finely chopped

1 small (130/4½ oz) zucchini (courgette), finely grated

1 large (150 g/5½ oz) carrot, peeled and finely grated

1 small (170 g/5¾ oz) capsicum (pepper), seeds removed and finely chopped

400 g (14 oz) no-added-salt tomato passata (puréed tomatoes)

½ cup (130 g) no-added-salt tomato paste (concentrated purée)

1 teaspoon dried oregano

1 teaspoon dried basil

Pinch of freshly ground black pepper (optional)

½–1 cup (125–250 ml) low-salt vegetable stock or homemade broth (optional)

Serving suggestions

Potato mash

Cooked brown rice pasta

Soft-cooked quinoa

Heat the oil in a large frying pan over medium heat. Add the onion, garlic and celery and sauté for about 3–4 minutes, or until softened.

Stir in the zucchini and carrot, then the capsicum and cook, stirring occasionally, for another 5 minutes, until the veggies start to soften.

Pour in the passata, tomato paste, oregano, basil and pepper (if using). Stir to combine, then bring the sauce to a simmer. Reduce the heat to low and simmer, stirring occasionally, for 15–20 minutes, or until the vegetables are tender and the sauce has thickened slightly. If you want a thinner sauce, add some stock or broth until the desired consistency is achieved.

Blend the sauce in a blender until smooth and stir it through mashed potato, pasta or quinoa for a gentle texture. For babies practising self-feeding, mix the sauce with soft pasta shapes.

Make it ...

Seasonal Swap vegetables for seasonal vegetables of choice.

Hearty Stir in cooked lentils, shredded chicken or crumbled tofu – adds more protein too!

Family friendly (2+) Serve over gluten-free pasta and sprinkled with a little parmesan (if dairy free isn't necessary), spiralised veggies or as a rich pizza sauce.

Leftovers Store in an airtight container in the fridge for up to 3 days or freeze for up to 3 months.

10+ months

Serves 6–8

Prep 25 mins

Cook 1 hr 5 mins

Cheesy tuna & veggie lasagne

Egg free

Peanut free

Sesame free

Soy free

Tree nut free

This cheesy lasagne is inspired by my mum. We used to love her creamy, flavour-packed bake loaded with protein-rich tuna, fibre-filled veggies and smooth, cheesy béchamel sauce. With a few tweaks and healthy overhauls, I adapted it for my little ones, and it soon became a family favourite that we still eat today. Mum has now made the same adaptations to her version too. The soft layers of pasta make it easy to eat, while the golden, bubbly cheese topping adds extra appeal to the nutrient-dense ingredients.

- 1 small (100 g/3½ oz) brown onion, chopped
- 2 garlic cloves
- 2 (80 g/2¾ oz) celery stalks, chopped
- 1 medium (120 g/4¼ oz) carrot, peeled and chopped
- 1 medium (190 g/6¾ oz) zucchini (courgette), chopped
- 1 tablespoon extra virgin olive oil
- 700 g (1 lb 9 oz) tomato passata (puréed tomatoes)
- ¼ cup (65 g) no-added-salt tomato paste (concentrated purée)
- 425 g (15 oz) can tuna in springwater (skipjack tuna preferable), drained
- 2 teaspoons dried oregano
- 2 cups (60 g) baby spinach, finely chopped
- ¼ cup (20 g) flat-leaf parsley leaves, finely chopped
- 8 dried wholemeal lasagne sheets
- ½ cup (50 g) grated low-salt cheese
- 1 tablespoon chia seeds

Preheat the oven to 180°C (350°F).

Place the onion, garlic, celery, carrot and zucchini in a food processor and process until finely grated, scraping down the side once or twice to help grate evenly.

Heat the oil in a large saucepan over medium heat. Add the vegetable mixture and sauté, stirring frequently, for 4–5 minutes, or until softened.

Add the passata, tomato paste, tuna and oregano. Reduce the heat to low and cook, covered but stirring occasionally, for about 15 minutes, or until the sauce has thickened slightly and the flavours have developed. Stir through the spinach and parsley, then remove from the heat.

Meanwhile, make the béchamel sauce. Melt the butter in a medium saucepan over medium heat. Remove from the heat, then add the flour and whisk for about 30 seconds, or until well blended. Place the pan back over low heat and slowly whisk in the milk, 1 cup (250 ml) at a time. Cook, whisking continuously, for 6–8 minutes, or until thickened. If it becomes too thick, add a little extra milk. Stir in the cheese and remove from the heat.

To assemble, spread about 1 cup tuna mixture over the base of a large casserole dish, then cover with lasagne sheets, trimming to fit if needed. Layer with 1½ cups of tuna mixture (or enough to cover the pasta), then 1 cup béchamel sauce. Repeat layering with the remaining lasagne sheets, tuna mixture and béchamel, finishing with a layer of béchamel. (You will have 4 layers of pasta.)

Sprinkle with the cheese and chia seeds and bake for 40–45 minutes, or until golden brown and pasta is cooked.

Cut the lasagne into small, soft pieces or mash slightly to suit your child's stage of eating. Serve with a spoon or allow self-feeding with bite-sized portions.

Béchamel sauce

60 g (2¼ oz) unsalted butter

⅓ cup (40 g) wholemeal spelt flour

3 cups (750 ml) milk of choice, plus extra if needed

1 cup (100 g) grated low-salt cheese

Make it ...

Dairy free Swap butter for extra virgin olive oil and milk for a dairy-free alternative, such as coconut, oat or soy milk, omit cheese and stir ½ cup (30 g) nutritional yeast flakes into béchamel.

Gluten free Swap lasagne sheets for gluten-free rice lasagne sheets and swap flour for cornflour, arrowroot or a gluten-free flour blend.

Seasonal Swap spinach for greens of choice.

Boosted Add any grated vegetables of choice, such as mushroom, parsnip and capsicum (pepper).

Different Swap béchamel sauce for a white sauce (see page 236); swap canned fish for fresh, low-mercury fish fillets – cook at the same time as vegetable mixture, adding to one side of pan until browned on both sides. Remove from pan.

Fussy-eater proof Make sure all vegetables are finely puréed before adding tuna to sauce.

Family friendly (2+) Serve with a side salad or steamed veggies.

Leftovers Store in an airtight container in the fridge for up to 3 days or freeze for up to 3 months.

8+ months

Serves 4–6

Prep 15 mins (+ 30 mins marinating)

Cook 30 mins

Butter chicken

 Egg free

 Fish free

 Gluten free

 Peanut free

 Sesame free

Soy free

 Tree nut free

Curry might not be the first thing you think of when wondering what to cook for your baby, but it really can be a great option from 8 months onwards. Here, the chicken is marinated in yoghurt and mild spices that won't overwhelm young palates. And the creamy coconut base has children coming back for more. It's one of the recipes I always recommend to encourage babies to explore new flavours.

600 g (1 lb 5 oz) pasture-raised or organic skinless, boneless chicken thighs, trimmed

½ small (50 g/1¾ oz) brown onion, quartered

2 garlic cloves

1 medium (100 g/3½ oz) carrot, peeled and roughly chopped

1 (40 g/1½ oz) celery stalk, chopped

2 tablespoons extra virgin olive oil

½ cup (130 g) no-added-salt tomato paste (concentrated purée)

1 cup (250 ml) canned coconut milk

1 cup (250 ml) low-salt chicken stock or homemade broth (salt free for babies)

Marinade

¾ cup (195 g) natural unsweetened yoghurt

1 tablespoon finely grated fresh ginger

1 teaspoon garam masala

1 teaspoon ground cumin

1 teaspoon mild paprika powder

1 teaspoon ground turmeric

Freshly ground black pepper, to taste (optional)

Serving suggestions

Soft-cooked brown rice

Soft-cooked quinoa or wholemeal couscous

Steamed veggies

Soft naan (see page 230)

Combine all the marinade ingredients in a bowl.

Cut the chicken into bite-sized pieces and toss through the marinade. Cover and refrigerate for 30 minutes or overnight.

Place the onion, garlic, carrot and celery in a food processor and process until finely chopped, scraping down the side once or twice to help blend evenly.

In a large saucepan, heat the oil over medium heat. Add the vegetable mixture to the pan and cook for 3–4 minutes, or until softened. Add the marinated chicken, reserving any marinade left in the bowl, and cook until the chicken is browned.

Add the tomato paste, coconut milk, stock or broth and reserved marinade and cook for 20–25 minutes, or until the chicken is tender.

Shred the chicken into small, soft pieces and mix with extra sauce to keep it moist. Serve with mashed rice, quinoa or couscous for easy eating. For babies practising baby-led weaning, offer tender chicken pieces with a spoonful of sauce and steamed veggies or naan for dipping.

Make it …

Dairy free Swap yoghurt for natural unsweetened coconut, soy or oat yoghurt.

Vegetarian Swap chicken for legumes of choice or tofu and swap stock for vegetable stock.

Seasonal Swap celery and carrot for seasonal vegetables of choice.

Fussy-eater proof Serve chicken separate from sauce and rice.

Family friendly (2+) Add 1 extra teaspoon garam masala and a pinch of ground chilli to marinade for richer flavour; serve with basmati or brown rice, warm Soft naan (see page 230) and a sprinkle of coriander (cilantro) leaves.

Leftovers Store in an airtight container in the fridge for up to 3 days or freeze for up to 3 months.

8+ months

Serves 8

Prep 25 mins (+ cooling)

Cook 50 mins

 Vegetarian

 Egg free

 Fish free

 Gluten free

 Peanut free

 Sesame free

 Soy free

 Tree nut free

Lentil & veggie cottage pie

There are so many simple ways to pack more goodness into kids' meals, and this pie is one of my absolute favourites. I've added cauliflower to the creamy mash topping (a little trick I come back to often) and boosted the flavour and fibre of the lentil filling with plenty of veggies and fresh herbs. It's always a hearty hit in my place. Plus, it's easy to switch up the veggies depending on what's in season or hanging out in your crisper.

1 tablespoon extra virgin olive oil

1 small (100 g/3½ oz) brown onion, roughly chopped

3 garlic cloves

1 (40 g/1½ oz) celery stalk, roughly chopped

1 large (140 g/5 oz) carrot, peeled and chopped

2 × 400 g (14 oz) cans lentils, drained and rinsed

¼ cup (65 g) no-added-salt tomato paste (concentrated purée)

1 tablespoon finely chopped thyme leaves

1 tablespoon finely chopped rosemary leaves

1 cup (250 ml) low-salt vegetable stock or homemade broth (salt free for babies), plus extra if needed

2 tablespoons nutritional yeast flakes

Freshly ground black pepper, to taste (optional)

Mashed potato topping

700 g (1 lb 9 oz) potatoes, peeled and diced

400 g (14 oz) cauliflower florets

40 g (1½ oz) unsalted butter

½ cup (125 ml) milk of choice

½ cup (50 g) grated low-salt cheese

Preheat the oven to 200°C (400°F).

Heat the oil in a large saucepan over medium heat. Add the onion, garlic, celery and carrot. Sauté for 5–7 minutes, or until the vegetables are softened.

Stir in the lentils, tomato paste, thyme and rosemary. Cook for another 2–3 minutes. Pour in the stock or broth and bring to a simmer. Add more stock or broth if needed to reach a desired consistency.

Stir in the nutritional yeast and season with pepper (if using). Cook for 10–15 minutes, or until the flavours meld together and the sauce thickens slightly. Transfer the lentil base to a baking dish.

Meanwhile, make the mashed potato topping. Place the potato and cauliflower in a large saucepan of boiling water. Cook for 15–20 minutes, or until the vegetables are tender.

Drain well, then pat dry the cauliflower. Return the vegetables to the pan. Add the butter, milk and cheese. Mash until smooth and creamy. Season with pepper (if using).

Spread the mashed topping evenly over the lentil base in the dish. Use a fork to create ridges on the surface to help the topping crisp up in the oven.

Bake the pie for 20–25 minutes, or until the top is golden brown and crispy. Allow to cool slightly.

To serve, mash or blend the pie for a smoother texture or serve in small manageable pieces for self-feeding.

the
little
bunny

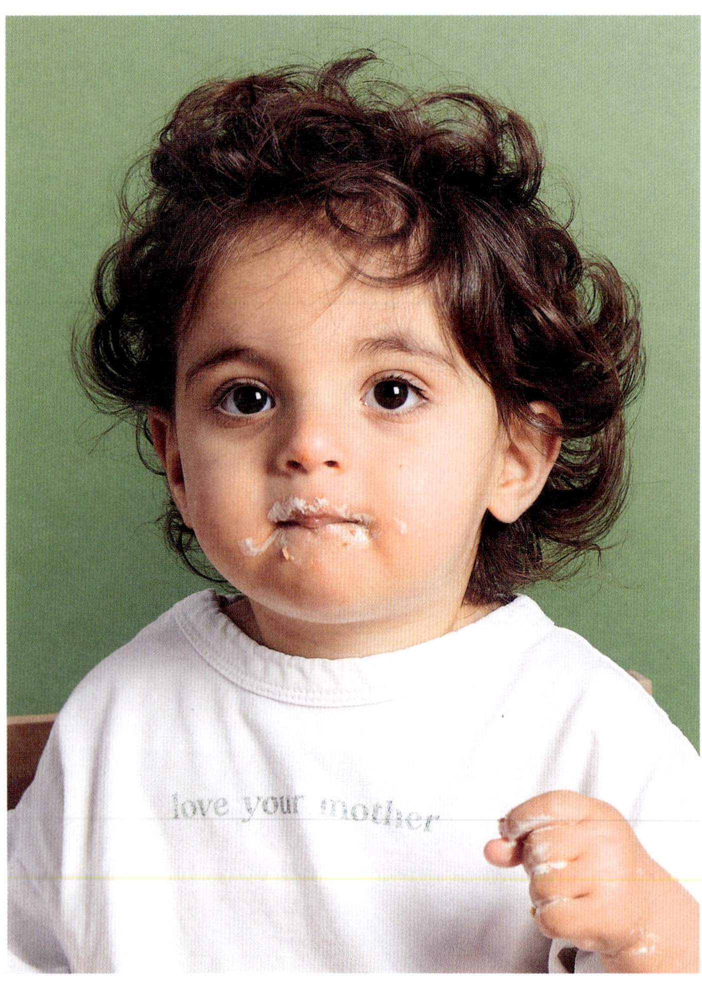

Make it ...

Dairy free In topping, swap butter for extra virgin olive oil, swap cheese for 2 tablespoons nutritional yeast flakes (or to taste), use a plant-based milk.

Seasonal Swap vegetables in lentil base for seasonal vegetables of choice; swap cauliflower in topping for sweet potato or parsnip.

Boosted Add extra roughly chopped or grated vegetables to the lentil base (such as zucchini/courgette, capsicum/pepper or more of the same).

Faster Grate all vegetables for lentil base in a food processor before frying.

Fussy-eater proof Deconstruct meal by serving mash topping separate from lentil base.

Family friendly (2+) Stir in 1 tablespoon tamari when adding lentils; serve with a garden salad for a main meal.

School friendly Pack warm in a thermos for lunch.

Leftovers Store in an airtight container in the fridge for up to 3 days or freeze for up to 3 months.

6+ months

Serves 4

Prep 15 mins

Cook 25 mins

Coconut fish curry

- Dairy free
- Egg free
-  Gluten free
-  Peanut free
-  Sesame free
-  Soy free
-  Tree nut free

This was the first fish curry I made for my baby, and it quickly became loved by the whole gang. Mild, creamy and gently spiced, it's a great way to introduce new flavours without overwhelming tiny tastebuds. The soft white fish, sweet potato and coconut sauce create a comfort-filled bowl that can be blended, mashed or served as finger food. This is one of those recipes that proves real food can be both adventurous and baby friendly – and, yes, the grown-ups will love it too.

1½ tablespoons coconut oil

3 spring onions (scallions), white part only, thinly sliced

1 garlic clove, crushed

½ teaspoon finely grated fresh ginger

1 teaspoon mild curry powder (optional)

1 tablespoon no added salt tomato paste (concentrated purée)

1–2 tablespoons fresh lemon juice, to taste

1 medium (200 g/7 oz) sweet potato, peeled and finely diced

1 medium (80 g/2¾ oz) carrot, peeled and finely diced

1 cup (250 ml) coconut cream or coconut milk

1 cup (250 ml) low-salt vegetable stock or homemade broth (salt free for babies) or water

450–600 g (1–1 lb 5 oz) low-mercury, sustainably sourced skinless, boneless cod fillets, chopped

1 cup (30 g) baby spinach, chopped (optional)

2 tablespoons finely chopped coriander (cilantro) leaves

Serving suggestions

Potato mash

Soft-cooked brown rice or quinoa

Melt the oil in a large frying pan over medium heat. Add the spring onion, garlic, ginger, curry powder, tomato paste and lemon juice. Sauté for 2–3 minutes, or until fragrant and softened.

Stir in the sweet potato and carrot and cook for another 2 minutes. Pour in the coconut cream or milk and stock or broth or water. Bring to a gentle simmer and cook for 15 minutes, or until the vegetables are soft.

Add the fish and spinach (if using). Cook for another 5 minutes, or until the fish is cooked through. Sprinkle with the coriander.

Serve puréed, mashed or as finger food by separating the fish and vegetables, alongside mashed potato, rice or quinoa.

Make it ...

Different Swap cod for any low-mercury fish of choice.

Seasonal Swap carrot for any root vegetables of choice.

Freezer friendly Use frozen low-mercury fish fillets and bake at 200°C (400°F) for 10–15 minutes before adding to curry mixture to avoid it being too 'fishy' for children.

Family friendly (2+) Serve with a sprinkle of coriander (cilantro) leaves for added flavour; pair with warm Soft naan (see page 230) or roti (if gluten free isn't necessary).

Leftovers Store in an airtight container in the fridge for up to 3 days or freeze for up to 3 months.

- 10+ months
- Serves 4–5
- Prep 15 mins (+ 10 mins standing)
- Cook 55 mins

One-pot chicken & tomato risotto

 Egg free

 Fish free

 Gluten free

 Peanut free

 Sesame free

 Soy free

 Tree nut free

Enjoy this easy, creamy rice bake together as a family, then pop any leftovers in a thermos for tomorrow's lunch box. It beats a Vegemite sandwich any day, and it's a brilliant way to introduce little ones to warm, hearty meals early on. Not only is it more nourishing, it also helps boost their veggie and protein intake from the start. The best part? I reckon it's not standing at the stove stirring. Just add the stock or broth, bake and you're done. Nutritious, satisfying and on the table without the fuss.

- 1½ tablespoons extra virgin olive oil
- 1 small (100 g/3½ oz) brown onion, finely chopped
- 1–2 garlic cloves, crushed
- 1 small (90 g/3¼ oz) carrot, peeled and grated
- ¾ cup (100 g) peeled and grated pumpkin (squash)
- 5 (520 g/1 lb 2 oz) pasture raised or organic skinless, boneless chicken thighs, trimmed and cut into 2 cm (¾ in) pieces
- 1½ cups (315 g) brown rice
- 300 g (10½ oz) tomato passata (puréed tomatoes)
- 3 cups (750 ml) low-salt vegetable stock or homemade broth (salt free for babies), plus extra if needed
- 1½ tablespoons finely chopped basil leaves

Serving suggestion

Mushy peas

Preheat the oven to 180°C (350°F).

Heat the oil in a large ovenproof skillet or pan with a lid over medium heat. Add the onion, garlic, carrot and pumpkin and sauté for 3 minutes, or until softened. Add the chicken and cook for 3–4 minutes, or until browned. Add the rice and cook, stirring, for another 2 minutes.

Pour in the tomatoes and stock or broth and stir until well combined. Bring to a simmer, cover and place in the oven. Cook, stirring halfway through, for 40–45 minutes, or until most of the liquid is absorbed. Add extra stock or broth if all the liquid has been absorbed but the rice is still not soft.

Remove the skillet from the oven and sit for 10 minutes, then fold through the basil.

Serve mashed in small portions or shape the rice mixture into soft, scoopable mounds with mushy peas. Or you can mash the rice mixture with a fork and shred the chicken into small, soft pieces for easier chewing.

For babies 6–9 months, purée the risotto, if preferred.

Make it ...

Dairy free Omit parmesan and drizzle with coconut milk or coconut cream at the end.

Vegetarian Swap chicken for cubed tofu.

Seasonal Swap carrot and pumpkin for vegetables of choice.

Fussy-eater proof Mash vegetables before adding chicken, so they are undetected.

Family friendly (2+) Add ⅓ cup (30 g) grated parmesan with the basil.

School friendly Pack warm in a thermos.

Leftovers Store in an airtight container in the fridge for up to 3 days or freeze for up to 3 months.

Tip If you don't have an ovenproof skillet with a lid, cook in a frying pan, then transfer mixture to a large deep roasting dish. Cover with foil to bake.

Creamy pumpkin mac'n'cheese

10+ months

Serves 6

Prep 15 mins

Cook 35 mins

Vegetarian

Egg free

Fish free

Gluten free

Peanut free

Sesame free

Tree nut free

Blend roasted pumpkin, silken tofu and coconut and you've created the smoothest, most velvety sauce for mac'n'cheese. Extra cheese on top is always requested in our house, and why not? Knowing this version is full of nutrients, I feel reassured I'm still feeding my children a healthy, wholesome dinner, with extra veggies snuck in!

350 g (12 oz) dried brown rice spiral pasta

30 g (1 oz) unsalted butter

1 tablespoon arrowroot

2 garlic cloves, crushed

2 cups (500 ml) coconut milk

1½ cups (300 g) roasted pumpkin (squash)

680 g (1 lb 8 oz) non-GMO silken tofu

1 cup (100 g) grated low-salt cheese, plus extra 1 cup (100 g, optional)

1 cup (30 g) baby spinach, chopped

Serving suggestion

Steamed veggies

Preheat the oven to 180°C (350°F).

Cook the pasta according to package instructions. Drain and set aside.

Meanwhile, in a large saucepan, melt the butter over medium heat. Add the arrowroot and whisk until well incorporated. Add the garlic and cook for about 2 minutes. Pour in the coconut milk and cook, stirring continuously, for 2–3 minutes, or until it thickens up.

Add the pumpkin, tofu and cheese and whisk to combine. Using a stick blender, blend until smooth. (Alternatively, place the sauce in a high-speed blender and blend until smooth and creamy.)

Add the spinach and cooked pasta and stir until everything is coated in the sauce evenly. Transfer to a large casserole dish, sprinkle with the extra cheese (if using) and bake for 15–20 minutes, or until golden. (Alternatively, place under the oven grill/broiler on medium for 8–10 minutes.)

For babies still developing chewing skills, leave out the baking step and mash the pasta mixture slightly or serve in soft, manageable pieces with steamed veggies on the side.

Make it …

Dairy free Swap butter for olive oil and cheese for 1 cup (60 g) nutritional yeast flakes.

Seasonal Swap pumpkin for sweet potato.

Family friendly (2+) Add extra grated low-salt cheese on top before baking for a richer, golden crust; serve with a green salad or roasted vegetables for a hearty and balanced family dinner.

School friendly Delicious cold as a pasta salad or pack warm in a thermos for lunch.

Leftovers Store in an airtight container in the fridge for up to 3 days or freeze leftover sauce for up to 3 months.

6+ months

Serves 12

Prep 15 min (+ cooling)

Cook 30 mins

Rainbow veggie frittata

 Vegetarian

 Dairy free

 Fish free

Gluten free

 Peanut free

 Sesame free

 Soy free

 Tree nut free

From babies learning to self-feed to big kids coming home hungry, this fluffy vegetarian frittata is a nourishing go-to for the whole gang. Packed with high-quality protein from eggs and made extra light and creamy with dairy-free coconut cream, it's both satisfying and gentle on little tummies. Serve it warm or cold, in fingers or wedges; there are so many easy ways to make it lunch-box friendly. I serve it as a quick meal at home for the kids and me.

- 1 tablespoon extra virgin olive oil
- 1 small (100 g/3½ oz) brown onion, finely diced
- 1 garlic clove, crushed
- ½ small (90 g/3¼ oz) red capsicum (pepper), seeds removed and finely diced
- 100 g (3¾ oz) broccoli florets, finely chopped
- 1 small (100 g/3¾ oz) carrot, peeled and grated
- ½ cup (60 g) frozen green peas
- 6 large pasture-raised or organic eggs
- ¾ cup (185 ml) coconut cream
- 2 tablespoons soft herb leaves of choice (such as dill, flat-leaf parsley or chives), finely chopped

Serving suggestions

Mashed avocado

Steamed veggies

Preheat the oven to 180°C (350°F) and line a 18 × 26 cm (7 × 10½ in) baking dish with baking paper.

Heat the oil in a frying pan over medium heat and sauté the onion for 2–3 minutes. Add the garlic, capsicum and broccoli and cook for another 3–4 minutes, or until the vegetables have softened. Add the carrot and peas and cook for 2 minutes. Remove from the heat and allow to cool.

Place the vegetable mixture in a food processor and process until finely crushed or puréed, scraping down the side once or twice to help blend evenly.

In a large bowl, combine the eggs, coconut cream and herbs. Stir in the vegetable mixture until combined, then pour the mixture into the prepared dish. Bake for 25–30 minutes, or until cooked through.

Cut the frittata into soft, manageable finger-sized pieces for easy grasping.

For babies still developing chewing skills, mash the frittata. Serve with avocado or steamed veggies for added texture and nutrients.

Make it ...

Seasonal Swap vegetables for seasonal vegetables of choice.

Cheesy Swap half the coconut cream for grated low-salt cheese.

Fussy-eater proof Steam and purée vegetables before adding to egg mixture for a smoother consistency.

Family friendly (2+) Serve warm/cold with wholemeal toast, salad or steamed veggies; sprinkle over grated low-salt cheese on top before baking.

School friendly Delicious in wraps or sandwiches or pack slice/s for a protein-rich snack.

Leftovers Store in an airtight container in the fridge for up to 3 days or freeze for up to 3 months.

6+ months

Makes 16

Prep 15 min (+ cooling)

Cook 20 mins

Iron-boosting beef & lentil patties

 Dairy free

 Fish free

 Gluten free

 Peanut free

 Sesame free

Soy free

 Tree nut free

Adding canned lentils to patties is such a simple way to boost your child's intake of fibre and essential nutrients that support growth and development. If you don't have any on hand, no problem. Just switch for any legumes you've got in the pantry. Baking these patties instead of frying makes them easier to prepare, with less mess in the kitchen and no need to stand over a hot pan. A fuss-free, nourishing option for your busy family.

½ cup (90 g) canned/cooked brown lentils, well drained

1 small (80 g/2¾ oz) carrot, peeled and finely chopped

1 small (130 g/4½ oz) zucchini (courgette), finely chopped

½ small (55 g/2 oz) brown onion, chopped

1 tablespoon finely chopped flat-leaf parsley leaves

1 pasture-raised or organic egg yolk

500 g (1 lb 2 oz) grass-fed minced (ground) beef

2 tablespoons chickpea flour (besan)

1 tablespoon extra virgin olive oil

Serving suggestion

Steamed or baked vegetables

Preheat the oven to 180°C (350°F) and line a baking tray with baking paper.

Place the lentils, carrot, zucchini, onion, parsley and egg yolk in a food processor and process until smooth or finely crushed, scraping down the side once or twice to help blend evenly.

Add the beef, flour and vegetable mixture to a large bowl and mix well until everything is evenly combined. Shape small portions into mini patties.

Place the patties on the prepared tray, brush lightly with the oil and bake, flipping halfway, for 15–20 minutes, or until cooked through.

Allow the patties to cool slightly before serving.

For babies still developing chewing skills, cut into small pieces and serve as finger food or mashed with a side of steamed or baked vegetables.

Make it ...

Egg free Swap egg for a store-bought egg replacer, or a flax egg (1 egg = 1 tablespoon ground flaxseed + 45 ml/1½ fl oz warm water) or a chia egg (1 egg = 1 tablespoon chia seed meal + ¼ cup/60 ml water).

Different Swap mince for lamb mince.

Pantry friendly Swap lentils for legumes of choice.

Fussy-eater proof Make sure vegetable mixture is blended thoroughly before adding beef to ensure it can't be detected.

Family friendly (2+) Use in wraps and serve with Tomato sauce (see page 239).

Leftovers Store in an airtight container in the fridge for up to 3 days or freeze for up to 3 months.

6+ months

Makes 20

Prep 20 mins (+ cooling)

Cook 15 mins

Easy veggie fritters

I like to call these 'first-bite fritters' as the soft centre and lightly crisp exterior make them easy for little hands to hold, helping to encourage self-feeding and develop motor skills. My babies always enjoyed these with creamy avocado and yoghurt – mostly for the mess they had fun making! Mealtimes in the early stages are just as much about exploring food by touch and smell as they are about actually eating. Offer a variety of textures – like the serving suggestions I've included here – to help them on their adventure!

Vegetarian

Dairy free

Fish free

Gluten free

Peanut free

Sesame free

Soy free

Tree nut free

- 1 small (170 g/5¾ oz) zucchini (courgette), grated, then excess moisture squeezed out
- 1 small (140 g/5 oz) carrot, peeled and grated
- ½ cup (80 g) corn kernels (fresh or frozen)
- 2 pasture-raised or organic eggs
- ½ cup, tightly packed (about 160 g) mashed sweet potato, cooled
- ¼ teaspoon pure garlic powder
- ¼ teaspoon ground cumin
- ¼ teaspoon ground turmeric
- ¼ cup (35 g) chickpea flour (besan)
- 2 tablespoons extra virgin olive oil

Serving suggestions

- Avocado
- Natural unsweetened coconut yoghurt
- Steamed veggies

Place the zucchini, carrot and corn in a food processor and pulse until finely chopped, scraping down the side once or twice to help blend evenly.

In a large bowl, whisk the eggs. Add the vegetable mixture, sweet potato and spices. Stir in the flour until well combined. The mixture should hold together but be slightly sticky.

Heat 1 tablespoon oil in a frying pan over medium heat. In batches, add spoonfuls of the mixture into the pan, pressing down slightly to form small patties. Cook for 3–4 minutes each side, until golden brown and crispy. Add more oil if necessary for the next batch.

Allow the fritters to cool slightly before serving.

Cut into strips or mash for easier handling.

For babies 9+ months, serve whole as soft finger food or cut into bite-sized pieces alongside avocado fingers, yoghurt or steamed veggies for a balanced meal.

Make it ...

Egg free Swap egg for a store-bought egg replacer, or a flax egg (1 egg = 1 tablespoon ground flaxseed + 45 ml/1½ fl oz warm water) or a chia egg (1 egg = 1 tablespoon chia seed meal + ¼ cup/60 ml water).

Seasonal Swap vegetables for seasonal vegetables of choice.

Boosted Add 1 tablespoon chia seeds to mixture.

Different Add herbs of choice to mixture.

Pantry friendly Swap flour for a gluten-free flour of choice or wholemeal spelt flour (if gluten free isn't necessary).

Family friendly (2+) Add ½ cup (50 g) grated low-salt cheese to mixture (if dairy free isn't necessary); serve with a garden salad or in a wrap.

School friendly Pack cold or warm in a thermos for lunch.

Leftovers Store in an airtight container in the fridge for up to 3 days or freeze for up to 3 months.

6+ months

Makes 20

Prep 25 mins (+ cooling)

Cook 40 mins

Salmon & quinoa patties

One of my favourite ways to support brain development and growth is by serving up salmon – it's naturally rich in omega-3 fatty acids and nourishing fats that little bodies thrive on. The delicate flavour of the fish pairs beautifully with the nutty texture of quinoa, making this dish as delicious as it is nutrient dense. It's one of those meals that feels special but is so simple to put together.

Egg free

Gluten free

Peanut free

Sesame free

Soy free

Tree nut free

- 2 teaspoons extra virgin olive oil, plus extra 1–2 tablespoons
- 380 g (13½ oz) low-mercury, sustainably sourced skinless, boneless salmon fillets
- ½ cup (80 g) cooked fresh corn kernels
- 1 medium (100 g/3½ oz) carrot, peeled and chopped
- 1 large (130 g/4½ oz) leek, white part only, chopped
- 2 tablespoons fresh orange juice
- ¼ cup (40 g) brown rice flour
- ½ teaspoon dried mixed herbs
- 1 cup (180 g) soft-cooked quinoa (see tip)

Serving suggestions

Tzatziki dip (see page 238)

Steamed veggies

Preheat the oven to 180°C (350°F) and line a large baking tray with baking paper.

Heat the oil in a medium frying pan over medium heat. Cook the salmon for 5–6 minutes, or until cooked when tested with a fork. Remove from the pan and allow to cool.

Place the salmon, corn, carrot, leek and orange juice in a food processor and process until smooth, scraping down the side once or twice to help blend evenly. Add the flour and herbs and process until well combined. Add the quinoa and pulse to combine.

With slightly moistened hands, shape ¼ cupfuls of the mixture into mini patties (or smaller if preferred) and place on the prepared tray. Drizzle with extra oil, then bake for 30 minutes, or until golden brown.

Allow to cool, then cut into smaller pieces or mash for younger babies and serve with tzatziki and steamed veggies.

Make it ...

Crispy Instead of baking patties, pan-fry for 3–4 minutes each side; coat with Gluten-free crumb mix (see page 243) before baking.

Different Swap salmon for boneless white fish or use canned salmon.

Boosted Add fresh soft herbs and 1 cup (30 g) baby spinach to food processor with other ingredients.

Family friendly (2+) Add 1–2 tablespoons of good-quality Dijon mustard to mixture; serve with roasted vegetables and pesto; for a lighter meal, serve with a garden salad.

School friendly Pack warm in a thermos for lunch.

Tip You will need ⅓ cup (65 g) uncooked quinoa to make the required 1 cup cooked for this recipe.

Leftovers Store in an airtight container in the fridge for up to 3 days or freeze for up to 3 months.

Lamb cutlets

6+ months

Serves 4

Prep 5 mins

Cook 8-10 mins

 Dairy free

 Egg free

 Fish free

 Gluten free

 Peanut free

 Sesame free

 Soy free

 Tree nut free

These tender, juicy lamb cutlets were one of the first ways I introduced lamb to my babies. They quickly became a menu mainstay. The gentle hint of lemon and orange juice adds a subtle sweetness while also helping little tummies absorb iron – something I always felt reassured about when preparing this meal. These cutlets also helped my children become familiar with the taste and texture of red meat from an early age, making it more likely they'd accept it as they grew. Whether I shredded the meat into soft bites or let my babies hold the cutlet to gnaw on, it made for a nourishing, mess-filled meal we all enjoyed together – and still do.

- 2 tablespoons extra virgin olive oil
- 1 small (100 g/3½ oz) brown onion, thinly sliced
- 2 garlic cloves, crushed
- 8 grass-fed lamb cutlets
- Juice of 1 (150 g/5½ oz) orange
- Juice of 1 (90 g/3¼ oz) lemon
- 2 tablespoons mixed herb leaves (optional)
- Freshly ground black pepper, to taste (optional)

Serving suggestions

- Sweet potato or pumpkin (squash) mash
- Mushy peas

Heat the oil in a large frying pan over medium heat. Sauté the onion for 2–3 minutes, or until it begins to soften, then stir in the garlic and cook for another minute, or until fragrant.

Add the cutlets and sear for 3–4 minutes each side, or until nicely browned.

Add the orange and lemon juice and herbs and sizzle for a minute or two to enhance the flavour.

Cook the cutlets for another 2–3 minutes each side. Remove from the heat and transfer the cutlets to a plate for 5 minutes to rest. Season with pepper (if using).

Offer the cutlets whole (with the bone for grip) for baby-led weaning, ensuring the meat is soft and tender for safe chewing. Omit the onion mixture or just drizzle over the pan juices.

For babies 8–10 months, offer the whole cutlet (with the bone for grip) without the onion mixture or just drizzle over the pan juices; or serve the lamb and the onion thinly sliced, alongside mash or mushy peas.

Make it ...

Seasonal Swap mixed herbs for herbs of choice.

Family friendly (2+) Serve cutlets whole with roasted potatoes, side salad or steamed greens and a drizzle of citrusy pan juices; slice lamb and serve in warm wraps with Tzatziki dip (see page 238), cucumber sticks and cherry tomatoes.

Leftovers Store in an airtight container in the fridge for up to 3 days or freeze for up to 3 months.

8+ months

Serves 8

Prep 10 mins (+ cooling)

Cook 40 mins

 Vegan

 Dairy free

Egg free

 Fish free

 Peanut free

 Sesame free

 Soy free

 Tree nut free

Hearty minestrone soup

Don't discount soup as a meal option for little ones - it's a slurpalicious way to let baby try to 'catch' the pieces of pasta and veggies, and feed themselves. This bowl is swimming with nourishing ingredients, including cannellini beans, sweet potato and kale, so there are plenty of shapes and colours to choose from. It's gently seasoned with dried herbs to ensure it's full of flavour without being overpowering.

- 3 garlic cloves
- 1 small (100 g/3½ oz) brown onion, quartered
- ½ (90 g/3¼ oz) leek, white part only, roughly chopped
- 2 (80 g/2¾ oz) celery sticks, roughly chopped
- 1 tablespoon extra virgin olive oil
- 1 medium (120 g/4¼ oz) carrot, peeled and diced
- 1 large (160 g/5½ oz) zucchini (courgette), diced
- 1 small (300 g/10½ oz) sweet potato, peeled and diced
- 400 g (14 oz) can cannellini beans, drained and rinsed
- 400 g (14 oz) can butter beans, drained and rinsed
- 700 g (1 lb 9 oz) tomato passata (puréed tomatoes)
- ½ teaspoon dried oregano
- 6 cups (1.5 litres) low-salt vegetable stock or homemade broth (salt free for babies)
- 1¼ cups (125 g) dried wholegrain spirals (or pasta of choice)
- 1 cup (30 g) finely shredded kale leaves
- Freshly ground black pepper, to taste (optional)

Place the garlic, onion, leek and celery in a food processor and process until finely grated, scraping down the side once or twice to help grate evenly.

Heat the oil in a large saucepan or stockpot. Add the vegetable mixture. Sauté for 3–4 minutes, or until softened. Add the carrot, zucchini and sweet potato and cook for 3–4 minutes, or until they begin to break down.

Add the cannellini and butter beans, passata, oregano and stock or broth and bring to the boil. Cover, reduce the heat to low and simmer for 20 minutes, or until the vegetables have softened.

Add the pasta and kale and season with pepper (if using). Cook for another 10 minutes, or until the pasta is al dente.

Mash the vegetables and pasta to serve. Always allow the soup to cool to a safe temperature before serving.

Make it ...

Gluten free Swap wholegrain spirals for gluten-free pasta.

Seasonal Use seasonal vegetables of choice, such as green beans, fennel, pumpkin (squash), cauliflower, broccoli or peas.

Pantry friendly Swap cannellini and butters beans for legumes of choice.

Fussy-eater proof Purée sauce until smooth before adding pasta and kale; omit kale.

Family friendly (2+) Serve sprinkled with grated parmesan.

Leftovers Store in an airtight container in the fridge for up to 3 days or freeze for up to 3 months.

6+ months

Serves 6

Prep 10 mins (+ cooling)

Cook 35 mins

Creamy pumpkin & coconut soup

 Vegan

 Dairy free

 Fish free

 Gluten free

 Peanut free

 Sesame free

Soy free

 Tree nut free

Neither of my babies were big fans of plain pumpkin, so I created this as a way to encourage them. It started as a sweet potato soup, but the first time I swapped in pumpkin, it was a winner. The natural sweetness, paired with creamy coconut milk and warming cinnamon, completely transformed the flavour. Suddenly, the kids couldn't get enough. Now it's a comfort-food favourite. It's nourishing, velvety and packed with vitamin A from the pumpkin to support healthy eyes, skin and immunity. The coconut milk adds healthy fats that help little bodies absorb nutrients and stay fuller for longer, while the gentle spices are soothing on tummies.

1 tablespoon coconut oil

1 small (100 g/3½ oz) brown onion, sliced

1 (180 g/6 oz) leek, white part only, thinly sliced

3 garlic cloves, crushed

4 cups (500 g) peeled and finely chopped or grated pumpkin (squash)

1¼ cups (310 ml) low-salt vegetable stock or homemade broth (salt free for babies)

400 ml (14 fl oz) can coconut milk

1–2 teaspoons ground cinnamon, to taste

Serving suggestion

Dippers, such as steamed veggie fingers

In a large saucepan, heat the oil over medium heat. Add the onion, leek and garlic and sauté for 3–4 minutes, or until softened and translucent.

Stir in the remaining ingredients and bring to the boil. Reduce the heat to low and simmer gently for 25–30 minutes, or until the vegetables are soft. Remove from the heat and allow to cool slightly.

Blend with a stick blender or transfer the mixture to a food processor and process until a smooth and creamy texture is achieved, scraping down the side once or twice to help blend evenly.

Once cooled, serve in a baby-friendly open cup or feed with a preloaded spoon, gently guiding the spoon to the baby's mouth, or offer soup with dippers, such as steamed veggie fingers.

Make it ...

Hearty For a thicker soup, reduce to 200–250 ml (7–9 fl oz).

Seasonal Swap pumpkin for sweet potato, parsnip, cauliflower or broccoli.

Family friendly (2+) Serve with Cheesy butter crackers (see page 185), Soft naan (see page 230), sourdough toast or brown rice.

Leftovers Store in an airtight container in the fridge for up to 3 days or freeze for up to 3 months.

6+ months

Serves 8 (makes 16)

Prep 15 mins

Cook 15 mins

Lamb & vegetable koftas

 Dairy free

 Gluten free

 Fish free

 Peanut free

 Sesame free

 Soy free

 Tree nut free

Introduce your baby to the rich, savoury taste of lamb with these tender, nutrient-packed koftas. I developed this recipe for my babies to ensure they received the iron they needed to thrive. With a gentle blend of spices and hidden veggies, these koftas are a delicious way to expand your baby's palate while ensuring they get the nourishment they need.

1 large (150 g/5½ oz) leek, white part only, roughly chopped

1 medium (130 g/4½ oz) carrot, peeled and roughly chopped

2 (30 g/1 oz) pitted soft medjool dates

1 garlic clove

1 pasture-raised or organic egg

500 g (1 lb 2 oz) grass-fed minced (ground) lamb

½ teaspoon ground cinnamon

¼ teaspoon ground cumin

Extra virgin olive oil, for frying

Serving suggestion

Sweet potato mash

Place the leek, carrot, dates, garlic and egg in a food processor and process until smooth, scraping down the side once or twice to help blend evenly.

Transfer the mixture to a large bowl, then add the lamb, cinnamon and cumin. Mix well until fully combined. Shape the mixture into small koftas, using oiled hands or gloves to prevent sticking.

Heat oil in a frying pan over medium heat. In batches, cook the koftas, turning every 3–5 minutes, or until evenly browned and cooked through. (Alternatively, arrange them on a lined baking tray, drizzle with oil and bake at 180°C (350°F) for 25 minutes.)

Serve the koftas mashed, or whole as a finger food if they can safely grasp and chew or offer in finger-sized strips alongside mashed sweet potato.

Make it ...

Egg free Omit egg.

Vegetarian Swap lamb for canned/cooked chickpeas.

Different Swap mince for beef mince.

Boosted Add 2 cups (60 g) baby spinach to food processor with other ingredients.

Family friendly (2+) Serve with brown rice or sweet potato wedges and baked vegetables.

School friendly Delicious in wraps or pack warm in a thermos or on their own for lunch.

Leftovers Store in an airtight container in the fridge for up to 3 days or freeze for up to 3 months.

10+ months

Serves 4–6

Prep 15 mins

Cook 30 mins

Protein-packed chicken nuggets

 Fish free

 Gluten free

 Peanut free

 Sesame free

Soy free

 Tree nut free

These crunchy nuggets are a delicious, nutritious take on the fast-food fave, packed with protein-rich chicken and veggies for added goodness. It's almost impossible to find healthy store-bought options. That's why I developed this recipe, as an alternative for fussy little eaters and to ensure that babies do not get introduced to salty, additive-filled and ultra-processed food from the supermarket. My nuggets are golden and crispy, designed for little hands to grasp and self-feed, while offering a great source of protein, zinc and iron – key nutrients for babies and toddlers. The mild seasoning adds flavour without being overpowering. They are perfect for fussy babies, toddlers and children too.

500 g (1 lb 2 oz) pasture-raised or organic minced (ground) chicken

1 small (120 g/4¼ oz) carrot, peeled and finely grated

1 small (160 g/5½ oz) zucchini (courgette), finely grated and squeezed to remove excess water

1 garlic clove, crushed

1 small (100 g/3½ oz) brown onion, finely grated or diced

1 pasture-raised or organic egg

½ cup (75 g) Gluten-free crumb mix or Rice 'breadcrumbs' (see page 243), plus extra for coating

1 tablespoon grated parmesan (optional)

1 teaspoon sweet paprika

½ teaspoon dried oregano or mixed herbs

Extra virgin olive oil, to drizzle

Serving suggestions

Homemade dip, such as Hummus or Tzatziki (see pages 224 and 238)

Steamed veggies

Sweet potato mash

Preheat the oven to 200°C (400°F) and line a baking tray with baking paper.

In a large bowl, combine the chicken, carrot, zucchini, garlic, onion, egg, crumbs, parmesan (if using), paprika and herbs. Mix thoroughly until well combined.

Shape tablespoonfuls of the mixture into nugget-sized pieces. Roll each piece in extra crumbs to coat lightly for a crispy finish.

Place the nuggets on the prepared tray, spacing them slightly apart. Lightly drizzle with oil to enhance crispiness.

Bake, flipping halfway through, for 25–30 minutes, or until golden brown and cooked through.

Serve mashed, broken into soft, bite-sized pieces or offer as finger food alongside a dip, soft steamed veggies or mashed sweet potato.

Make it ...

Dairy free Swap parmesan for nutritional yeast flakes or omit.

Egg free Swap egg for a store-bought egg replacer, or a flax egg (1 egg = 1 tablespoon ground flaxseed + 45 ml/1½ fl oz warm water) or a chia egg (1 egg = 1 tablespoon chia seed meal + ¼ cup/60 ml water).

Seasonal Swap zucchini for pumpkin (squash), parsnip or sweet potato.

Pantry friendly Swap crumb mix or rice 'breadcrumbs' for Wholemeal sourdough breadcrumbs (see page 242).

Family friendly (2+) Add garlic and herbs for flavour; serve with potato wedges and Tomato sauce (see page 239).

Leftovers Store in an airtight container in the fridge for up to 3 days or freeze for up to 3 months.

Falafel balls

8+ months

Makes 14

Prep 10 mins
(+ 30 mins chilling & cooling)

Cook 20 mins

 Vegan

 Dairy free

 Egg free

 Fish free

 Gluten free

 Peanut free

 Sesame free

 Soy free

 Tree nut free

Turning a family favourite into a baby-friendly meal has never been easier! These vegan falafels are soft and bursting with gentle flavours. Blended with iron-rich spinach, chickpeas for fibre and protein, and fragrant herbs for added taste, they're full of new textures while supporting your little one's development. Serve with creamy Hummus (see page 224) or mashed avocado for a wholesome meal to enjoy, no matter their age or stage.

1½ cups (235 g) cooked chickpeas (or 400 g/ 14 oz can chickpeas, drained and rinsed)

½ medium (75 g/2½ oz) brown onion, roughly chopped

1 garlic clove

1 cup (40 g) baby spinach, roughly chopped

¼ cup (20 g) finely chopped flat-leaf parsley leaves, chopped

1 tablespoon extra virgin olive oil

½ teaspoon ground cumin

½ teaspoon ground coriander

⅓ cup (45 g) chickpea flour (besan)

Extra virgin olive oil or coconut oil, for frying

Serving suggestion

Homemade dip, such as Hummus (if sesame free isn't necessary; see page 224) or Tzatziki (if dairy free isn't necessary; see page 238)

Place the chickpeas, onion, garlic, spinach, parsley and olive oil in a food processor and process until smooth, scraping down the side once or twice to help blend evenly.

Add the spices and flour and stir to combine. Refrigerate the mixture for 30 minutes.

Scoop out 1 heaped tablespoon of the mixture and gently shape into a small patty or ball suitable for baby's size and age. Repeat with the remaining mixture.

Heat a non-stick frying pan over medium heat and add a little oil. In batches, add the falafels and cook for 3–4 minutes each side, or until golden brown and cooked through. Use caution when flipping to ensure they hold their shape.

Allow the falafels to cool slightly before serving to your baby. You can serve them as finger food or mash them for younger babies who are starting solids, with a dip on the side.

Make it ...

Seasonal Swap spinach for kale or greens of choice.

Boosted Mix 2 tablespoons ground seeds of choice (see tip 180) into mixture.

Family friendly (2+) Serve in wraps, pita pockets or alongside a fresh salad with a dollop of Tzatziki dip (see page 238) or Hummus (see page 224).

School friendly Pack with veggie sticks and a homemade dip for recess.

Leftovers Store in an airtight container in the fridge for up to 3 days or freeze for up to 3 months.

12+ months

Makes 1

Prep 15 mins (+ cooling)

Cook 30 mins

Vegetarian

Egg free

Fish free

Peanut free

Sesame free

Soy free

Tree nut free

Pumpkin patch pizza

This pizza (pictured on page 50) is my pick for celebrating your little one's birthday in a wholesome way. Made with a nourishing base of sweet potato and pumpkin, this pizza base is naturally sweet, packed with nutrients and has a soft texture. With its vibrant colour and gentle flavours, it's a guaranteed hit with both babies and adults. Plus, these bases can also be used as flatbreads or wraps.

Dough

1 cup (250 g) steamed and mashed sweet potato, cooled

½ cup (125 g) steamed and mashed kent pumpkin (squash), cooled

1½ cups (210 g) wholemeal spelt flour

2 teaspoons baking powder

Pinch of sea salt

1 tablespoon extra virgin olive oil, plus extra for greasing

Toppings

1 cup (260 g) no-added-salt tomato paste (concentrated purée) or tomato passata (puréed tomatoes)

2 cups (200 g) grated low-salt cheese (gouda, mozzarella or goat's cheese)

1 teaspoon dried oregano

Optional toppings

Basil leaves

Sliced mushroom, capsicum (pepper) and/or tomato

Pitted olives

Grated carrot and/or zucchini

Leftovers Store in an airtight container in the fridge for up to 3 days or freeze for up to 3 months.

Preheat the oven to 200°C (400°F). Line a pizza pan or baking tray with baking paper.

To make the dough, place all the ingredients in a food processor and process until well combined, scraping down the side once or twice to help blend evenly. (Alternatively, knead together in a large bowl with your hands until the mixture is well combined, smooth and doughy.)

Press out the dough into a large circle on the prepared pan or tray. If it's too sticky, oil your hands with extra oil. To achieve a crispy base, the dough should be about a 0.5 cm (¼ in) thick.

Bake for 15–20 minutes, or until the edge is browned slightly. (Cook for 20 minutes for a crispy base.) Remove from the oven, spread over the tomato paste or passata, then scatter over the cheese, oregano and any of the optional toppings.

Turn the oven to grill (broiler) on high. Grill for 5–8 minutes, or until the cheese is melted. Keep a close eye to prevent burning.

Remove from the oven and allow to cool.

For babies 8–12 months, cut the pizza into small squares or thin strips to make it easy for little hands to grasp and self-feed.

Make it ...

Gluten free Swap flour for almond meal (if tree nut free isn't necessary), a cassava and millet flour mix or a gluten-free flour blend.

Dairy free Swap cheese for crumbled tofu or omit.

Batch cooked Shape and pre-bake smaller bases, then freeze in airtight containers for up to 4 months to have as a quick dinner or lunch-box meal.

Party tip Turn your baby's pizza into a vibrant party platter by using colourful veggie toppings and cutting the pizza into fun shapes with cookie cutters shaped like stars, hearts or the number one for their first birthday. You can also make mini pizzas.

10+ months

Makes 1

Prep 10 mins (+ cooling)

Cook 25 mins

Easy hidden-chickpea pizza

Vegetarian

Fish free

Gluten free

Peanut free

Sesame free

Soy free

Tree nut free

This chickpea pizza base is a wholesome, protein-rich alternative to traditional pizza dough. Made with chickpeas and chickpea flour (besan), it's naturally gluten free, packed with fibre and has a gentle flavour. The soft yet sturdy texture can hold lots of delicious toppings, from classic tomato and cheese to baby-friendly veg. It's a simple, nutritious option for both quick family meals and special occasions.

400 g (14 oz) can no-added-salt chickpeas, drained and rinsed

1 tablespoon extra virgin olive oil, plus extra for greasing

1 large pasture-raised or organic egg

½ cup, tightly packed (85 g) chickpea flour (besan), plus extra for dusting

Toppings

⅓ cup (80 ml) no-added-salt tomato passata (puréed tomatoes)

1 teaspoon chopped oregano leaves or dried oregano (optional)

1 cup (100 g) grated low-salt cheese

Handful of basil leaves, chopped (optional)

Preheat the oven to 180°C (350°F) and line a baking tray or pizza pan with baking paper.

Place the chickpeas, oil and egg in a high-speed blender and blend until smooth, scraping down the side once or twice to help blend evenly.

Add the flour and process until well combined. The dough will still be sticky to the touch.

Sprinkle the dough with some extra flour, and oil your hands. Shape the dough into a round pizza shape, pressing it down onto the prepared tray until approx. 0.5–1 cm (¼–½ in) thick. Bake for 15 minutes.

Take out of the oven. Spread the pizza base with passata and sprinkle with cheese and oregano (if using).

Increase the oven temperature to 200°C (400°F) and bake the pizza for another 5–10 minutes, or until the cheese is melted.

Allow to cool completely. Sprinkle with basil (if using).

Cut the pizza into soft, manageable strips or bite-sized pieces to encourage self-feeding.

Make it ...

Dairy free Omit cheese.

Boosted Top pizza with sliced vegetables, such as capsicum (pepper), mushroom, tomato, corn and spinach.

Different Use toppings of choice.

Family friendly (2+) Season base with ½ teaspoon salt or to taste; serve with salad for a balanced, wholesome meal.

School friendly Pack slice/s in lunch box.

Tip Shape and bake smaller bases, then freeze in airtight containers for a quick dinner or lunch-box option.

Leftovers Store in an airtight container in the fridge for up to 3 days or freeze for up to 3 months.

8+ months

Serves 6

Prep 15 mins (+ cooling)

Cook 35 mins

Sneaky veggie chicken noodle soup

 Dairy free

 Egg free

 Fish free

 Gluten free

 Peanut free

Sesame free

 Soy free

 Tree nut free

All kids love chicken noodle soup, and this one holds a special place in my heart because it was my baby's first. I wanted to create a nourishing version that was packed with hidden veggies yet still comforting and delicious. Blending the vegetables into the broth makes it smooth and creamy, which gives it a baby-friendly texture boosted with vitamins and fibre in every spoonful. With tender chicken for protein and iron, soft noodles for energy and a soothing, hydrating broth, it's a complete and balanced meal that supports growth, digestion and immunity.

1 tablespoon extra virgin olive oil

1 small (100 g/3½ oz) brown onion, finely chopped

1 (40 g/1½ oz) celery stalk, chopped

2 garlic cloves, crushed

1 large (160 g/5½ oz) carrot, peeled and chopped

1 small (160 g/5½ oz) zucchini (courgette), chopped

1 small (120 g/4¼ oz) potato, peeled and diced

Pinch of ground turmeric

Pinch of freshly ground black pepper (optional)

4 cups (1 litres) low-salt vegetable or chicken stock or homemade broth (salt free for babies)

180 g (6 oz) gluten-free dried spaghetti, broken into quarters

250 g (9 oz) pasture-raised or organic cooked shredded chicken breast (steamed, roasted or grilled)

Heat the oil in a large saucepan over medium heat. Add the onion, celery, garlic, carrot, zucchini, potato, turmeric and pepper (if using) and sauté for 3–4 minutes, or until slightly softened.

Pour in the stock or broth and 4 cups (1 litres) water. Bring to the boil, then reduce the heat to low and simmer for 20 minutes, or until the veggies are really soft.

Using a stick blender, blend the mixture until smooth to create a creamy, nutrient-rich base.

Stir in the pasta and chicken and cook, stirring occasionally, for 8–10 minutes, or until the pasta is al dente and the chicken is heated through. Remove from the heat and allow to cool slightly before serving.

Mash the spaghetti into smaller, softer pieces or offer small spoonfuls of the soup.

For babies 10–12 months, serve in a bowl with soft pieces of chicken and pasta for self-feeding.

Make it ...

Seasonal Swap carrot, zucchini and potato for seasonal vegetables of choice.

Pantry friendly Swap spaghetti for brown rice, quinoa, barley or gluten-free spaghetti.

Family friendly (2+) Skip the blending.

Leftovers Store in an airtight container in the fridge for up to 3 days or freeze for up to 3 months.

Tip If you don't have any leftover chicken, you can cook 300–350 g (10½–12 oz) raw chicken directly in the soup. Add it (whole or diced) to the pan with the stock and simmer for 20–25 minutes, or until fully cooked through. Remove the chicken, shred or chop, then return it to the soup before adding the pasta.

Snacks

8+ months

Makes 30

Prep 20 mins (+ cooling)

Cook 25 mins

Crunchy broccoli nuggets

- Vegetarian
- Fish free
- Gluten free
- Peanut free
- Soy free
- Tree nut free

Getting little ones to eat can feel like a daily battle, especially when green things are involved. I created these nuggets during one of those phases when my own kids refused anything that looked remotely 'leafy'. I wrapped the nuggets in a golden, cheesy coating and shaped them just the right size for little hands, and something shifted – suddenly greens weren't so scary anymore! These crispy nuggets are a delicious and approachable way to introduce veggies. They're perfect for baby-led weaning and help support pincer grasp development, while exposing kids to new textures. Bonus: they're freezer and lunch-box friendly, and always a win with a side of mashed avocado or a dip.

3 cups (240 g) raw broccoli florets

¼ cup tightly packed (20 g) baby spinach, roughly chopped

1 tablespoon flat-leaf parsley leaves, chopped

2 pasture-raised or organic eggs

¼ small (30 g/1 oz) brown onion, quartered (optional)

⅓ cup (35 g) grated low-salt cheese

2 tablespoons extra virgin olive oil, plus extra for drizzling

½ cup (75 g) Gluten-free crumb mix or Rice 'breadcrumbs' (see page 243)

½ cup (80 g) sesame seeds (optional)

Serving suggestion

Homemade dip, such as Hummus or Tzatziki (see pages 224 and 238)

Preheat the oven to 180°C (350°F) and line a baking tray with baking paper.

Pat-dry the broccoli and place in a food processor. Process until finely chopped and the consistency resembles rice. Add the spinach, parsley, eggs, onion (if using), cheese and oil and process until smooth. Add the breadcrumbs and sesame seeds and pulse to combine.

Shape the mixture into small logs and place on the prepared tray. Drizzle with a little extra oil and bake for 20–25 minutes, or until golden brown and crispy on top.

Allow to cool completely before serving mashed, as finger food or cut into small bite-sized pieces, alongside a dip, such as hummus or tzatziki, or natural yoghurt.

Make it ...

Egg free Swap egg for a store-bought egg replacer, or a flax egg (1 egg = 1 tablespoon ground flaxseed + 45 ml/1½ fl oz warm water) or a chia egg (1 egg = 1 tablespoon chia seed meal + ¼ cup/60 ml water).

Seasonal Swap broccoli for cauliflower, spinach for greens of choice and/or parsley for herbs of choice.

Boosted Add 1 tablespoon chia seeds to mixture before baking.

Faster Press mixture into a lined baking dish and bake for 25–30 minutes. Once cooled, cut into small bites.

Pantry friendly Swap crumb mix or rice 'breadcrumbs' for Wholemeal sourdough breadcrumbs (if gluten free isn't necessary; see page 242); swap sesame seeds for seeds of choice.

Fussy-eater proof Coat nuggets in more crumbs and fry in extra virgin olive oil; swap broccoli for cauliflower and potato and omit spinach.

Tip If your little one is new to finger foods, you can shape these into flatter patties to make them even easier to hold.

Leftovers Store in an airtight container in the fridge for up to 3 days or freeze for up to 3 months.

6+ months

Makes 12

Prep 10 mins (+ cooling)

Cook 25 mins

Nourishing herby fish bites

 Dairy free

 Gluten free

 Peanut free

 Sesame free

Soy free

 Tree nut free

Most babies aren't born fussy eaters. Sometimes it's our own reactions that shape theirs. When introduced early as part of a real-food approach, even strong-flavoured ingredients like sardines can become staples. Both my children loved these snacks from the start, and I've seen the same again and again with families I've supported. These bites are the perfect entry point: gently herbed, soft in texture and surprisingly subtle in flavour. Sardines are one of the most nutrient-dense sources of omega-3s and incredibly budget friendly. They're a simple and wholesome way to raise a confident, adventurous eater.

1 cup (170 g) soft-cooked millet, cooled

120 g (4¼ oz) can sardines in spring water, drained

1 medium (100 g/3½ oz) finely grated carrot

1 pasture-raised or organic egg

2 tablespoons finely chopped coriander (cilantro) leaves

Zest of 1 (90 g/3¼ oz) lemon

1 tablespoon fresh lemon juice

½ teaspoon dried oregano

½ teaspoon crushed garlic or pure garlic powder (optional)

2–3 tablespoons Gluten-free crumb mix or Rice 'breadcrumbs' (see page 243)

Extra virgin olive oil, for cooking

Serving suggestions

Steamed veggies

Sliced avocado

Preheat the oven to 180°C (350°F) and line a baking tray with baking paper.

Place the millet, sardines, carrot, egg, coriander, lemon zest and juice, dried oregano and garlic or garlic powder (if using) in a food processor and process until finely crushed or puréed, scraping down the side once or twice to help blend evenly.

Add 2 tablespoons crumbs and gently stir through until combined. Add the remaining 1 tablespoon if the mixture feels too wet. Form small patties using your hands and place on the prepared tray. Drizzle with oil and bake for 20–25 minutes, or until golden. (Alternatively, fry them in a frying pan for about 3–4 minutes each side.)

Allow them to cool slightly before serving.

Serve mashed or for finger-food practice alongside steamed veggies and avocado slices.

Make it ...

Seasonal Swap carrot for pumpkin (squash) or sweet potato.

Faster Mash everything together, except oil, in a large bowl, then shape into patties.

Pantry friendly Swap sardines for canned tuna or salmon; swap crumb mix for oat flour or Wholemeal sourdough breadcrumbs (if gluten free isn't necessary; see page 242).

Family friendly (2+) Serve with Tzatziki dip (see page 238) or add to wraps with cucumber, cherry tomatoes and a drizzle of lemon juice for a light lunch; pair with sweet potato wedges and a green salad.

Leftovers Store in an airtight container in the fridge for up to 3 days or freeze for up to 3 months.

8+ months

Makes 20

Prep 15 mins (+ cooling)

Cook 20 mins

Cheesy veggie muffins

Vegetarian

Fish free

Peanut free

Sesame free

Soy free

Tree nut free

Finding a veggie-filled muffin that works for babies starting solids and still gets a thumbs up from fussy eaters and older kids is not easy. Packed with zucchini, carrot, protein-rich eggs and calcium-loaded cheese, these muffins are soft and suited for little hands and developing tastebuds. Whether you're navigating baby-led weaning, lunch-box prep or after-school hunger, these muffins tick every box. Enjoy them warm, freeze them for later or serve with a dollop of tomato sauce for an extra burst of flavour. One batch, multiple wins.

- 1 large (260 g/9¼ oz) zucchini (courgette), finely grated
- 1 large (150 g/5½ oz) carrot, peeled and finely grated
- 2 cups (300 g) wholemeal spelt flour
- 1 teaspoon baking powder
- ½ teaspoon bicarbonate of soda (baking soda)
- 1½ cups (150 g) low-salt cheese, grated
- ½ cup (125 ml) milk of choice
- ¼ cup (65 g) natural unsweetened yoghurt
- ¼ cup (60 ml) extra virgin olive oil
- 2 pasture-raised or organic eggs

Serving suggestion

Tomato sauce (see page 239)

Preheat oven to 180°C (350°F) and line a mini muffin tray with paper cases.

Place the zucchini and carrot in a clean tea (dish) towel and squeeze out any excess water.

Add all the ingredients to a food processor and process until smooth.

Spoon the batter into the prepared muffin cases and bake for 15–20 minutes, or until a cake tester or skewer inserted comes out clean.

Allow to cool before serving mashed or as finger food, with tomato sauce on the side.

Make it ...

Dairy free Omit cheese; use coconut, oat or soy milk; swap yoghurt for natural unsweetened coconut yoghurt.

Gluten free Swap flour for brown rice flour, buckwheat flour, millet flour or a gluten-free flour blend.

Egg free Swap egg for a store-bought egg replacer, or a flax egg (1 egg = 1 tablespoon ground flaxseed + 45 ml/1½ fl oz warm water) or a chia egg (1 egg = 1 tablespoon chia seed meal + ¼ cup/60 ml water).

Seasonal Swap vegetables for any seasonal root vegetables.

Different Swap cheese for goat's cheese or mozzarella.

Faster Finely grate zucchini and carrot in food processor.

Fussy-eater proof Peel zucchini before grating.

School friendly This is an excellent bento-style lunch option for toddlers or a quick and filling snack for recess.

Leftovers Store in an airtight container in the fridge for up to 3 days or freeze for up to 3 months.

8+ months

Makes 12

Prep 10 mins (+ cooling)

Cook 25 mins

Cheesy savoury blondies

Vegetarian

Fish free

Gluten free

Peanut free

Sesame free

Soy free

Tree nut free

I developed this recipe after the success of my sweet Nourishing blondies (see page 205) – proof that chickpeas are one of the most versatile pantry staples. They're affordable and an excellent source of plant-based protein and fibre. This savoury version is packed with grated veggies and makes a nourishing, fuss-free option for breakfast, as a lunch-box snack, or turn it into a main with steamed veggies and a homemade dip, like hummus, mashed avo or natural yoghurt. I often bake it in batches and freeze portions for those days when time is tight, but you still want something wholesome on the table. It'll be ready when you are.

- 400 g (14 oz) can chickpeas, rinsed and drained
- 3 pasture-raised or organic eggs
- ¼ cup (60 ml) extra virgin olive oil
- ½ cup (50 g) grated low-salt cheese, plus extra ⅓ cup (35 g)
- 1½ tablespoons coconut flour
- 1 teaspoon baking powder
- 1 cup (250 g) leftover roast vegetables of choice (such as pumpkin/squash, sweet potato, carrot, cauliflower and broccoli)

Preheat the oven to 180°C (350°F) and line the base and sides of a 20 cm (8 in) square cake tin with baking paper.

Place the chickpeas, eggs and oil in a food processor and process until smooth, scraping down the side once or twice to help blend evenly.

Add the cheese, flour and baking powder and process until well combined. Add the roast vegetables and pulse to combine. Transfer the mixture to the prepared tin and sprinkle with extra cheese. Bake for 20–25 minutes.

Allow to cool before cutting into squares.

Cut the blondies into soft, finger-sized pieces or mash them for easier handling.

Make it …

Dairy free Swap cheese for nutritional yeast flakes, coconut cream or silken tofu.

Pantry friendly Swap chickpeas for cannellini or navy beans; swap coconut flour for flour of choice.

Fussy-eater proof Make sure beans and vegetables are processed very smoothly.

Family friendly (2+) Top with crumbled feta instead of grated cheese; serve as a snack or side dish with Tzatziki dip (see page 238) and steamed veggies.

Leftovers Store in an airtight container in the fridge for up to 3 days or freeze for up to 3 months.

Chickpea & pumpkin bites

8+ months

Serves 4 (makes 12)

Prep 15 mins

Cook 30 mins

 Vegetarian

 Dairy free

 Fish free

Gluten free

 Peanut free

 Sesame free

 Soy free

 Tree nut free

These are the ultimate nutrient-packed finger food – soft on the inside, lightly crisp on the outside and bursting with flavour! Made with fibre-rich chickpeas, vitamin-packed pumpkin and energy-boosting brown rice, they're made for little hands and growing appetites. Try these for baby-led weaning to introduce a gentle hint of cumin for extra flavour while being easy to chew and digest. Serve them with a dip, like mashed avocado or yoghurt, or pair with steamed veggies for a wholesome meal.

- 2 garlic cloves
- 2 spring onions (scallions), chopped
- ½ cup (115 g) steamed or roasted pumpkin (squash)
- 1 pasture-raised or organic egg
- 2 tablespoons coriander (cilantro) leaves
- ½ teaspoon ground cumin
- 1 cup (180 g) soft-cooked brown rice
- 400 g (14 oz) can chickpeas, drained and rinsed
- ⅓ cup (45 g) Rice 'breadcrumbs' (see page 243)
- 2 tablespoons extra virgin olive oil

Optional toppings

- Tzatziki dip (if dairy free isn't necessary; see page 238)
- Hummus (if sesame free isn't necessary; see page 224)
- Natural unsweetened coconut yoghurt

Preheat the oven to 180°C (350°F) and line a baking tray with baking paper.

In a food processor, blend the garlic, spring onion, pumpkin, egg, coriander and cumin until smooth.

Add the rice and chickpeas, then pulse a few times until the mixture is combined. Mix in the crumbs with two or three more pulses.

Shape into small patties, about 1.5 cm (⅝ in) thick and place on the prepared tray. Drizzle with the oil. Bake for 30 minutes, or until golden.

Mash the patties with a little tzatziki, hummus or yoghurt for a soft, creamy texture. For babies practising self-feeding, cut the patties into small, soft strips or offer as whole patties for them to grasp.

Make it ...

Egg free Swap egg for a store-bought egg replacer, or a flax egg (1 egg = 1 tablespoon ground flaxseed + 45 ml/1½ fl oz warm water) or a chia egg (1 egg = 1 tablespoon chia seed meal + ¼ cup/60 ml water).

Seasonal Swap pumpkin for sweet potato.

Boosted Add ¼ cup (35 g) pumpkin or sunflower seed meal to batter.

Pantry friendly Swap chickpeas for beans of choice.

Fussy-eater proof Make sure mixture has very smooth consistency.

School friendly Delicious in a wrap or sandwich or warm in a thermos for lunch.

Leftovers Store in an airtight container in the fridge for up to 3 days or freeze for up to 3 months.

8+ months

Makes 12–16

Prep 20 mins

Cook 30 mins

Golden lentil & pumpkin cakes

 Vegetarian

 Fish free

 Gluten free

 Peanut free

 Sesame free

 Soy free

 Tree nut free

Creating a plant-based patty that both my babies and I genuinely enjoyed took some trial and error, but this one was a success. As a busy working mum, I needed something quick to prep, freezable, protein rich and filling enough for the whole family. When my daughter started solids, having these stocked in the freezer was a lifesaver. We could all sit down to the same meal, my baby, my 3-year-old son and I, which in those chaotic early years felt like the biggest win. These bites became part of our weekly rhythm, and I hope they become a favourite in your home too.

¾ cup (150 g) steamed or roasted pumpkin (squash)

400 g (14 oz) can lentils, drained and rinsed

1 large pasture-raised or organic egg

1 cup, tightly packed (120 g) grated low-salt cheese

¼ cup (30 g) coconut flour

¼ cup (35 g) Rice 'breadcrumbs' (see page 243)

2 tablespoons extra virgin olive oil, for drizzling

Optional toppings

Pesto or Hummus (if sesame free isn't necessary; see page 224)

Preheat the oven to 180°C (350°F) and line a baking tray with baking paper.

In a food processor, combine the pumpkin, lentils, egg and cheese until the lentils are broken down and the mixture is well combined (be careful not to over-process).

Add the flour and crumbs and pulse until combined.

Shape heaped tablespoons of the mixture into small patties and place on the prepared tray. Drizzle with the oil and bake, flipping halfway through, for 20–30 minutes, or until golden brown.

Serve mashed or as finger food on their own or with a side of pesto or hummus.

Make it ...

Dairy free Swap cheese for ½ cup (15 g) nutritional yeast flakes or omit.

Egg free Swap egg for a store-bought egg replacer, or a flax egg (1 egg = 1 tablespoon ground flaxseed + 45 ml/1½ fl oz warm water) or a chia egg (1 egg = 1 tablespoon chia seed meal + ¼ cup/60 ml water).

Boosted Add soft herb leaves, such as basil or oregano, and/or 1 cup (30 g) baby spinach to food processor along with the other ingredients.

Pantry friendly Swap lentils for legumes of choice; swap flour for almond meal or flour of choice; swap rice 'breadcrumbs' for Wholemeal sourdough breadcrumbs (if gluten free isn't necessary; see page 242).

Family friendly (2+) Add soft herb leaves to mixture, such as basil or oregano.

Tip These patties store well in the freezer, making them a great meal-prep option for busy days. Just reheat and you're done!

Leftovers Store in an airtight container in the fridge for up to 3 days or freeze for up to 3 months.

10+ months

Makes 12

Prep 15 mins (+ cooling)

Cook 25 mins

 Vegetarian

 Egg free

 Fish free

 Peanut free

 Sesame free

 Soy free

 Tree nut free

Pizza scrolls

It's no surprise that little ones gravitate towards bready foods. Soft textures, familiar flavours and easy-to-grasp shapes make them a go-to for babies and toddlers. But the reality is, many bakery-style snacks that look wholesome are anything but. Most are loaded with hidden sodium, additives, seed oils and preservatives that don't belong in a baby's or young child's diet. I developed these scrolls as an alternative to satisfy bread-loving cravings without compromising on health. Help shape lifelong food preferences with real food over the ultra-processed options.

Dough

- 2 cups (300 g) wholemeal spelt flour, plus extra for dusting
- 1 cup (260 g) natural unsweetened Greek-style yoghurt, plus extra if needed
- 1 teaspoon baking powder
- ¼ teaspoon bicarbonate of soda (baking soda)

Filling

- ¼ cup (60 ml) tomato passata (puréed tomatoes)
- ¼ cup (65 g) pumpkin (squash) or carrot purée
- 1 teaspoon dried oregano
- ⅓ cup (35 g) grated low-salt cheese

Preheat the oven to 180°C (350°F) and line a large baking tray with baking paper.

In a food processor, combine all the dough ingredients and blend until smooth. Transfer the dough to a work surface and shape into a ball. Add a little extra yoghurt if the dough is too dry; add extra flour if too wet. Place between two sheets of baking paper. If the dough is too sticky, lightly dust the paper and dough with extra flour. Roll out the dough into a rectangle, about 25 × 40 cm (10 × 16 in) and 0.5–1 cm (¼–½ in) thick. Remove the top sheet of paper.

For the filling, mix the passata and vegetable purée until well combined.

Evenly spread the passata mixture over the dough, then sprinkle with the oregano and cheese.

Cut the dough into long strips lengthways, then halve each strip crossways. Roll each strip into a snail shape and arrange them on the prepared tray 2 cm (¾ in) apart. Bake for 20–25 minutes, or until golden.

Allow to cool on a wire rack before serving.

Slice the scrolls into bite-sized pieces or offer halves. These are soft enough for self-feeding and sturdy enough for little hands to grasp.

Leftovers Store in an airtight container in the fridge for up to 3 days or freeze for up to 3 months.

Make it ...

Dairy free Swap yoghurt for natural unsweetened coconut, oat or soy yoghurt and omit cheese.

Gluten free Swap flour for a blend of 1½ cups (180 g) buckwheat flour, 1 cup (120 g) almond flour and 1 teaspoon psyllium husk powder (if tree nut free isn't necessary).

Pantry friendly Swap flour for wholemeal flour.

Family friendly (2+) Season dough with a pinch of sea salt; serve alongside a salad or roasted veggies for a balanced meal; boost flavour by adding finely chopped basil leaves or olives to filling.

School friendly Pack in lunch box or reheat as a quick after-school snack.

8+ months

Serves 15

Prep 15 mins (+ cooling)

Cook 1 hr

Pumpkin zucchini loaf

 Vegetarian

 Dairy free

 Fish free

 Gluten free

 Peanut free

 Sesame free

 Soy free

 Tree nut free

This is a soft, nutrient-rich loaf packed with wholesome pumpkin and zucchini (courgette). It's naturally moist and full of fibre, making it gentle on tiny tummies. The seed meal provides a boost of protein, healthy fats and essential minerals like zinc, while coconut flour keeps it light and gluten free. Its mildly sweet, earthy flavour makes it a great option for breakfast, snacks or even as a side with savoury meals.

2 cups (250 g) peeled and finely grated butternut pumpkin (squash)

1 cup (180 g) peeled and finely grated zucchini (courgette)

½ cup (125 ml) extra virgin olive oil

4 large pasture-raised or organic eggs

2 cups (240 g) seed meal (see box, below)

½ cup (60 g) coconut flour

1 cup (120 g) arrowroot

2 teaspoons baking powder

Serving suggestions

Natural unsweetened coconut yoghurt

Mashed avocado

Preheat the oven to 180°C (350°F) and line the base and sides of a loaf tin with baking paper.

Place the pumpkin and zucchini in a clean tea (dish) towel and squeeze out any excess liquid.

Place the grated vegetables, oil and eggs in a food processor and process until smooth. Add the remaining ingredients and process until combined.

Pour the mixture into the prepared tin and bake for 55–60 minutes, or until a cake tester or skewer inserted comes out clean.

Allow to cool on a wire rack before slicing.

Serve warm in soft strips or small bite-sized pieces for self-feeding babies, or mash lightly for younger eaters. Spread with yoghurt or mashed avocado for added nourishment.

Make it ...

Egg free Swap egg for a store-bought egg replacer, or a flax egg (1 egg = 1 tablespoon ground flaxseed + 45 ml/1½ fl oz warm water) or a chia egg (1 egg = 1 tablespoon chia seed meal + ¼ cup/60 ml water).

Seasonal Swap pumpkin for carrot.

Boosted Spread nut butter of choice (if nut free isn't necessary) over a slice for a protein-boosted snack.

Faster Finely grate pumpkin and zucchini in food processor.

Pantry friendly Swap seed meal for almond meal (if nut free isn't necessary).

Family friendly (2+) Season batter with salt and pepper; add ½ cup (40 g) grated parmesan to batter.

Leftovers Store in an airtight container in the fridge for up to 3 days or freeze for up to 3 months.

How to make seed meal

Place seeds of choice, such as pepitas (pumpkin seeds), sunflower seeds and flaxseeds, in a food processor or high-speed blender and blend until a flour consistency is reached.

8+ months

Serves 15–20

Prep 20 mins (+ cooling)

Cook 40 mins

 Vegetarian

 Egg free

 Fish free

Peanut free

 Sesame free

 Soy free

 Tree nut free

Sweet potato & broccoli slice

This easy, veggie-packed slice isn't just nutritious; it's a parenting win you'll feel good about. Making baby snacks from scratch doesn't have to be complicated and this recipe proves it. In just one batch, you've made a lunch-box staple, a freezer backup and a nourishing snack for your little one. Sweet potato delivers slow-burning energy and immune-boosting beta-carotene, while broccoli adds gut-friendly fibre and key nutrients for growth. Add a little cheese for comfort and flavour, and you've got a slice that feels familiar but does far more for your child's development than anything store-bought.

1⅓ cups, tightly packed (240 g) peeled and steamed sweet potato

½ cup (80 g) steamed broccoli florets

½ cup (50 g) grated low-salt cheese

⅔ cup (100 g) wholemeal spelt flour

1 tablespoon chia seeds

¼ cup, tightly packed (40 g) chickpea flour (besan)

½ cup (125 ml) milk of choice

1 tablespoon extra virgin olive oil

Serving suggestions

Steamed veggies

Mashed avocado

Preheat the oven to 180°C (350°F) and line a baking dish with baking paper.

Place all the ingredients in a food processor and process until well combined. Transfer to the prepared dish and spread evenly. Bake for 30–40 minutes, or until firm and golden.

Allow to cool completely before cutting into slices.

Serve in soft, finger-sized strips or small cubes for easy self-feeding and offer alongside soft, steamed veggies or mashed avocado.

Make it ...

Dairy free Swap cheese for nutritional yeast flakes and use coconut, oat or soy milk.

Gluten free Swap flour with brown rice flour, buckwheat flour or chickpea flour.

Seasonal Swap sweet potato for pumpkin (squash) and/or broccoli for cauliflower.

Fussy-eater proof Blend mixture until smooth.

Family friendly (2+) Serve warm or cold with a dollop of natural unsweetened Greek-style yoghurt or Hummus (see page 224) for added creaminess; pair with a side salad, roasted vegetables or grilled chicken for a complete and nourishing family meal.

School friendly Perfect lunch-box filler for recess or on-the-go snack.

Leftovers Store in an airtight container in the fridge for up to 3 days or freeze for up to 3 months.

8+ months

Makes 14–16

Prep 10 mins (+ cooling)

Cook 15 mins

Vegetarian

Egg free

Fish free

Gluten free

 Peanut free

 Sesame free

 Soy free

 Tree nut free

Green goodness bites

These bites are a delicious way to introduce more variety and vegetarian-powered nutrition into your family's week. Offering a wide range of plant-based flavours and textures helps expand little tastebuds and builds acceptance for a broader range of foods. By adding more colour and variety to your meals, you're supporting gut health and immunity, and creating strong, healthy food foundations for everyone around the table.

- ½ cup (90 g) soft-cooked quinoa
- ½ cup (90 g) soft-cooked brown rice
- ½ cup (45 g) sautéed spinach, finely chopped
- ¼ cup (25 g) grated carrot
- ¼ cup (45 g) grated zucchini (courgette)
- 2 tablespoons chickpea flour (besan)
- 1 tablespoon flaxseed meal
- 1 tablespoon grated low-salt cheese (optional)
- ½ teaspoon pure garlic powder
- ½ teaspoon dried oregano
- 1 tablespoon extra virgin olive oil, plus extra if frying

Serving suggestions

- Steamed veggies
- Sweet potato or pumpkin mash
- Homemade dip, such as Tzatziki dip (see page 238) or Hummus (if sesame free isn't necessary; see page 224)

Preheat the oven to 180°C (350°F) and line a baking tray with baking paper.

Place the quinoa, rice, spinach, carrot and zucchini in a food processor and process until finely chopped or mashed. Add the flour, flaxseed meal, cheese (if using), garlic powder and oregano and pulse to combine.

Scoop up level tablespoon portions and roll into bite-sized balls. Place on the prepared tray and lightly press to flatten (for younger babies). Drizzle with the oil, then bake for 15 minutes, or until slightly golden and firm enough to hold together. (Alternatively, cook in a frying pan with the oil – you might need a bit extra.)

Allow to cool before serving.

Serve mashed or as finger food alongside steamed veggies or mashed sweet potato or pumpkin and a dip.

Make it ...

Dairy free Omit cheese or swap for coconut cream.

Pantry friendly Swap quinoa for more brown rice or grain of choice.

Family friendly (2+) Serve in a wrap or create a delicious salad bowl and drizzle with tahini or Tzatziki dip (see page 238).

School friendly Delicious in a wrap or sandwich or for an after-school snack.

Leftovers Store in an airtight container in the fridge for up to 3 days or freeze for up to 3 months.

10+ months

Makes 16

Prep 20 mins (+ cooling)

Cook 25 mins

Veggie-loaded scones

 Vegetarian

 Egg free

 Fish free

 Peanut free

 Sesame free

 Soy free

 Tree nut free

- ½ cup (80 g) mixed seeds (we used 30 g/1 oz pepitas/pumpkin seeds, 30 g/1 oz sunflower seeds and 20 g/¾ oz flaxseeds)
- 1⅔ cups (250 g) wholemeal spelt flour, plus extra for dusting
- ½ teaspoon bicarbonate of soda (baking soda)
- ½ teaspoon baking powder
- 60 g (2 oz) unsalted butter, cold and chopped
- ¾ cup (75 g) grated low-salt yellow cheese, plus extra ½ cup (50 g)
- 1 large (150 g/5½ oz) carrot, peeled and finely grated
- 1 small (130 g) zucchini (courgette), peeled and finely grated
- 1 cup (260 g) natural unsweetened Greek-style yoghurt, plus extra if needed

Serving suggestions

Natural unsweetened Greek-style yoghurt

Mashed avocado

Homemade soup

These savoury scones are one of those hidden gems I kept coming back to during the toddler years. They're the kind of snack that lets you tick the 'veggies' box without the daily mealtime battles. I loved watching my kids happily devour them, unaware of just how many nutrients were packed into each bite. Serve them warm from the oven, broken into fingers for baby-led weaning or with yoghurt for older kids. These have been a real win in our kitchen and I hope they'll become a go-to in yours too.

Preheat the oven 180°C (350°F) and line a baking tray with baking paper.

Place the seeds in a food processor and process until a flour consistency is reached. Add the flour, bicarb, baking powder, butter and cheese and process until a breadcrumb consistency is reached.

Place the carrot and zucchini in a clean tea (dish) towel and squeeze out any excess liquid. Transfer to a large bowl and mix in the yoghurt.

Add the flour mixture to the vegetable mixture. Using your hands or a wooden spoon, mix until the dough comes together. Add a little extra yoghurt if the dough is too dry; add extra flour if too wet.

On a lightly floured benchtop, roll and shape the dough into a 4–5 cm (1½–2 in) thick log. Slice into 16 pieces, 1–1.5cm (½–⅝ in) thick. Arrange close together on the prepared tray. Top with the extra cheese. Bake for 20–25 minutes, or until golden brown and cooked through.

Allow to cool, then crumble the scones into soft, bite-sized pieces and serve with a dollop of yoghurt or mashed avocado for added creaminess.

For 12+ months babies, serve warm alongside soup for a hearty and balanced meal.

Leftovers Store in an airtight container in the fridge for up to 3 days or freeze for up to 3 months.

Make it ...

Dairy free Swap butter for coconut oil or extra virgin olive oil, yoghurt for natural unsweetened coconut yoghurt and omit cheese.

Gluten free Swap flour for brown rice flour, buckwheat flour, millet flour or a gluten-free flour blend.

Seasonal Swap carrot and zucchini for pumpkin (squash) or sweet potato.

Faster Bake in a lined loaf tin and cut into slices once baked.

Pantry friendly Swap seeds for almond meal (if nut free isn't necessary); swap seeds for more flour.

Fussy-eater proof Purée carrot and zucchini before adding to dough.

Family friendly (2+) Add a pinch of salt and some grated parmesan to dough; perfect addition for family meals and pairs well with a soup or salad.

School friendly Pack in lunch box with a slice of cheese, Hummus (see page 224) or mashed avocado.

10+ months

Makes 20

Prep 15 mins
(+ 30 mins chilling & cooling)

Cook 25 mins

Cheesy butter crackers

Vegetarian

Egg free

Fish free

Peanut free

Sesame free

Soy free

Tree nut free

These homemade cheesy crackers are a fantastic snack for little ones and the whole family. Packed with wholesome ingredients like wholemeal spelt flour, flaxseed meal and cheese, they offer a deliciously savoury crunch without the additives often found in store-bought crackers. The combination of healthy fats and fibre makes them ideal for growing babies, while their buttery, cheesy flavour ensures they're a hit with older children too. Perfect for lunch boxes, afternoon snacks or as a side to your favourite dips.

90 g (3 oz) unsalted butter

1⅓ cups (200 g) wholemeal spelt flour

2 tablespoons flaxseed meal

1¼ cups (125 g) grated low-salt cheese

½ teaspoon baking powder

Serving suggestions

Homemade dip, like Hummus (if sesame free isn't necessary; see page 224) or mashed avocado or egg

Steamed veggie sticks

Preheat the oven to 180°C (350°F) and line a baking tray with baking paper.

In a food processor, blend all the ingredients until a dough forms. Transfer to a bowl, cover and refrigerate for 30 minutes.

Place the chilled dough between two sheets of baking paper and roll out until 3–5 mm (⅛–2 in) thick. Remove the top sheet of paper and use a cookie cutter to cut out circles and arrange on the prepared tray. (Alternatively, you can bake the entire sheet of dough and break into pieces once cooled. Or use a sharp knife to cut it into squares before baking.)

Bake for 20–25 minutes, depending on the thickness.

Allow the crackers cool completely. They will crisp up as they cool.

Break the crackers into manageable pieces or serve with a homemade dip and steamed veggie sticks.

Leftovers Store in an airtight container in the fridge for up to 14 days or freeze for up to 3 months.

Make it ...

Dairy free Swap butter for coconut oil and cheese for ½ cup (30 g) nutritional yeast.

Gluten free Swap flour for brown rice flour, buckwheat flour, millet flour or a gluten-free flour blend.

Boosted Add 2 tablespoons chia seeds to batter.

Fussy-eater proof Cut out fun shapes using cookie cutters.

Family friendly (2+) An excellent addition to a family snack platter – pair with low-salt cheese slices, Hummus (see page 224) or veggie sticks for a balanced and satisfying snack.

School friendly Perfect lunch-box filler for recess.

6+ months

Makes 24

Prep 20 mins (+ cooling)

Cook 20 mins

Pumpkin spice muffins

Vegetarian

Dairy free

Fish free

Peanut free

Sesame free

Soy free

Tree nut free

Soft, gently spiced and naturally sweetened with pumpkin and dates, these mini muffins are a perfect first bake for little hands. The warm blend of cinnamon, nutmeg and ginger introduces babies to new flavours while keeping things gentle on tiny tummies. Whether served as a self-feeding snack or mashed, your baby will love these muffins and so will you!

- 1½ cups (300 g) steamed or roasted pumpkin (squash), cooled
- 2 pasture-raised or organic eggs
- 9 (135 g/4¾ oz) pitted soft medjool dates (see tip) or ½ cup (140 g) Date & cinnamon paste (see page 227)
- ¼ cup (60 ml) melted coconut oil
- 1 teaspoon pure vanilla extract or powder
- 1 cup (150 g) wholemeal spelt flour
- ½ teaspoon baking powder
- ½ teaspoon bicarbonate of soda (baking soda)
- ½ teaspoon ground cinnamon
- ¼ teaspoon ground nutmeg
- ¼ teaspoon ground ginger

Preheat the oven to 180°C (350°F) and line a mini muffin tray with paper cases.

Place the pumpkin, eggs, dates or date paste, oil and vanilla in a food processor and process until smooth. Add the remaining ingredients and process until just combined.

Spoon the batter into the prepared muffin cases and bake for 15–20 minutes, or until a cake tester or skewer inserted comes out clean.

Allow to cool before serving.

Offer mashed or break into manageable pieces for your baby to practise self-feeding.

Tip If using medjool dates and they aren't soft, soak them in hot water for 10 minutes, then drain before adding to the food processor.

Make it ...

Gluten free Swap flour for brown rice flour, chickpea flour/besan (+ 1 tablespoon flaxseed meal) or a gluten-free flour blend.

Egg free Swap egg for a store-bought egg replacer, or a flax egg (1 egg = 1 tablespoon ground flaxseed + 45 ml/1½ fl oz warm water) or a chia egg (1 egg = 1 tablespoon chia seed meal + ¼ cup/60 ml water).

Seasonal Swap pumpkin for sweet potato; if using paste, swap for Apricot & pear or Apple & fig (see page 233).

Pantry friendly Swap oil for unsalted butter or ghee (if dairy free isn't necessary).

Family friendly (2+) To sweeten, add ¼–⅓ cup pure maple syrup (60–80 ml), or coconut sugar (35–50 g), or ⅓ cup (50 g) sliced sulphur-free sultanas or dried fruit to batter.

Leftovers Store in an airtight container in the fridge for up to a week or freeze for up to 3 months.

12+ months

Serves 12

Prep 30 mins
(+ overnight chilling & cooling)

Cook 30 mins

Vegetarian

Fish free

Peanut free

Sesame free

Soy free

Tree nut free

Vanilla cake with coconut cream frosting

Celebrate your little one's first milestones with this vanilla cake (pictured on page 50). It is a naturally sweetened, wholesome alternative to traditional, sugar-laden birthday cakes. Sweetened with date and cinnamon paste instead of refined sugar, it's rich in fibre and gentle on tummies. Bub will love the soft, moist texture and the frosting, which adds a creamy finish without the need for processed icing. For older children, this can be adapted into a larger cake with fun toppings.

- 1⅔ cups (250 g) wholemeal spelt flour
- 2 teaspoons baking powder
- ½ teaspoon bicarbonate of soda (baking soda)
- Pinch of sea salt (optional)
- 3 pasture-raised or organic eggs
- 1 cup (280 g) Date & cinnamon paste (see page 227)
- ½ cup (125 ml) milk of choice
- 140 g (5 oz) unsalted butter, melted
- 1 teaspoon pure vanilla extract or powder
- 2 teaspoons fresh lemon juice

Whipped coconut cream frosting

- 2 × 400 ml (14 fl oz) cans coconut cream, chilled in the fridge overnight
- 2 teaspoons pure vanilla extract or powder
- ½–1 teaspoon ground cinnamon (optional)

Preheat the oven to 180°C (350°F) and grease or line the base and sides of two 15 cm (6 in) cake tins with baking paper.

Combine the flour, baking powder, bicarb and salt (if using) in a bowl.

In a large bowl, whisk together the eggs, date paste, milk, butter, vanilla and lemon juice until smooth. Stir the dry mixture into the wet mixture.

Divide the batter evenly between the prepared tins and bake for 25–30 minutes, or until a cake tester or skewer inserted comes out clean.

Allow the cakes to cool in the tins for 5 minutes, before transferring to a wire rack to cool completely.

Meanwhile, make the frosting. Open the coconut cream tins. Only the thick, creamy part is needed, so carefully drain the liquid (reserve for other uses). Transfer the thick coconut cream to a stand mixer. Whisk on medium speed for 1–2 minutes, or until smooth and creamy. Add the vanilla and cinnamon and whisk until combined. Chill to thicken more or use immediately.

Trim the cake tops flat. Spread some frosting over one cake, then stack the other cake on top. Top with more frosting. If desired, frost the side too for a finished look. Slice the cake into soft, manageable pieces or mash for early eaters. Avoid adding frosting if your baby prefers a simpler texture.

Leftovers Store in an airtight container in the fridge for up to 5 days (iced) or freeze cake bases (un-iced) for up to 3 months.

Make it ...

Dairy free Swap milk with unsweetened coconut, soy or oat yoghurt and butter with coconut oil.

Gluten free Swap flour for gluten-free flour blend.

Egg free Swap egg for a store-bought egg replacer, or a flax egg (1 egg = 1 tablespoon ground flaxseed + 45 ml/1½ fl oz warm water) or a chia egg (1 egg = 1 tablespoon chia seed meal + ¼ cup/60 ml water).

Seasonal Swap date paste for Apricot & pear or Apple & fig paste (see page 233).

Pantry friendly Swap paste for 1 cup (240 g) pitted soft medjool dates.

Family friendly (2+) To sweeten, swap date paste for ½–1 cup (125–250 ml) pure maple syrup and add 1–2 tablespoons maple syrup or raw honey to frosting.

10+ months

Makes 36

Prep 20 mins (+ cooling)

Cook 15 mins

Choc zucchini muffins

Vegetarian

 Dairy free

 Fish free

 Peanut free

 Sesame free

 Soy free

 Tree nut free

- 3 pasture-raised or organic eggs
- 14 (210 g/7½ oz) pitted soft medjool dates or ¾ cup (210 g) Date & cinnamon paste (see page 227)
- ¾ cup (185 ml) melted coconut oil
- ¼ cup (60 ml) unsweetened coconut milk
- 1 teaspoon pure vanilla extract or powder
- 2 cups (300 g) wholemeal spelt flour
- ¼ cup (25 g) raw cacao powder
- 2 tablespoons carob powder
- 2 teaspoons bicarbonate of soda (baking soda)
- 2 cups (360 g) grated zucchini (courgette), from about 2 zucchini

Optional toppings

- Natural unsweetened coconut yoghurt
- Grated fruit

I originally created these for my first child – he loved them. But when his little sister came along, I created a version without added sugars. Although maple syrup is a natural added sugar, under the age of 2, it's not necessary, so this wholesome recipe was born. Naturally sweetened with dates and packed with fibre-rich zucchini, these muffins offer the chocolatey flavour kids crave, minus the sugar highs and crashes. I keep a stash ready for morning tea, lunch boxes or those hungry afternoon moments.

Preheat the oven to 180°C (350°F) and line three mini muffin trays with paper cases.

Place the eggs, dates or date paste, oil, milk and vanilla in a food processor and process until smooth. Add the flour, cacao, carob and bicarb and process until well combined. Add the zucchini and process until just combined.

Spoon 1 tablespoon of batter into each muffin case. Bake for 12–15 minutes, or until a cake tester or skewer inserted comes out clean.

Allow to cool completely.

Serve the muffins sliced into soft, finger-friendly pieces or mashed for younger eaters.

For babies 10+ months, pair with a dollop of yoghurt or a sprinkle of grated fruit for added freshness.

Make it ...

Gluten free Swap flour for brown rice flour, buckwheat flour, millet flour or a gluten-free flour blend.

Egg free Swap egg for a store-bought egg replacer, or a flax egg (1 egg = 1 tablespoon ground flaxseed + 45 ml/1½ fl oz warm water) or a chia egg (1 egg = 1 tablespoon chia seed meal + ¼ cup/60 ml water).

Seasonal If using paste, swap for Apricot & pear or Apple & fig (see page 233).

Boosted Add 1 tablespoon chia seeds to batter.

Fussy-eater proof Encourage your little one to help make them.

Family friendly (2+) To sweeten, swap dates for ½–¾ cup (80–120 g) coconut sugar to batter.

Leftovers Store in an airtight container in the fridge for up to a week or freeze for up to 3 months.

10+ months

Serves 24

Prep 10 mins (+ cooling)

Cook 45 mins

Little pumpkin raisin loaf

Vegetarian

 Dairy free

 Fish free

 Peanut free

 Sesame free

 Soy free

 Tree nut free

It's easy to grab a loaf of raisin bread from the supermarket – marketed as wholesome, but often filled with refined sugars, preservatives and unnecessary additives. This loaf turns everyday ingredients into a naturally sweet, wholesome alternative. It's soft enough for little fingers, free from added sugar and loaded with flavour, fibre and feel-good nutrition. There's something satisfying about baking this loaf from scratch. You know exactly what's inside and it's a choice that feels good on every level.

- 1¼ cups (250 g) steamed or roasted pumpkin (squash), cooled
- 1 large pasture-raised or organic egg
- ½ cup (125 ml) melted coconut oil
- 9 (135 g/4¾ oz) pitted soft medjool dates or ½ cup (140 g) Date & cinnamon paste (see page 227)
- ¼ cup (60 ml) coconut milk
- 1 teaspoon pure vanilla extract or powder
- 1½ cups (220 g) wholemeal spelt flour
- 1 teaspoon baking powder
- ¼ teaspoon bicarbonate of soda (baking soda)
- 1 teaspoon ground cinnamon
- ½ cup (80 g) sulphur-free raisins or sultanas, finely chopped

Preheat the oven to 180°C (350°F). Grease and line the base and sides of a 20 × 10 cm (8 × 4 in) loaf tin with baking paper.

Place the pumpkin, egg, oil, dates or date paste, milk and vanilla in a food processor and process until smooth. Add the flour, baking powder, bicarb and cinnamon and mix until combined. Gently fold in the raisins or sultanas.

Pour the batter into the prepared tin. Bake for 40–45 minutes, or until a cake tester or skewer inserted comes out clean.

Allow to cool in the tin before slicing.

Serve mashed or cut into finger-sized strips to encourage self-feeding.

Tip If time is tight, this is when a 100 per cent organic fruit pouch can be used as a sweetener instead of the dates or date paste. Choose 100 per cent apple or pear. It will add sweetness without the additives or added sugar.

Make it ...

Gluten free Swap flour for brown rice flour, buckwheat flour or a gluten-free flour blend.

Egg free Swap egg for a store-bought egg replacer, or a flax egg (1 egg = 1 tablespoon ground flaxseed + 45 ml/1½ fl oz warm water) or a chia egg (1 egg = 1 tablespoon chia seed meal + ¼ cup/60 ml water).

Seasonal Swap pumpkin for sweet potato; if using paste, swap for Apricot & pear or Apple & fig (see page 233).

Pantry friendly Swap coconut oil for unsalted butter or ghee; swap raisins/sultanas for sulphur-free dried fruit of choice.

Boosted Add 1–2 tablespoons chia seeds to batter.

Family friendly (2+) To sweeten, add ¼–⅓ cup pure maple syrup (60–80 ml) or coconut sugar (35–50 g) to batter.

Leftovers Store in an airtight container in the fridge for up to 10 days or freeze for up to 3 months.

Chocolate cupcakes

12+ months

Makes 40

Prep 30 mins (+ cooling, 10 mins soaking & 30 mins chilling)

Cook 15 mins

 Vegetarian

 Fish free

 Peanut free

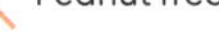 Sesame free

 Soy free

 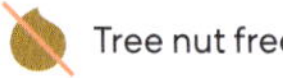 Tree nut free

½ cup (120 g) pitted soft medjool dates or ⅔ cup (180 g) Date & cinnamon paste (see page 227)

1 cup (250 ml) milk of choice

3 pasture-raised or organic eggs

¼ cup (60 ml) melted unsalted butter

1 teaspoon pure vanilla extract or powder

1¾ cups (265 g) wholemeal spelt flour

2 tablespoons raw cacao powder

1 tablespoon carob powder

1 teaspoon baking powder

½ teaspoon bicarbonate of soda (baking soda)

Choc date frosting

2 cups (480 g) pitted soft medjool dates

1 cup (250 ml) boiling water

⅓ cup (80 ml) coconut cream

2 tablespoons melted coconut oil

⅓ cup (30 g) raw cacao powder

2 tablespoons carob powder

1 teaspoon pure vanilla extract or powder

Optional toppings

Desiccated coconut

Fresh berries

Leftovers Store in an airtight container in the fridge for up to 4 days or freeze for up to 3 months.

These cupcakes (pictured on page 51) are everything a party food should be: soft and chocolatey without relying on refined sugar or ultra-processed ingredients. Whether you're packing them for a daycare celebration, baking for a birthday or just creating something special for a family afternoon tea, this recipe lets you offer a moment of joy as well as a meaningful nutrition win. From the cake to the frosting, feel reassured knowing it's 100 per cent real food and 0 per cent nasties.

Preheat the oven to 180°C (350°F) and line three or four mini muffin trays with paper cases (or bake in batches, if you don't have this many trays).

Whisk together the dates or date paste, milk, eggs, butter and vanilla in a large bowl until smooth. In another bowl, combine the flour, cacao, carob, baking powder and bicarb, then stir into the wet mixture until smooth.

Spoon the batter into the prepared muffin cases until three-quarters full. Bake for 12–15 minutes, or until a cake tester or skewer inserted comes out clean. Allow to cool in the trays for 5 minutes, before transferring to a wire rack to cool completely.

While the cupcakes cool, make the frosting. Place the dates and boiling water in a high-speed blender and allow to soak for 10 minutes. Add the remaining frosting ingredients and blend until smooth and creamy. Refrigerate for 30 minutes or longer if frosting seems too runny.

Spread or pipe 1–2 tablespoons of frosting onto each cupcake. Sprinkle with desiccated coconut or top each with a berry for a fun twist.

Make it ...

Dairy free Use almond, coconut or oat milk and swap butter for coconut oil.

Gluten free Swap flour for brown rice, flour, chickpea flour (besan) or a gluten-free flour blend.

Egg free Swap egg for a store-bought egg replacer, or a flax egg (1 egg = 1 tablespoon ground flaxseed + 45 ml/1½ fl oz warm water) or a chia egg (1 egg = 1 tablespoon chia seed meal + ¼ cup/60 ml water).

Boosted Add 1 cup (130 g) grated sweet potato or pumpkin (squash) or mashed banana to batter.

Pantry friendly Swap dates or paste for Apricot & pear or Apple & fig paste (see page 233); swap carob for more cacao.

Family friendly (2+) To sweeten, swap paste for ½ cup (125 ml) pure maple syrup to batter.

Tip Instead of cupcakes, you can bake as bigger cakes. Line the base and sides of two 15 cm (6 in) round cake tins. Spoon in the batter and bake for 25–30 minutes, or until a cake tester or skewer inserted comes out clean.

10+ months

Makes 36

Prep 20 mins

Cook 15 mins

Blueberry lemon muffins

Vegetarian

Fish free

Peanut free

Sesame free

Soy free

Tree nut free

There's something magical about baking with your kids, especially when they get to stir the batter and sneak a few blueberries along the way. These mini muffins were such a joy to make with my little ones. We picked our favourite berries, added a sprinkle of lemon zest and enjoyed them warm from the oven with a little butter melted on top. They're the kind of muffin that makes you wonder why store-bought ever became the norm. Made with simple pantry staples, they pack in real nourishment without the additives or refined sugars. Perfect for baby-led weaning, lunch boxes or morning tea, this is the feel-good baking that brings us together.

100 g (3½ oz) unsalted butter, melted

½ cup (130 g) natural unsweetened yoghurt

1 teaspoon lemon zest

2 pasture-raised or organic eggs

4 (60 g/2¼ oz) pitted soft medjool dates

½ cup (135 g) unsweetened 100 per cent apple purée (homemade or store-bought)

1¼ cups (190 g) wholemeal spelt flour

1 teaspoon baking powder

½ teaspoon bicarbonate of soda (baking soda)

1 cup (160 g) blueberries (fresh or frozen)

Preheat the oven to 180°C (350°F) and line a mini muffin tray with paper cases.

Mix together the butter, yoghurt and lemon zest in a bowl, then transfer to a food processor along with the eggs, dates and apple purée. Process until creamy. Add the flour, baking powder and bicarb and process until combined. Gently fold through the blueberries.

Spoon the batter into the prepared muffin cases, filling each about three-quarters full. Bake for 15 minutes, or until a cake tester or skewer inserted comes out clean.

Allow to cool slightly, then serve mashed, in small bite-sized pieces or whole for baby-led weaning.

Make it ...

Dairy free Swap butter for coconut oil and yoghurt with natural unsweetened coconut, soy or oat yoghurt.

Gluten free Swap flour for a gluten-free flour blend.

Egg free Swap egg for a store-bought egg replacer, or a flax egg (1 egg = 1 tablespoon ground flaxseed + 45 ml/1½ fl oz warm water) or a chia egg (1 egg = 1 tablespoon chia seed meal + ¼ cup/60 ml water).

Seasonal Swap dates for ¼ cup (70 g) Date & cinnamon, Apricot & pear or Fig & apple paste (see pages 227 and 233); swap blueberries for berries of choice.

Family friendly (2+) To sweeten, swap dates for ½–¾ cup (80–120 g) coconut sugar to batter.

Leftovers Store in an airtight container in the fridge for up to 6 days or freeze for up to 3 months.

10+ months

Makes 10

Prep 20 mins

Cook 35 mins

Sweet potato & apricot scrolls

Vegetarian

Egg free

Fish free

Gluten free

Peanut free

Sesame free

Soy free

Tree nut free

Coconut oil, for greasing

⅓ cup (90 g) Apricot & pear paste (see page 233)

Pinch of ground cinnamon

Dough

2 cups (400 g) steamed purple or white sweet potato, cooled and mashed (see tip)

¾ cup (90 g) cassava flour or gluten-free flour blend, plus extra if needed

1 teaspoon pure vanilla extract or powder

½ teaspoon baking powder

Natural unsweetened Greek-style yoghurt, if needed

Optional toppings

Natural unsweetened coconut yoghurt

Mashed banana

Store-bought scrolls often contain around 6 teaspoons of added sugar in a single serve! When you make your own, you're not just reducing sugar, but modelling real-food habits from the very first bite. These are ideal for early eaters and toddlers alike and, let's be honest, adults can enjoy them too. Whether served fresh, packed in a lunch box or pulled from the freezer, these scrolls are a reminder of what's possible with just a few ingredients and a little planning.

Preheat the oven to 180°C (350°F) and grease a muffin tray with oil.

Place all the dough ingredients, except the yoghurt, in a food processor and process until a dough forms. Add a little yoghurt if the dough is too dry; add extra flour if too wet.

Place the dough on a large piece of baking paper, rolling or pressing it out into a large rectangle (about 0.5–1 cm/¼–½ in thickness).

Spread a thin layer of the apricot paste evenly over the dough, then sprinkle with the cinnamon. Use the paper to help roll up the dough into a tight log, then cut the log into 10 rolls.

Place the rolls in the prepared muffin trays and bake for 30–35 minutes, or until golden.

Serve warm for a soft texture. Cut the scrolls into small, manageable pieces and pair with yoghurt or mashed banana for added moisture and flavour.

Make it ...

Nutty Swap paste for nut butter.

Dairy free Swap yoghurt for natural unsweetened coconut yoghurt.

Pantry friendly Swap paste for Date & cinnamon paste (see page 227), pitted and chopped soft medjool dates, Berry chia jam (see page 228) or butter spiced with ground cinnamon.

Leftovers Store in an airtight container in the fridge for up to 4 days or freeze for up to 3 months.

Tip Purple sweet potato has purple or white skin with white flesh inside, while white sweet potato has purple or tan skin. Fussy eaters may prefer the white variety. When steaming the sweet potato, cook until tender – do not overcook. Otherwise it will be too watery for the dough. Also make sure the mash is cold before making the dough. It's best to prep the day before and refrigerate overnight.

6+ months

Makes 24

Prep 15 mins (+ cooling)

Cook 20 mins

Wholesome banana muffins

 Vegetarian

 Dairy free

 Fish free

 Gluten free

 Peanut free

Sesame free

 Soy free

 Tree nut free

- 2 medium (220 g/7¾ oz) ripe bananas
- 3 pasture-raised or organic eggs
- ½ cup (125 ml) coconut milk
- 2 tablespoons coconut oil
- 5 (75 g/2½ oz) pitted soft medjool dates or ⅓ cup (90 g) Date & cinnamon paste (see page 227)
- ¾ cup (90 g) buckwheat flour
- ¼ cup (30 g) arrowroot
- 1 teaspoon baking powder
- ½ teaspoon bicarbonate of soda (baking soda)
- 1 teaspoon ground cinnamon

These naturally sweet, fluffy mini muffins were a hit from the very first bite – and not just with my babies. Try them when baby is transitioning from purées to finger foods. Made with banana, dates and wholesome flours, they skip added sugar while still delivering that soft, comforting baked-goods feel we all love. Whether you serve them mashed, whole or cut into finger-sized pieces, these muffins are freezer friendly, allergy conscious and easy to adapt.

Preheat the oven to 180°C (350°F) and line a mini muffin tray with paper cases.

Place the bananas, eggs, milk, oil and dates or date paste in a food processor and process until smooth. Add the remaining ingredients and process again until the mixture is well combined.

Spoon the batter into the prepared muffin cases, filling each with about 1–2 tablespoons of the batter. Bake for 15–20 minutes, or until the muffins are golden and firm to the touch.

Transfer to a wire rack and allow to cool completely.

Serve mashed or in finger food–sized pieces, depending on your baby's stage of eating.

Make it ...

Egg free Swap egg for a store-bought egg replacer, or a flax egg (1 egg = 1 tablespoon ground flaxseed + 45 ml/1½ fl oz warm water) or a chia egg (1 egg = 1 tablespoon chia seed meal + ¼ cup/60 ml water).

Seasonal If using paste, swap for Apricot & pear or Apple & fig (see page 233).

Boosted Add 1 tablespoon chia seeds to batter.

Faster Swap dates or paste for unsweetened 100 per cent apple or pear purée (homemade or store-bought).

Pantry friendly Swap milk for milk of choice; swap flour and arrowroot for wholemeal spelt flour (if gluten free isn't necessary).

Family friendly (2+) To sweeten, add ¼–½ cup (60–125 ml) raw honey or pure maple syrup to batter.

Leftovers Store in an airtight container in the fridge for up to a week or freeze for up to 3 months.

12+ months

Serves 15

Prep 40 mins

 Vegan

 Dairy free

 Egg free

 Fish free

 Gluten free

 Peanut free

 Sesame free

 Soy free

 Tree nut free

Birthday fruit cake

This vibrant birthday cake made of fruit (pictured on page 51) is a refreshing and naturally sweet alternative to traditional cakes – a first or second birthday masterpiece! With cleverly assembled colourful fruits, this is rich in essential vitamins, antioxidants and hydration, making it a fun yet healthy way to mark special occasions. With no added sugar, gluten, dairy or nuts, it's ideal for allergy-friendly celebrations while still feeling festive and exciting. It's an excellent allergy-free option for childcare birthdays too!

- 1 large (9 kg/19 lb 13 oz) seedless watermelon (for the base)
- 1 small (450 g/1 lb) rockmelon, peeled
- 1 small (2 kg/4 lb 8 oz) honeydew melon, peeled
- 1 cup (160 g) strawberries, hulled and halved or quartered lengthways, plus extra for garnishing
- 1 cup (160 g) blueberries, quartered for safety, plus extra for garnishing
- 1 cup (160 g) raspberries, plus extra for garnishing
- 1 cup (150 g) seedless grapes, halved for safety
- 1 (100 g/3½ oz) kiwi, peeled and quartered lengthways
- 1 medium (110 g/3 ¾ oz) banana, sliced (optional)
- Mint leaves, for garnishing

Frosting (optional)

- 400 ml (14 fl oz) can full-fat coconut cream, chilled in the fridge overnight

Slice off both ends of the watermelon to create a flat surface. Carefully trim the rind, shaping the watermelon into a large cylinder (this will be your main cake layer). Alternatively, to make a three-layer cake, cut the watermelon into three 8 cm (3¼ in) thick rounds: the first 20 cm (8 in) in diameter; the second 17 cm (6½ in); and the third 13 cm (5 in), and stack.

If making the frosting, open the coconut cream tin. Only the thick, creamy part of the coconut cream is needed for this recipe, so carefully drain the liquid (reserve for other recipes or discard). Transfer the thick coconut cream to a stand mixer and whisk on medium speed for 1–2 minutes, or until smooth and creamy. Pat the surface of the watermelon as dry as you can with paper towel before gently spreading or piping on the frosting. This helps the frosting stick properly.

Cut the rockmelon and honeydew into thin slices or fun shapes (using cookie cutters). Arrange the melon, strawberries, blueberries, raspberries, grapes, kiwi and banana (if using) around or on the cake for a colourful design. Use small fruit skewers or straws cut into short segments (3–5 cm/1¼–2 in) to secure the fruit decorations if needed.

Garnish with mint and extra berries. Serve immediately or chill until ready to celebrate! Before serving, ensure all skewers and straws have been removed.

Tip Make sure all berries and grapes are halved or quartered for safety.

Make it ...

Seasonal Swap fruit used for decorating for other fruits of choice.

Different Swap coconut cream for natural unsweetened Greek-style yoghurt (if dairy free isn't necessary).

Family friendly (2+) Offer yoghurt alongside for dipping; let older children build their own mini kebabs using cut fruit for a hands-on, engaging activity.

Leftovers Store in an airtight container in the fridge for up to 2 days. It's best to ice it just before serving.

Elephant
m
Insect
Cake

10+ months

Makes 12

Prep 10 mins (+ cooling)

Cook 15 mins

Peanut butter cookies

These melt-in-the-mouth PB cookies are a great snack for little ones learning to self-feed, and they're a delicious option for older siblings and parents too. Enjoy them as a baby-friendly morsel or in an on-the-go snack pack.

Vegan

Dairy free

Egg free

Fish free

Gluten free

Sesame free

Soy free

- ½ cup (140 g) smooth natural peanut butter
- 3 (45 g/1½ oz) pitted soft medjool dates
- 1 medium (110 g/3 ¾ oz) ripe banana
- 1 teaspoon pure vanilla extract or powder
- 1½ cups (180 g) almond meal
- ¼ teaspoon ground cinnamon (optional)
- Coconut oil, for greasing hands

Preheat the oven to 180°C (350°F) and line a baking tray with baking paper.

Place the peanut butter, dates, banana and vanilla in a food processor and process until smooth. Add the almond meal and cinnamon (if using) and pulse until a dough forms.

Using a tablespoon and your hands (greasing with coconut oil to prevent sticking), shape the dough into small balls and place on the prepared tray. Use a fork or your hand to flatten into cookies. Bake for 15 minutes.

Allow to cool, then serve.

Offer the cookies whole or in strips to grasp and chew.

Make it ...

Pantry friendly Swap peanut butter for nut butter of choice.

Family friendly (2+) Turn these into a decadent choc PB cookie by swapping dates and banana for ¼ cup (60 ml) pure maple syrup and adding 2 tablespoons dark chocolate chips to dough.

School friendly Swap almond meal for pumpkin seed meal and peanut butter for tahini or sunflower seed butter.

Leftovers Store in an airtight container for up to 2 weeks or freeze for up to 3 months.

10+ months

Makes 15

Prep 10 mins (+ cooling)

Cook 30 mins

Choc beetroot brownies

Vegetarian

Dairy free

Fish free

Gluten free

Sesame free

Soy free

Small, simple swaps to baked goodies can make all the difference. Here, I've packed brownies with black beans and beetroot. Rich cacao and carob create a deep flavour without the need for refined sugar, and dates make these brownies naturally sweet. It's a delicious way to keep nutrition front and centre!

- 400 g (14 oz) can black beans, drained and rinsed
- 2 large pasture-raised or organic eggs
- 1 cup (245 g) roasted or steamed beetroot
- 8 (120 g/4¼ oz) pitted soft medjool dates or ½ cup (140 g) Date & cinnamon paste (see page 227)
- ¼ cup (60 ml) melted coconut oil
- 2 teaspoons pure vanilla extract or powder
- ¼ cup (25 g) raw cacao powder
- ¼ cup (25 g) carob powder
- ¼ cup (40 g) brown rice flour
- ¼ cup (30 g) almond meal
- 1 teaspoon baking powder

Preheat the oven to 180°C (350°F) and line the base and sides of a 20 cm (8 in) square cake tin with baking paper.

Place the black beans, eggs, beetroot, dates or date paste, oil and vanilla in a food processor and blend until smooth. Add the remaining ingredients and blend again until well combined.

Pour the mixture into the prepared dish and smooth the top. Bake for 25–30 minutes, or until the edges are set but the centre is still slightly soft.

Allow to cool completely before slicing. The brownies will firm up as they cool.

Make it ...

Nut free Swap almond meal for coconut flour or seed meal.

Sweeter Choose sweet beetroot (taste raw to check) and avoid bland/bitter tasting ones.

Seasonal If using paste, swap for Apricot & pear or Apple & fig (see page 233).

Boosted Sprinkle crushed nuts or seeds on top before baking.

Pantry friendly Swap flour with oat flour or wholemeal flour of choice (if gluten free isn't necessary).

Family friendly (2+) To sweeten, add ¼–½ cup (35–75 g) coconut sugar or extra dates or paste to batter.

Leftovers Store in an airtight container in the fridge for up to a week or freeze for up to 3 months.

Vanilla bean bliss cookies

10+ months

Makes 12–14

Prep 10 mins (+ cooling)

Cook 20 mins

Vegan

 Dairy free

 Egg free

 Fish free

 Sesame free

 Soy free

Store-bought baby cookies are often filled with refined flour and concentrated fruit sugars. If you can spare 30 minutes, try these – they're a much better option. Made with creamy white beans, smooth almond butter and sweet medjool dates, they're rich in fibre, protein and essential nutrients to support your baby's growth. The hint of vanilla and cinnamon adds a gentle warmth designed for tiny tastebuds. Plus, they're free from dairy, egg and wheat!

- 1 cup (180 g) cooked or canned cannellini beans, drained and rinsed
- ¼ cup (70 g) almond butter
- 4 (60 g/2¼ oz) pitted soft medjool dates
- 1 teaspoon pure vanilla extract or powder
- ¼ cup (25 g) rolled or quick oats
- 2 tablespoons coconut flour
- ½ teaspoon baking powder
- ¼ teaspoon bicarbonate of soda (baking soda)
- Pinch of cinnamon
- Coconut oil, for greasing if needed

Optional extras

- Finely chopped sulphur-free dried apricots or sultanas

Preheat the oven to 180°C (350°F) and line a baking tray with baking paper.

Place the beans, almond butter, dates and vanilla in a food processor and process until smooth and creamy. Add the oats, flour, baking powder, bicarb and cinnamon. Pulse until a soft dough forms. Stir in the dried fruit (if using).

Scoop up small tablespoons of dough and roll them into balls. If the dough seems too sticky, grease your hands with coconut oil before working with the dough. Flatten slightly to form cookie shapes, then arrange on the prepared tray.

Bake for 15 minutes, or until the edges are lightly golden. The cookies will be soft but firm up as they cool. If you prefer a crunchier cookie, bake for an additional 5 minutes.

Allow the cookies to cool completely before serving.

Serve whole as soft finger food or break into smaller pieces for easier handling and safer eating.

Make it ...

Pantry friendly Swap beans for beans of choice; swap almond butter for nut butter of choice.

Family friendly (2+) Swap dates for ¼ cup (60 ml) pure maple syrup and mix dark chocolate chips into dough.

School friendly Swap almond butter for seed butter or tahini.

Leftovers Store in an airtight container in the fridge for up to 2 weeks or freeze for up to 3 months.

10+ months

Makes 16

Prep 10 mins (+ cooling)

Cook 25 mins

Fudgy brownies

Vegetarian

Dairy free

Fish free

Gluten free

Peanut free

Sesame free

Soy free

Tree nut free

I first developed these veggie-loaded, fudgy brownies while working one-on-one with a family whose little fussy eater refused beans and vegetables. They quickly became a staple in my own home too. This upgraded version is naturally sweetened with dates and packed with black beans for fibre and protein, making them a smart choice for babies and growing kids alike. Plus, they're perfect lunch-box snacks. Add a pop of juicy colour by serving them with fresh raspberries. They look and taste like a classic brownie, but with ingredients you can feel good about.

- 400 g (14 oz) can black beans, drained and rinsed
- 6 (90 g/3¼ oz) pitted soft medjool dates or ⅓ cup (90 g) Date & cinnamon paste (see page 227)
- 3 pasture-raised or organic eggs
- ¼ cup (60 ml) melted coconut oil
- ⅓ cup (30 g) raw cacao powder
- 2 tablespoons carob powder
- 2 teaspoons pure vanilla extract or powder
- 1 teaspoon baking powder

Preheat the oven to 180°C (350°F) and line the base and sides of a 20 cm (8 in) square cake tin with baking paper.

Place the black beans, dates or date paste and eggs in a food processor and process until smooth, scraping down the side once or twice to help blend evenly. Add the remaining ingredients and process until well combined and smooth.

Pour the mixture into the prepared tin and smooth the top. Bake for 20–25 minutes, or until a cake tester or skewer inserted comes out clean.

Allow to cool before cutting into small, soft bite-sized pieces that baby can grasp (pea-sized for pincer grasp or strips for self-feeding) or mashing with a fork.

Make it ...

Egg-free Swap eggs for 3 medium (330 g/11½ oz) ripe bananas.

Seasonal If using paste, swap for Apricot pear or Apple & fig paste (see page 233).

Boosted Add 1 tablespoons chia seeds to batter; sprinkle crushed seeds or raspberries (fresh or frozen) on top before baking.

Pantry friendly Swap black beans for canned adzuki beans or kidney beans.

Fussy-eater proof Make sure batter is processed until very smooth.

Family friendly (2+) To sweeten, swap half the dates for ¼–½ cup (40–75 g) coconut sugar.

Leftovers Store in an airtight container in the fridge for up to 4 days or freeze for up to 3 months.

Banana oat cookies

6+ months

Makes 8

Prep 10 mins (+ cooling)

Cook 12 mins

- Vegan
- Dairy free
- Egg free
- Fish free
- Peanut free
- Sesame free
- Soy free
- Tree nut free

Made with just four simple ingredients, these are so easy to make without a trip to the shops. Free from dairy and egg and with no added sugar, there's a lot to love about these bickies. Offer when your baby gets hungry in the pram or alongside breakfast – you're ensuring every bite counts!

1 medium (110 g/3 ¾ oz) ripe banana, mashed

½ cup (55 g) rolled or quick oats

¼ teaspoon ground cinnamon

1 tablespoon melted coconut oil

Preheat the oven to 180°C (350°F) and line a baking tray with baking paper.

In a bowl, mix all the ingredients until well combined.

Scoop small spoonfuls onto the prepared tray, flattening slightly into cookie shapes. Bake for 10–12 minutes, or until lightly golden.

Allow to cool completely before serving.

For babies that are not self-feeding confidently, lightly mash or crumble.

Make it ...

Gluten free Swap oats for brown rice or quinoa flakes or certified gluten-free oats.

Nutty Add 1 teaspoon–1 tablespoon peanut butter or nut butter to batter to introduce these ingredients.

Pantry friendly Swap oil for unsalted butter or ghee.

Leftovers Store in an airtight container in the fridge for up to 4 days or freeze for up to 3 months.

10+ months

Makes 12

Prep 10 mins (+ cooling)

Cook 25 mins

Nourishing blondies

This recipe started in my clinic kitchen when I was supporting a very fussy toddler and their family. I needed something naturally sweet, full of nutrients and soft that still felt like a real snack. These simple ingredients deliver protein, fibre and natural sweetness in every mouthful. There's no refined sugar and no fuss – just a smart way to feed your child with confidence.

Vegetarian

Dairy free

Fish free

Gluten free

Peanut free

Sesame free

Soy free

Tree nut free

- 400 g (14 oz) can chickpeas, drained and rinsed
- 3 large pasture-raised or organic eggs
- 6 (90 g/3¼ oz) pitted soft medjool dates or ⅓ cup (90 g) Date & cinnamon paste (see page 227)
- ¼ cup (60 ml) melted coconut oil
- 2 teaspoons pure vanilla extract or powder
- 1½ tablespoons coconut flour
- 1 teaspoon baking powder
- ¼ cup (40 g) frozen raspberries

Preheat the oven to 180°C (350°F) and line the base and sides of a 20 cm (8 in) square cake tin with baking paper.

Place the chickpeas, eggs, dates or date paste, oil and vanilla in a food processor and process until smooth, scraping down the side once or twice to help blend evenly. Add the flour and baking powder and process until smooth.

Pour the mixture into the prepared tin. Sprinkle with the raspberries. Bake for 25 minutes, or until a cake tester or skewer inserted comes out clean.

Allow to cool before cutting into small, soft bite-sized pieces that the baby can grasp (pea-sized for pincer grasp or strips for self-feeding) or mash with a fork.

Make it ...

Egg free Swap eggs for 2 medium (220 g/7¾ oz) ripe bananas.

Seasonal If using paste, swap for Apricot & pear or Fig & apple paste (see page 233); swap raspberries for berries, fresh fruit or dried fruit of choice.

Pantry friendly Swap chickpeas for canned cannellini or navy beans.

Fussy-eater proof Make sure batter is processed until very smooth.

Family friendly (2+) To sweeten, swap dates for ¼–½ cup (60–125 ml) pure maple syrup.

Leftovers Store in an airtight container in the fridge for up to 4 days or freeze for up to 3 months.

10+ months

Makes 24

Prep 15 mins (+ 3 hrs freezing & cooling)

Cook 25 mins

Frozen yoghurt granola bars

 Vegetarian

 Egg free

 Fish free

 Peanut free

 Sesame free

 Soy free

These frozen yoghurt granola bars are more than just a snack, they're a lifesaver for hot days and sore little gums. I first made these for a teething baby who refused warm foods, and the soothing coldness quickly worked its magic. Layered with creamy banana yoghurt and a vibrant berry swirl, they're visually appealing. Good for babies learning to self-feed and older siblings looking for something 'fun' in the freezer.

Base

1 cup (240 g) pitted soft medjool dates

2 cups (220 g) rolled or quick oats

1 cup (280 g) almond butter

¼ cup (25 g) shredded coconut

Pinch of ground cinnamon

Berry filling

2 cups (320 g) frozen berries of choice, lightly mashed

Yoghurt layer

1 cup (260 g) natural unsweetened yoghurt

1 teaspoon pure vanilla extract or powder

1 medium (110 g/3 ¾ oz) ripe banana, mashed

Line the base and sides of a 20–30 cm (8–12 in) baking dish with baking paper.

Place all the base ingredients in a food processor and process until well combined. Press the mixture evenly into the prepared dish and flatten with a spatula. Place in the freezer while preparing the other layers.

To make the berry filling, place the berries in a small saucepan over medium heat. Simmer for 5–10 minutes, then remove from the heat and allow to cool for a few minutes. Pour evenly over the base.

To make the yoghurt layer, combine all the ingredients in a small bowl until smooth. Spread evenly on top of the berry filling and place in the freezer for 2–3 hours to set.

Allow to soften slightly at room temperature for 5–10 minutes before serving. Cut into small, manageable pieces or mash the softened bars with a fork for easier eating.

Tip It's best to prep these a day ahead and set in the freezer overnight.

Make it ...

Dairy free Swap yoghurt for natural unsweetened coconut yoghurt.

Gluten free Swap oats for brown rice or quinoa flakes, or certified gluten-free oats.

Nut free Swap almond butter for seed butter or tahini.

Seasonal Swap berries for banana, mango or other fruit of choice.

Pantry friendly Swap almond butter for nut butter of choice.

Fussy-eater proof Purée berries and yoghurt layer ingredients until smooth and pour over base for even texture.

Family friendly (2+) To sweeten, add 2 teaspoons raw honey or pure maple syrup to base and 2 teaspoons maple syrup or honey to yoghurt layer.

Leftovers Store in an airtight container in the freezer for up to 3 months.

10+ months

Makes 10–12

Prep 15 mins

Apricot & coconut bliss balls

Vegan

Dairy free

Egg free

Fish free

Gluten free

Peanut free

Sesame free

Soy free

These naturally sweet bliss balls are a nutrient-dense snack for babies under 1, as well as the whole family. Made with soft dried apricots, nourishing coconut and healthy fats, they provide a gentle energy boost without added sugars or artificial ingredients. Their soft texture makes them easy for little ones to chew, while the fibre and essential vitamins support digestion and overall growth. Whether served as a finger food for babies, a lunch-box addition or a quick family snack, these bliss balls are a simple, wholesome alternative to store-bought options – free from additives but full of goodness.

- 1 cup, tightly packed (200 g) sulphur-free dried apricots
- 1 cup (80 g) desiccated coconut, plus extra 1 cup (80 g) for rolling
- 1 cup (120 g) almond meal
- 1 tablespoon chia seeds
- 1 teaspoon pure vanilla extract or powder
- 1 tablespoon melted coconut oil

Line a baking tray with baking paper.

Place all the ingredients in a food processor and process until everything is well combined and a dough forms.

Roll the mixture into small balls, then roll in the extra coconut. Place on the prepared tray and refrigerate until set or eat straight away.

Serve mashed, whole or in finger food–sized pieces.

Make it ...

Nut free Swap almond meal for ground seeds (see tip 180) or oat flour.

Pantry friendly Swap apricots for pitted soft medjool dates.

Family friendly (2+) These should be sweet enough, but to sweeten further, add 1–2 tablespoons pure maple syrup or dip or drizzle in melted dark chocolate.

Leftovers Store in an airtight container in the fridge for up to a week or freeze for up to 3 months.

10+ months

Makes 35

Prep 20 mins (+ 1½ hrs chilling)

Powerhouse choc bliss balls

 Vegan

 Dairy free

 Egg free

 Fish free

 Gluten free

 Peanut free

 Sesame free

 Soy free

These baby-friendly bites (pictured on page 210) are packed with essential vitamins, minerals, healthy fats and fibre. With ingredients such as hemp seeds, almond meal, kale, banana and dates, they offer a natural source of plant-based protein, iron and omega-3s to support your little one's growth and development. And they'll keep kids going, thanks to the long-lasting energy they provide.

- 1½ medium (165 g/5¾ oz) ripe bananas
- 10 (150 g/5½ oz) pitted soft medjool dates
- ½ cup, tightly packed (30 g) chopped kale leaves
- 1¾ cups (210 g) almond meal
- 1 cup (80 g) desiccated coconut
- 2 tablespoons raw cacao powder
- 2 tablespoons hemp seeds
- 1 teaspoon pure vanilla extract or powder
- 1 tablespoon melted coconut oil

Line a tray with baking paper.

Place the banana, dates and kale in a food processor and process until smooth. Add the remaining ingredients and process until well combined.

If the dough seems too sticky, place it in the fridge for 30 minutes.

Roll level tablespoons of the mixture into small balls and arrange on the prepared tray. Refrigerate for 1 hour.

Serve mashed, whole or in finger food–sized pieces.

Make it ...

Nut free Swap almond meal for pumpkin seed meal.

Seasonal Swap kale for baby spinach.

Different Roll in extra desiccated coconut, almond meal or pumpkin seed meal.

Pantry friendly Swap hemp seeds for flaxseed meal.

Family friendly (2+) Dip or drizzle in melted dark chocolate.

Leftovers Store in an airtight container in the fridge for up to a week or freeze for up to 6 months.

Strawberry yoghurt marshmallows (see page 214)

Banana, choc and cinnamon smoothie (see page 220)

Powerhouse choc bliss balls (see page 209)

Hidden veggie fruit gummies three ways (see page 212)

8+ months

Makes 24

Prep 10 mins (+ 2 hrs chilling)

Cook 5 mins

Hidden veggie fruit gummies three ways

These veggie and fruit gummies (pictured on the previous page) are a fun, nutritious way to serve up real veggies in a form that little ones love. While babies don't need vegetables to be hidden, these soft, wobbly gummies will tempt even the fussiest toddlers. Each of the three versions blends naturally sweet fruit with gentle vegetables like spinach, pumpkin or cauliflower – creating colourful bites rich in vitamin C and gut-supportive gelatine.

Dairy free

Egg free

Fish free

Gluten free

Peanut free

Sesame free

Soy free

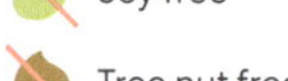
Tree nut free

1½ tablespoons gelatine powder

Combine the gelatine with ¼ cup (60 ml) juice for your chosen variation in a small bowl and whisk until combined.

Place the fruit and vegetables for your chosen variation in a high-speed blender with the remaining juice. Blend until smooth.

Transfer the purée to a small saucepan. Pour in the gelatine mixture and bring to a gentle boil over medium heat. Whisk continuously until the gelatine dissolves.

Pour the mixture into moulds of choice and refrigerate for 2 hours, or until firm.

Cut the gummies into small, soft pieces for easy self-feeding.

For babies 12+ months, serve whole as a healthy afternoon snack or as a fun snack alongside fresh fruit for added variety.

Make it ...

Seasonal Swap mango for pineapple or blueberries; swap spinach for greens of choice; swap strawberries for berries of choice; swap cauliflower for carrot, broccoli or parsnip; swap pumpkin for sweet potato.

Faster Pour mixture into a shallow baking dish, allow to set in the fridge or freezer (for quicker setting time), then cut into small cubes.

Fussy-eater proof Use fun-shaped moulds.

Family friendly (2+) To sweeten further, add 2 tablespoons raw honey or pure maple syrup to mixture.

Leftovers Store in an airtight container in the fridge for up to 5 days or in the freezer for up to 3 months.

1. Mango & spinach

100 ml (3½ fl oz) fresh orange juice

1 cup (150 g) chopped mango (fresh or frozen)

Handful of baby spinach

2. Strawberry & cauliflower

100 ml (3½ fl oz) fresh apple juice

1 cup (160 g) strawberries, (fresh or frozen)

½ cup (40 g) steamed cauliflower florets, cooled

3. Mango & pumpkin

½ cup (125 ml) fresh orange juice

½ cup (75 g) chopped mango (fresh or frozen)

½ cup (100 g) steamed or roasted pumpkin (squash), cooled

10+ months

Makes 16

Prep 10 mins (+ cooling & 2 hrs chilling)

Cook 5 mins

Strawberry yoghurt marshmallows

 Egg free

 Fish free

 Gluten free

 Peanut free

Sesame free

 Soy free

 Tree nut free

Who doesn't love a marshmallow? Children's eyes always widen when the squishy treats appear! Ditch the store-bought for homemade (pictured on page 210) – they're easy and, of course, much better for your baby. I've naturally sweetened these ones with juicy strawberries. Plus, Greek-style yoghurt and gelatine are beneficial for gut health.

2 tablespoons gelatine powder

⅓ cup (80 ml) fresh apple juice or water

2 cups (320 g) frozen strawberries

1 teaspoon pure vanilla extract or powder

1 cup (200 g) natural unsweetened Greek-style yoghurt

Line a 15 × 20 cm (6 × 8 in) glass dish with baking paper.

In a small bowl, whisk the gelatine and juice, then set aside to bloom.

Place the strawberries, vanilla and 2 tablespoons water in a small saucepan and bring to the boil over medium–high heat. Once simmering, stir in the gelatine mixture and whisk until dissolved. Remove from the heat and allow to cool for 15–20 minutes.

Transfer the mixture to a high-speed blender. Add the yoghurt and blend until smooth and fluffy.

Pour the mixture into the prepared dish and refrigerate for 1–2 hours, or until firm.

Serve in soft, bite-sized pieces for easy self-feeding.

Make it ...

Dairy free Swap yoghurt for natural unsweetened coconut yoghurt or coconut cream.

Sweeter Swap 2 tablespoons water for more apple juice.

Seasonal Swap strawberries for berries of choice.

Pantry friendly Swap apple juice for more water.

Fussy-eater proof Pour mixture into fun-shaped moulds or cut out shapes with cookie cutters.

Family friendly (2+) To sweeten further, add 2 tablespoons pure maple syrup or raw honey to mixture.

Leftovers Store in an airtight container in the fridge for up to 3 days or freeze for up to 3 months.

12+ months

Makes 10–12

Prep 5 mins

Healthy chocolate balls

- Vegan
- Dairy free
- Egg free
- Fish free
- Gluten free
- Sesame free
- Soy free

With an overseas long-haul flight ahead of us, where I knew I'd have my toddler balanced on one hip and a baby on the other, I came up with these (pictured on page 50). Easy to pack, these chocolate balls were satisfying for my toddler and for me when I needed something to nibble mid-breastfeed without the sugar crash. They've become my go-to travel and snack companion. Whether you're navigating a flight or a fussy afternoon, these chocolate balls deliver calm, comfort and nourishment in every bite.

- 1 cup, loosely packed (200 g) pitted soft medjool dates
- 1 cup (80 g) desiccated coconut
- ½ cup (60 g) LSA (flaxseeds, almonds, sunflower seeds)
- 1 tablespoon raw cacao powder
- 1 tablespoon carob powder (optional)
- 1 tablespoon melted coconut oil
- ½ cup carob powder (50 g) or desiccated coconut (40 g), for rolling

Place all the ingredients, except the carob or desiccated coconut, in a food processor and process until well combined and a dough forms.

Roll the mixture into small balls, then roll in the carob or desiccated coconut.

Place on the prepared tray and refrigerate until set or eat straight away.

Serve mashed, whole or in finger food–sized pieces.

Make it ...

Nut free Swap LSA for 1 cup mixed seeds (160 g) or oat flour (110 g).

Pantry friendly Swap dates for sulphur-free dried apricots.

Family friendly (2+) These should be sweet enough, but to sweeten further, add 1–2 tablespoons pure maple syrup or dip or drizzle in melted dark chocolate.

Leftovers Store in an airtight container in the fridge for up to a week or freeze for up to 3 months.

12+ months

Serves 13

Prep 5 mins (+ cooling)

Cook 20 mins

Blondie granola puffs

Vegetarian

Dairy free

Egg free

Fish free

Gluten free

Sesame free

Soy free

Say goodbye to store-bought puffs loaded with refined sugars and unnecessary additives. These blondie granola puffs are a much better alternative! Light, crispy and naturally sweetened with date paste, they're packed with nourishing ingredients, including creamy cashew butter and a hint of vanilla. They're a fantastic way to ditch processed cereals and puffed snacks in favour of a wholesome, homemade option. Sprinkle them over yoghurt, mix them into porridge, or enjoy straight from the jar – just be warned, they're seriously addictive.

5 cups (100 g) brown rice or quinoa puffs

½ teaspoon ground cinnamon (optional)

¼ cup (70 g) Date & cinnamon paste (see page 227)

2 tablespoons cashew butter

¼ cup (60 ml) melted coconut oil

1–2 teaspoons pure vanilla extract or powder, to taste

Optional toppings

Yoghurt or milk of choice

Preheat the oven to 150°C (300°F) and line a large baking tray with baking paper.

Place the puffs and cinnamon (if using) in a large bowl.

Place the date paste, cashew butter, oil and vanilla in a small saucepan over medium heat and stir until smooth and creamy. Remove from the heat and allow to cool for 10 minutes.

Pour the date mixture over the puff mixture and stir until the puffs are coated. Spread over the prepared tray and bake for 15–20 minutes, stirring halfway through.

Allow to cool completely on the tray. The puffs will crisp up as they cool.

Serve on their own as puffs or mix with yoghurt and/or milk of choice or use in any recipe that calls for rice puffs. Store in an airtight jar for an easy, crunchy snack anytime.

Make it ...

Nut free Swap cashew butter for tahini or sunflower seed butter.

Boosted Add 1 cup (about 140 g) crushed seeds or nuts to mixture.

Pantry friendly Swap paste for Apricot & pear or Apple & fig (see page 233).

Family friendly (2+) If transitioning kids off sugary cereals, add ¼ cup (60 ml) pure maple syrup to sweeten; swap date paste for pure maple syrup or raw honey.

Leftovers Store in an airtight container in a cool, dry spot in the pantry for up to 2 weeks.

8+ months

Makes 20

Prep 20 mins (+ 30 mins chilling)

Pumpkin pie bliss balls

 Vegan

 Dairy free

 Egg free

 Fish free

 Peanut free

 Sesame free

 Soy free

 Tree nut free

Mashed pumpkin is a great ingredient beyond just baby's first purées. Here it adds a soft, creamy texture as well as a boost of beta-carotene to support healthy vision and immunity. Lightly spicing the mixture with cinnamon, ginger and nutmeg really leans into the pumpkin pie flavours. These are the bliss balls to pack for an energy-boosting on-the-go snack.

- 6 (90 g/3¼ oz) pitted soft medjool dates
- 1 cup (110 g) rolled oats, plus extra if needed
- ½ cup (40 g) desiccated coconut, plus extra for rolling (optional)
- 2 teaspoons flaxseed meal
- 1 cup, tightly packed (260 g) steamed or roasted and mashed pumpkin (squash), plus extra if needed
- 1 teaspoon ground cinnamon
- ½ teaspoon ground ginger
- ¼ teaspoon ground nutmeg
- ½ teaspoon pure vanilla extract or powder

If the dates are firm, soften by soaking in warm water for 5–10 minutes, then drain.

Meanwhile, place the oats, coconut and flaxseed meal in a food processor and process until a flour consistency is reached.

Add the pumpkin, dates, spices and vanilla. Blend until the mixture comes together into a sticky dough. If too wet, add extra oats or coconut; if too dry, add a little more pumpkin or a splash of water.

Roll the mixture into small balls, then roll in extra coconut for more texture (if using). Refrigerate for at least 30 minutes to firm up before serving.

Serve mashed or in little bite-sized pieces.

Make it ...

Gluten free Swap oats for quinoa flakes.

Seasonal Swap pumpkin for sweet potato.

Boosted Add 1 tablespoon chia seeds to mixture.

Fussy-eater proof Make sure mixture is processed until very smooth.

Family friendly (2+) To sweeten, add 1–2 tablespoons raw honey or coconut sugar.

Leftovers Store in an airtight container in the fridge for up to 5 days or freeze for up to 3 months.

8+ months

Serves 20

Prep 20 mins (+ 1 hr freezing)

 Vegan

 Dairy free

 Egg free

 Fish free

 Gluten free

 Peanut free

 Sesame free

 Soy free

Carrot & beetroot date balls

I like to include veggies in these bliss balls as a fun way to introduce beetroot and carrot in a delicious, baby-friendly form. The soft texture makes them easy to mash or break apart for younger eaters, while older toddlers will enjoy grasping and nibbling on them independently.

- 1 cup (240 g) pitted soft medjool dates
- ½ cup, loosely packed (80 g) grated beetroot
- ¼ cup (25 g) grated carrot
- 1 cup (80 g) desiccated coconut, plus extra ½ cup (40 g) for rolling
- ⅓ cup (40 g) almond meal
- 2 tablespoons chia seeds

Line a baking tray with baking paper.

Place all the ingredients in a food processor and process until smooth.

Roll the mixture into small balls, then roll in extra coconut. Arrange on the prepared tray and place in the freezer for 1 hour to set.

Remove from the freezer at least 10 minutes before serving.

Serve mashed or broken into small, soft pieces for easy self-feeding.

Flatten the balls slightly to create a softer texture.

Make it ...

Nut free Swap almond meal for oats or extra desiccated coconut.

Seasonal Swap carrot for additional beetroot or vice versa.

Pantry friendly Swap chia seeds for flaxseeds, hemp seeds or pepitas (pumpkin seeds).

Faster Press mixture into a baking dish and freeze for 30 minutes. Cut into little squares to serve.

Fussy-eater proof Process dates and grated vegetables until puréed before adding remaining ingredients and making sure mixture is very smooth.

Leftovers Store in an airtight container in the freezer for up to 3 months.

8+ months

Serves 4

Prep 10 mins

 Vegan

 Dairy free

 Egg free

 Gluten free

 Fish free

 Peanut free

 Sesame free

Soy free

Banana, choc & cinnamon smoothie

This creamy banana, choc and cinnamon smoothie (pictured on page 210) is a gentle, nourishing way to introduce your baby and family to smoothies. It's made with simple, nutrient-rich ingredients, including banana, coconut milk, almond butter and pumpkin (but if you don't have any cooked pumpkin on hand, just leave it out). Tick off essential potassium, fibre, healthy fats and iron to support growing bodies – it's all in this cup!

- 2 medium (220 g/7¾ oz) ripe bananas, frozen
- 2 cups (500 ml) coconut milk, plus extra if needed
- 3 (45 g/1½ oz) pitted soft medjool dates
- 2 tablespoons almond butter
- ½ teaspoon ground cinnamon
- 1 teaspoon chia seeds
- 1–2 teaspoons carob powder, to taste
- ½ cup (100 g) steamed or baked pumpkin (squash) (optional)

Place all the ingredients in a high-speed blender and blend until smooth and creamy. If it's too thick for a straw, thin it out with some water or extra coconut milk.

Serve in small open cups or cups with a straw. Offer your baby ¼ cup (60 ml) to begin with and slowly increase to around ½ cup (125 ml) by 12 months (this is only a guide – your baby may drink more or less).

Make it ...

Nut free Swap almond butter for seed butter or omit.

Seasonal Swap pumpkin for sweet potato, zucchini (courgette), cauliflower or spinach.

Pantry friendly Swap milk for milk of choice.

Teething friendly Freeze into ice cubes for sore gums.

Family friendly (2+) Freeze into popsicle moulds; to sweeten, add 1 teaspoon pure maple syrup or raw honey.

Leftovers Store, covered, in the fridge for up to 2 days or freeze in popsicle moulds for up to 3 months.

8+ months

Serves 4

Prep 10 mins

Vegetarian

 Egg free

 Fish free

 Gluten free

 Peanut free

 Sesame free

 Soy free

 Tree nut free

Gut-friendly green smoothie

This green smoothie is as easy as throwing everything into a blender and blitzing. It's a nutrient-rich blend designed to nourish growing bodies while tasting naturally sweet and delicious. Packed with creamy avocado for healthy fats, spinach for essential vitamins and banana for natural sweetness, it's an ingenious way to add extra greens to your family's diet. Kefir or natural yoghurt boosts gut health, while coconut milk adds a rich, velvety texture that little ones love. Serve this smoothie at breakfast, snack time or as a refreshing post-playtime drink.

- 1 medium (110 g/3 ¾ oz) ripe banana, frozen
- ½ medium (70 g/2½ oz) ripe avocado
- 1 cup (30 g) baby spinach
- 1 teaspoon chia seeds
- ⅓ cup (85 g) natural unsweetened yoghurt or kefir
- 1½ cups (375 ml) coconut milk
- 4 (60 g/2¼ oz) pitted soft medjool dates

Place all the ingredients in a high-speed blender and blend until smooth and creamy.

Serve in small open cups or cups with a straw, or freeze in ice cube trays for a gum-soothing frozen treat.

Make it ...

Dairy free Swap yoghurt or kefir for natural unsweetened coconut yoghurt.

Seasonal Swap spinach for greens of choice.

Pantry friendly Swap milk for coconut water or water.

Boosted Add 2 teaspoons hemp seeds.

Family friendly (2+) Freeze into popsicle moulds; to sweeten, add 1 teaspoon pure maple syrup or raw honey.

Leftovers Store, covered, in the fridge for up to 2 days or freeze in popsicle moulds for up to 3 months.

Staples

6+ months

Makes 3.5–4L (118–135 fl oz)

Prep 10 mins

Cook 4 hours 15 mins (stove) or 18 hours 15 mins (slow cooker)

Bone broth

 Dairy free

 Egg free

 Fish free

 Gluten free

 Peanut free

 Sesame free

 Soy free

 Tree nut free

When I first started introducing bone broth to my babies, I knew I wanted a version that was rich in nutrients, yet gentle enough for their tiny tummies. This was the very first bone broth I made for them – simple, nourishing and designed for little ones. It's become a regular in my kitchen for adding to purées, spoonfeeding on its own or mixing into family meals. Unlike traditional bone broths that are often loaded with salt, this uses just a pinch of Himalayan rock salt to enhance the flavour without overwhelming delicate kidneys. Instead of relying completely on salt, I add apple cider vinegar, which helps draw out essential minerals, such as calcium, magnesium and phosphorus, from the bones. After hours of gentle simmering, the acidity softens, leaving a mild and soothing broth that's easy to digest.

- 1.5 kg (3 lb 5 oz) grass-fed beef or pasture-raised or organic chicken bones
- 1 medium (90 g) leek, white part only, thinly sliced
- 2 large (300 g/10½ oz) carrots, chopped
- 2 (80 g/2¾ oz) celery stalks, roughly chopped
- 2 tablespoons apple cider vinegar
- 1 teaspoon Himalayan rock salt
- 1 bunch flat-leaf parsley

Preheat the oven to 180°C (350°F) and roast the bones on a baking tray for about 30 minutes (optional, for added flavour and richness).

Transfer the bones to a large stockpot or slow cooker. Add the leek, carrot, celery, vinegar and salt, then cover with enough water to submerge the bones. If using a slow cooker, fill until three-quarters full.

If cooking in a pot, cook uncovered for at least 4 hours over low heat, adding more water if necessary. If using a slow cooker, set on low and cook for 12–18 hours. In the last 15 minutes of cooking, add the parsley.

Allow to cool, then remove the bones and strain the broth, discarding the bones and solids.

Store in small airtight containers. Freeze in silicone moulds for convenient, portion-sized broth cubes.

Tips For a clearer broth, skim off any foam or impurities that rise to the surface during cooking.

Use in purées, meat dishes, sauces or to add flavour to roast veggies, mashed potato, brown rice or pasta.

Make it ...

Different Use lamb bones; add extra herbs, such as thyme, rosemary or bay leaves for more flavour; add a handful of kale or spinach in the last 30 minutes of cooking.

Boosted Add garlic or ginger for an immune-boosting kick.

Leftovers Store in an airtight container in the fridge for up to 3 days or freeze for up to 3 months.

Hummus three ways

6+ months

Serves 10

Prep 15 mins

 Vegan

 Dairy free

 Egg free

 Fish free

Gluten free

 Peanut free

 Soy free

 Tree nut free

Dips and spreads are often one of the biggest hidden sources of sodium and additives in a child's diet, so creating a homemade version like this provides a clean, wholesome alternative. Both my babies absolutely loved this hummus! Each of the three flavour variations are worth a try. I love serving it as a dip for soft veggie sticks, spreading it on toast fingers or mixing it into mashed veggies for an extra flavour boost. The garlic, cumin and cinnamon give a gentle hint of spice.

1½ cups (270 g) cooked chickpeas or 400 g (14 oz) can chickpeas, drained and rinsed

¼–½ cup (60–125 ml) filtered, boiled and cooled water (optional, for desired consistency)

Place the chickpeas in a food processor. Add all the ingredients of your chosen flavour variation. Process until smooth, scraping down the side once or twice to help blend evenly. Add some (or all) of the water until your desired consistency is reached. Taste and adjust texture (with more water) or flavour (with more garlic, lemon juice and spices) if needed.

Leftovers Store in an airtight container or jar in the fridge for up to 4 days or freeze in small portions for up to 3 months.

Make it ...

Sesame free Omit tahini.

Nutty Swap tahini for smooth almond butter (if appropriate for your baby's age and nut free isn't necessary).

Seasonal Swap beetroot for pumpkin (squash), sweet potato or carrot; swap pumpkin for sweet potato.

Different Add a pinch of sweet paprika or mild soft herb leaves, such as parsley, for extra flavour.

Faster Use store-bought steamed organic beetroot to reduce prep time.

Fussy-eater proof Peel chickpeas by gently rubbing with a clean tea (dish) towel before blending; mix with natural unsweetened yoghurt for a creamier texture (if dairy free isn't necessary); serve with fun-shaped dippers or veggie fries to encourage self-feeding.

Pantry friendly Swap chickpeas for cannellini or butter beans.

Family friendly (2+) Serve with carrot or cucumber sticks or wholemeal crackers.

School friendly Spread on sandwiches or wraps with grilled chicken or roast veg.

Serving suggestions

6–9 months

- Serve as a smooth purée.
- Spread over soft bread fingers or steamed veggie sticks.
- Mix a small spoonful with mashed avocado for added creaminess.

9–12 months

- Spread over mini brown rice cakes, wholemeal toast fingers or Lebanese bread strips.
- Use as a dip for cooked wholemeal pasta spirals, roasted veggie sticks or soft sourdough bread soldiers.

12+ months

- Add to savoury muffins (see pages 103 and 173), falafels (see page 162), sandwiches, wraps or quesadillas.
- Stir into quinoa, couscous or potato mash for added nutrients.
- Serve with scrambled eggs, chicken or fish cakes for a balanced meal.

1. Classic

2 tablespoons hulled tahini

1 small garlic clove (optional, use a smaller amount for milder flavour)

2 tablespoons extra virgin olive oil

1 tablespoon fresh lemon juice

½ teaspoon ground cumin (optional)

2. Butternut

2 tablespoons extra virgin olive oil

1¼ cups (250 g) peeled and steamed butternut pumpkin (squash), cooled

⅓ cup (90 g) unsweetened 100 per cent apple purée (homemade or store-bought)

½ teaspoon ground cinnamon

3. Beetroot

250 g (9 oz) beetroot, peeled, roasted and cooled

¼ cup (60 g) hulled tahini

2 garlic cloves (optional, use a smaller amount for milder flavour)

¼ cup (60ml) extra virgin olive oil

1 tablespoon fresh lemon juice

1½ teaspoons ground cumin (optional)

One-ingredient buckwheat bread

8+ months

Makes 1 loaf

Prep 10 mins (+ 8 hrs soaking, 20 hrs fermenting & cooling)

Cook 1 hr 20 mins

 Vegan

 Dairy free

 Egg free

 Fish free

 Gluten free

 Peanut free

 Sesame free

 Soy free

 Tree nut free

2½ cups (475 g) unhulled buckwheat groats (not activated or toasted)

Optional extras

1 teaspoon ground caraway seeds

1 teaspoon ground fennel seeds

Pinch of sea salt (optional)

Optional toppings

1 tablespoon poppy seeds

1 tablespoon flaxseeds

1 tablespoon bigger seeds of choice (such as pepitas/pumpkin or sunflower)

This one-ingredient loaf is a naturally gluten-free and nutrient-dense alternative to traditional bread. Buckwheat is rich in fibre, protein and essential minerals, such as magnesium and iron, making it a fantastic option for supporting energy levels and healthy digestion. Unlike store-bought breads, which can be high in salt and additives, this homemade version is free from preservatives and can be easily customised with optional herbs and seeds for added flavour. The slow fermentation process makes it gentle on tummies, while the naturally chewy texture is great for baby-led weaning or family mealtimes.

Rinse the buckwheat groats thoroughly under running water. Transfer to a large bowl, cover with fresh water and soak for 7–8 hours.

Drain and rinse the buckwheat, then transfer to a high-speed blender. Blend with 200 ml (7 fl oz) water and any or all of the optional extras (if using) until smooth and creamy.

Pour the mixture into a clean bowl, cover with a clean tea (dish) towel and leave to ferment at room temperature for about 20 hours, or until it develops a slightly sour aroma.

Preheat the oven to 180°C (350°F). Line the base and sides of a loaf tin with baking paper.

Pour in the fermented batter. Sprinkle with the optional toppings (if using) and bake for 1 hour 20 minutes.

Allow to cool before slicing.

Cut the bread into soft strips or small bite-sized pieces for baby-led weaning. Pair with mashed avocado, Hummus (see page 224) or yoghurt for added nutrition.

For babies 12+ months, serve toasted with nut butter (if nut free isn't necessary), Berry chia jam (see page 228) or as a side to soups and stews.

Leftovers Store in a cool dry spot in a bread container for up to a week, in an airtight container in the fridge for up to 10 days or freeze for up to 3 months.

Tip Make sure you are using buckwheat groats that are unhulled and not activated or toasted.

8+ months

Makes 3 cups

Prep 5 mins (+ 15 mins soaking)

Date & cinnamon paste

 Vegan

 Dairy free

 Egg free

 Fish free

 Gluten free

 Peanut free

 Sesame free

 Soy free

 Tree nut free

This paste (pictured overleaf) is the hero sweetener of this book. Unlike refined sugars, syrups or fruit juices, it retains the fibre of whole dates, which helps slow the release of natural sugars and supports healthy digestion. It's also less sweet than using dates on their own, which makes it a gentle, baby-friendly way to introduce natural sweetness without being overwhelming. Dates are rich in essential nutrients, such as potassium, magnesium, iron and B vitamins; when blended into a paste with a touch of cinnamon and vanilla, they become a versatile, nourishing alternative to processed sweeteners. It's a wholesome, real-food choice that helps babies and toddlers develop a preference for less intensely sweet foods, setting them up for healthier eating habits long term.

- 400 g (14 oz) pitted soft medjool dates
- Pinch of ground cinnamon
- Seeds scraped from 1 vanilla pod, or 1 teaspoon pure vanilla extract or powder (optional)

Soak the dates in boiling water for 10–15 minutes to soften.

Drain the dates, reserving 300–400 ml (10½–14 fl oz) of the soaking water.

Place the dates, reserved soaking water, cinnamon and vanilla (if using) in a high-speed blender. Blend until smooth and creamy.

Stir into porridge or yoghurt, spread over toast or pancakes, or use as a natural sweetener in baby-friendly baking.

Make it ...

Pantry friendly This works best with medjool dates, but any dates will work.

Leftovers Store in an airtight container or jar in the fridge for up to 10 days or freeze for up to 3 months.

8+ months

Makes 1½ cups

Prep 5 mins (+ cooling & chilling)

Cook 10 mins

Berry chia jam

Vegan

 Dairy free

 Egg free

 Fish free

 Gluten free

 Peanut free

 Sesame free

 Soy free

 Tree nut free

Ditch the supermarket jam for a jar of this vibrant berry spread. It's naturally sweet and packed with antioxidant-rich berries and fibre-filled chia seeds. The whole family will get a hit of omega-3s and essential nutrients. With no added sugar, this is a great choice for babies from 8 months.

- 2 cups (320 g) frozen mixed berries
- 1 teaspoon pure vanilla extract or powder
- 2 tablespoons chia seeds

Place the berries, vanilla and ½ cup (125 ml) water in a medium saucepan. Bring to a simmer over medium heat and cook for 8–10 minutes, or until the fruit has softened and is jammy in consistency.

Use a potato masher to mash the fruit to the desired consistency. (Alternatively, use a high-speed blender if you prefer a smoother jam.) Sprinkle the chia seeds on top and stir to combine.

Transfer the jam to a heatproof bowl, cover, then allow to cool before refrigerating. Chill until the jam is set and the chia has thickened the jam.

Offer the jam in small amounts spread thinly on bread or toast, pancakes or pikelets, or mixed into porridge or yoghurt for added flavour.

For babies 6–7 months, ensure the jam is mashed or blended until smooth.

Make it ...

Seasonal Swap berries for fruit of choice.

Boosted Add some puréed veggies, such as carrot, pumpkin (squash) or sweet potato.

Family friendly (2+) To sweeten, add 1–2 tablespoons pure maple syrup or raw honey; enjoy stirred through overnight oats or layered in parfaits with natural unsweetened Greek-style yoghurt and granola; use as a filling for homemade pastries or cookies for a wholesome sweet snack.

Leftovers Store in an airtight container or jar in the fridge for up to 1 week.

8+ months

Makes 6

Prep 15 mins

Cook 20 mins

Vegetarian

Egg free

Fish free

Peanut free

Sesame free

Soy free

Tree nut free

Soft naan

This soft and fluffy naan is a crowd-pleaser, while also giving your baby new textures to explore. Made with just a handful of simple ingredients, they're easy to make and easy for little hands to hold and mouths to manage. The yoghurt base provides a boost of calcium and protein, while the option to add cumin or mild curry powder allows you to gradually introduce new flavours too. It's my go-to for encouraging self-feeding. Plus, it pairs beautifully with a variety of dips, spreads and family meals.

1 cup (150 g) wholemeal spelt flour, plus extra if needed

1 teaspoon baking powder

Pinch of cumin or mild curry powder (optional, for added flavour)

1 cup (260 g) natural unsweetened Greek-style yoghurt, plus extra if needed

1 tablespoon extra virgin olive oil (optional, for brushing)

In a bowl, combine the flour, baking powder and cumin or curry powder (if using). Add the yoghurt and mix until a soft dough forms. If the dough feels sticky, add a little extra flour. If the dough feels dry, add extra yoghurt.

Transfer the dough onto a lightly floured surface and knead for about 2–3 minutes, or until smooth.

Divide the dough into 6 equal balls and roll each one into a small oval or circle about 1 cm (½ in) thick.

Heat a dry non-stick frying pan over medium heat. In batches, cook each naan for 2–3 minutes each side, or until golden brown and slightly puffed.

For added flavour, brush with a little oil once cooked.

Cut the naan into soft strips for easy self-feeding and serve alongside mild curry, mashed avocado or yoghurt for dipping.

Make it ...

Dairy free Swap yoghurt for natural unsweetened coconut, oat or soy yoghurt.

Gluten free Swap flour for brown rice flour, buckwheat flour, millet flour or a gluten-free flour blend.

Pantry friendly Swap flour for wholemeal flour.

Family friendly (2+) Add a pinch of salt to batter; sprinkle with herbs for extra flavour; use naan as mini pizza bases or wraps.

Leftovers Store in an airtight container for 2 days or freeze for up to 2 months. Simply reheat in a dry pan or warm oven.

8+ months

Serves 18 (makes 1½ cups)

Prep 5 mins (+ 10 mins soaking)

Vegan

Dairy free

Egg free

Fish free

Gluten free

 Peanut free

 Soy free

 Tree nut free

Tahini & date spread

This is a versatile addition to your pantry that works beautifully on toast, brown rice cakes or as a dip for fresh fruit. With just two ingredients, it's packed with calcium, healthy fats and energy-boosting goodness. It can also be sent to school on a sandwich for older children.

1 cup (240 g) pitted soft medjool dates

⅓ cup (90 g) hulled tahini

Place the dates in a bowl and cover with boiling water. Let them soak for 10 minutes.

Drain the dates, reserving 2 tablespoons of the soaking liquid.

Place the dates, tahini and reserved soaking liquid in a high-speed blender. Blend until smooth.

Spread a thin layer over soft toast fingers or rice cakes, or mix into porridge for a gentle burst of flavour. You can also stir a spoonful into yoghurt or mashed banana for a creamy, nutrient-dense snack.

Make it ...

Different Add orange or lemon zest for a zesty twist; add a sprinkle of ground cinnamon.

Sesame free Use nut or seed butter instead of tahini.

Family friendly (2+) Use as a filling for sandwiches, drizzle over pancakes or swirl into smoothies for a delicious, naturally sweet boost; pairs beautifully with low-salt cheese and crackers for a wholesome afternoon snack.

Leftovers Store leftover spread in a jar or airtight container in the fridge for up to 1 week or freeze for up to 3 months.

6+ months

Makes 6

Prep 10 mins (+ 10 mins standing)

Cook 25 mins

Oat & quinoa wraps

 Vegan

 Dairy free

 Egg free

 Fish free

 Peanut free

 Sesame free

Soy free

 Tree nut free

½ cup (95 g) quinoa

¾ cup (95 g) rolled or quick oats

Pinch of pure garlic powder, ground cinnamon or cumin, or dried mixed herbs (optional)

Extra virgin olive oil or coconut oil, for frying

I went looking for an alternative to the high-sodium, store-bought wraps out there – they were too salty or full of ingredients not suitable for my children. My daughter had just started solids and I needed a gentle, nourishing base I could stuff with mashed veggies or soft fruit, and something I could grab for school lunches for my son. I still make a double batch of these wraps most weekends and freeze them for the week.

Place the quinoa in a sieve and rinse under cold water to remove any dirt or impurities.

Drain, then transfer the quinoa to a high-speed blender. Add the oats, 1 cup (250 ml) water and any desired flavourings (such as garlic powder). Blend for about 1 minute, or until smooth, scraping down the side once or twice to help blend evenly.

Transfer the batter to a bowl and let it sit for about 10 minutes to thicken.

Heat a non-stick frying pan over medium heat. Lightly brush with oil. Once the pan is hot, pour ¼ cup (60 ml) of batter into the centre of the pan. Use the back of a spoon or a measuring cup to gently spread the batter in a circular motion, forming a 13 cm (5 in) wrap. Cook for 2 minutes, then flip with a spatula and cook for another minute on the other side. Remove the wrap from the pan and allow to cool on a plate. Repeat with the remaining batter, re-greasing the pan between batches to prevent sticking.

Cut the wraps into soft, manageable strips for easy grasping. Spread with mashed avocado, soft-cooked veggies or Hummus (see page 224) for a nutrient-rich snack. Top with mashed pumpkin, banana slices or ricotta to create a soft, baby-friendly finger food.

Leftovers Store in an airtight container in the fridge for up to 4 days or freeze for up to 3 months.

Make it ...

Gluten free Swap oats with brown rice or quinoa flakes, or certified gluten-free oats.

Boosted Add 1 teaspoon flaxseed meal to batter.

Pantry friendly Swap quinoa for millet, extra oats or quinoa flakes (no need to rinse).

Fussy-eater proof Soak the uncooked quinoa in water for 2–3 hours to help reduce saponins, the natural compounds that give quinoa a bitter taste.

Family friendly (2+) Fill wraps with scrambled eggs, grilled chicken or roasted vegetables; for a quick, energy-boosting snack, spread with nut butter, Berry chia jam (see page 228) and berries.

School friendly Use as a base for school wraps or quesadillas.

8+ months

Makes 2 cups

Prep 10 mins (+ 30 mins soaking)

Cook 10 mins

 Vegan

 Dairy free

 Egg free

 Fish free

 Gluten free

 Peanut free

 Sesame free

 Soy free

 Tree nut free

Fruit paste two ways

I created these fruit pastes as a gentle, natural remedy for constipation when my little ones were struggling with tummy troubles. The combo of fibre-rich dried and fresh fruit helps support healthy digestion while also adding a soft, natural sweetness to meals. The apricot and pear version is light and tangy, while the apple and fig is rich and jammy. I'd stir a spoonful into porridge or yoghurt or spread it thinly on toast fingers, knowing I was offering a wholesome alternative to sugary spreads. It also helped keep things moving. Simple to make and freezer friendly, they quickly became a staple in my kitchen for both babies and the rest of the family.

1. Apricot & pear

2 cups (340 g) sulphur-free dried apricots

4 large (600 g) ripe pears, peeled, cored and chopped

1 teaspoon ground cinnamon (optional)

2. Apple & fig

2 cups (340 g) sulphur-free dried figs

4 medium (720 g) apples, peeled, cored and chopped

1 teaspoon ground cinnamon (optional)

Place the dried fruit of your chosen variation in a bowl and cover with hot water. Let soak for at least 30 minutes (or overnight for extra softness).

Drain, then transfer the soaked fruit to a high-speed blender. Set aside.

In a small saucepan, add the chopped fresh fruit of your chosen variation and ½ cup (125 ml) water. Bring to a simmer over low heat, then cook for 10 minutes, or until the fruit is soft. Transfer the mixture to the blender.

Add the cinnamon (if using) and blend until smooth, adding extra water if needed for the desired consistency.

Stir this paste into porridge, yoghurt or baby rice cereal for a naturally sweet flavour boost. Spread a thin layer over wholemeal toast or pancakes for a tasty finger-food option. Use as a natural sweetener in baby-friendly baking.

For babies 12+ months, use it as a fruit spread on wholegrain crackers or in sandwiches.

Make it ...

Fussy-eater proof Add to pancake batter or blend into smoothies for a naturally sweet flavour they'll love.

Leftovers Store in an airtight container or jar in the fridge for up to 7 days or freeze for up to 3 months.

8+ months

Makes 22

Prep 15 mins (+ cooling)

Cook 30 mins

Chamomile veggie rusks

 Vegan

 Dairy free

 Egg free

 Fish free

 Peanut free

 Sesame free

 Soy free

 Tree nut free

These homemade rusks are a soothing solution for little ones navigating the discomfort of teething. They're infused with chamomile tea, which offers gentle calming properties that can help ease irritability, while the firm texture massages sore gums. Free from added sugars, preservatives and unnecessary fillers, they're a wholesome alternative to store-bought rusks. Safety note: rusks should be firm, not crumbly.

1 chamomile teabag

180 g (6 oz) rolled oats

⅓ cup (55 g) pepitas (pumpkin seeds)

1 tablespoon melted coconut oil

½ cup, tightly packed (60 g) finely grated carrot

¾ cup (110 g) finely grated sweet potato

Brew a cup of chamomile tea with boiling water, allowing the tea bag to sit in the cup for 3–5 minutes. Remove the tea bag and allow it to cool completely (see tip).

Preheat the oven to 180°C (350°F) and line two baking trays with baking paper.

Place the oats and pepitas in a food processor and process until a flour consistency is reached.

Add the remaining ingredients and 1 tablespoon chamomile tea and process until a dough forms.

Transfer the dough to a lightly floured surface and roll into a long log about 1.5 cm (⅝ in) thick. Cut into fingers 5–7 cm (2–2¾ in) long and place on the prepared trays.

Bake for 25–30 minutes, or until crisp on the outside.

Allow to cool completely before serving. Never leave a baby unattended while chewing on teething rusks. Always supervise them to prevent choking. Offer in a safe highchair position and ensure the rusk is firm and not crumbling.

Tip To cool down the tea faster, add ice cubes to the cup or place in the fridge once cooled to room temperature.

Make it ...

Gluten free Swap oats with 1 cup chickpea flour (140 g) or brown rice flour (160 g).

Pantry friendly Swap oats for wholemeal spelt flour.

Leftovers Store in an airtight container in the fridge for up to a week or freeze for up to 3 months.

White sauce two ways

8+ months

Makes 1½ cups (ricotta), 2¾ cups (cauliflower)

Prep 10 mins

Cook 10 mins

 Vegetarian

 Egg free

 Fish free

 Gluten free

 Peanut free

 Sesame free

 Soy free

Tree nut free

1–2 tablespoons ghee or unsalted butter

1 tablespoon tapioca starch

1. Ricotta

1 cup (250 g) smooth ricotta

½ cup (125 ml) coconut milk

1 tablespoon nutritional yeast flakes or grated parmesan (optional, for extra flavour)

Pinch of ground nutmeg

Pinch of ground white pepper (optional)

2. Cauliflower

½ head (300 g/10½ oz) cauliflower, chopped into small florets

1½ cups (375 ml) coconut milk

Pinch of ground nutmeg

½ cup (50 g) grated low-salt cheese (optional)

Store-bought white sauces are often loaded with unnecessary additives, preservatives, sodium and hidden sugars, making them less than ideal for growing little ones. These homemade alternatives – a creamy ricotta and nutrient-rich cauliflower – are simple to make, wholesome and designed to ensure your baby can enjoy the same delicious family meals without compromising on flavour. The ricotta version is silky and mild, while the cauliflower one is a dairy-free spin, packed with fibre, vitamins and antioxidants. Both are quick to prepare and family friendly, so you can successfully tackle busy weeknights.

To make the ricotta version, combine the ricotta, milk, nutritional yeast or parmesan (if using), nutmeg and pepper (if using) in a medium bowl until smooth.

Heat 1 tablespoon ghee or butter in a saucepan over medium heat. Stir in the starch and cook, stirring constantly, for 1 minute to create a roux.

Gradually whisk in the ricotta mixture, ensuring there are no lumps. Simmer for 2–3 minutes, or until the sauce thickens.

Remove from the heat and use immediately or store in the fridge.

To make the cauliflower version, heat 2 tablespoons ghee or butter in a large frying pan over medium heat and sauté the cauliflower for about 5 minutes, or until softened.

Sprinkle the starch over the top and sauté for another minute. Pour in the milk and simmer for 2–3 minutes, or until the sauce thickens.

Add the nutmeg and cheese (if using). Allow to cool slightly, then pour the mixture into a high-speed blender. Blend until smooth and creamy. Use immediately or store in the fridge.

Blend the sauce with mashed vegetables or spoon it over soft finger foods to encourage self-feeding. Mix the sauce with soft-cooked brown rice pasta, steamed veggies or mashed potato for a creamy, nutrient-packed meal.

Make it ...

Dairy free Swap ricotta for coconut cream; swap ghee or butter for extra virgin olive oil or coconut oil; swap cheese for coconut cream or nutritional yeast flakes or omit.

Pantry friendly Swap tapioca starch for arrowroot or flour of choice (if gluten free isn't necessary).

Boosted Add 300 g (10½ oz) silken tofu for added protein.

Faster Blitz cauliflower in a food processor until cauli rice before sautéing.

Family friendly (2+) Stir through pasta, layer in lasagne or drizzle over roasted veggies; add a sprinkle of grated low-salt cheese or fresh soft herb leaves for extra flavour; cauliflower version works beautifully as a pizza sauce or creamy dip – boost veggie intake without fuss!

Leftovers Store in an airtight container in the fridge for up to 4 days or freeze for up to 3 months.

8+ months

Makes 1¼ cups

Prep 10 mins

 Vegetarian

 Fish free

 Gluten free

 Peanut free

Sesame free

 Soy free

 Tree nut free

Tzatziki dip

Made with Greek-style yoghurt for gut-friendly probiotics, cucumber for hydration and a hint of herbs for added flavour, this homemade dip is nutrient rich and refreshing. Unlike traditional tzatziki, this baby-friendly version keeps the seasoning mild and skips any excess salt, making it gentle on tiny tummies. Whether paired with soft veggie sticks, spread on toast fingers or served alongside grilled meats, this versatile dip is a great way to encourage self-feeding and healthy eating habits from an early age.

- 1 medium (150g/5½ oz) cucumber, peeled
- 1 cup (260 g) natural unsweetened Greek-style yoghurt
- 1 teaspoon fresh lemon juice
- 1 teaspoon extra virgin olive oil
- 1 tablespoon fresh dill or mint leaves, finely chopped
- 1 small garlic clove, crushed (optional)
- ½ teaspoon ground cumin (optional, for added flavour)

Grate the cucumber, then place in a clean tea (dish) towel or muslin (cheesecloth). Squeeze out as much excess liquid as possible.

In a bowl, combine the cucumber, yoghurt, lemon juice, oil, herbs, garlic and cumin. (For a milder flavour, particularly for babies under 12 months, add only a small amount of garlic and cumin or omit altogether.) Stir until well combined.

For a smoother, creamier consistency, briefly blend the mixture with a stick blender.

Serve immediately or chill in the fridge for 30 minutes to allow the flavours to develop.

Serve in a mild and baby-friendly way by stirring a small spoonful into mashed avocado, sweet potato or soft-cooked quinoa for added flavour and creaminess.

For babies 10+ months exploring finger foods, offer it as a dip alongside steamed veggie sticks. Always introduce new flavours gradually and adjust the garlic or herbs for a gentler taste, if needed.

Make it ...

Dairy free Swap yoghurt for natural unsweetened coconut yoghurt.

Milder Blend with a little mashed avocado.

Different Swap dill for mint or flat-leaf parsley for a different flavour profile.

Fussy-eater proof If your baby or toddler isn't a fan of the texture of raw cucumber, blend tzatziki until smooth.

Family friendly (2+) Spread on pita bread or wholemeal wraps with shredded chicken or lamb; use as a dip for cucumber sticks, capsicum (pepper) strips or steamed broccoli; stir through cooked quinoa or couscous for added creaminess and flavour.

Leftovers Store in an airtight container in the fridge for up to 3 days. Freezing is not recommended as the texture may change.

10+ months

Makes 3½ cups

Prep 10 mins (+ cooling)

Cook 15–20 mins

 Vegan

 Dairy free

 Egg free

Fish free

 Gluten free

 Peanut free

 Sesame free

 Soy free

 Tree nut free

Tomato sauce

One of the greatest benefits of starting your baby on a real-food approach is helping them develop a taste for natural flavours before sugary and salty sauces become the norm – preferences that can be harder to shift later. When I had my babies, I couldn't find a store-bought tomato sauce without added sugars or preservatives, so I made this one. Once you've experienced how easy, versatile and toddler-approved this condiment is – on everything from pasta to pizza to casseroles – you won't want to go back. It's a small effort with lasting rewards, and that's the kind of win every parent needs.

- 2 tablespoons extra virgin olive oil
- 1 medium (150 g/5½ oz) brown onion, finely chopped
- 2 garlic cloves, crushed
- 700 g (1 lb 9 oz) tomato passata (puréed tomatoes)
- 100 g (3½ oz) no-added-salt tomato paste (concentrated purée)
- 1 small (60 g) carrot, peeled and finely grated
- ½ cup (135 g) unsweetened 100 per cent apple purée (homemade or store-bought)
- 4 sulphur-free dried apricots, finely diced
- 1 teaspoon dried oregano
- 1 tablespoon arrowroot (optional, for thickening)

Heat the oil in a large saucepan over medium heat. Add the onion and garlic and sauté for 2–3 minutes, or until soft.

Add the passata, tomato paste, carrot, apple purée, apricot and oregano. Bring to the boil, then reduce the heat to low and simmer for 15 minutes, or until the sauce has thickened. If not thick enough, add the arrowroot and cook for a further 3 minutes.

Remove from the heat and allow to cool.

Place the mixture in a high-speed blender or food processor and blend until smooth, scraping down the side once or twice to help blend evenly.

Mix a small amount of this sauce with cooked pasta spirals or soft couscous for an easy meal. You can also use it as a dip for steamed veggie sticks or spoon it over mashed sweet potato for added flavour.

Tip Prepare a double batch of tomato sauce and freeze in small portions using large ice cube trays.

Make it ...

Seasonal Swap carrot for pumpkin (squash) or sweet potato.

Boosted Add 2 tablespoons chia seeds before blending.

Pantry friendly Swap apple purée for pear.

Fussy-eater proof Make sure sauce is puréed until very smooth.

Family friendly (2+) Makes a fantastic pizza base, pasta sauce or filling for homemade lasagne; add to meatballs, bakes or use it as a dip for homemade veggie nuggets or zucchini (courgette) fritters.

Leftovers Store in an airtight container in the fridge for up to 4 days or freeze for up to 3 months.

6+ months

Makes 2 cups

Prep 10 mins (+ cooling)

Cook 5 mins

 Vegan

 Dairy free

 Egg free

 Fish free

 Gluten free

 Peanut free

 Sesame free

Soy free

 Tree nut free

Creamy seed butter

Seed butters are a delicious and wholesome way to introduce healthy fats into your baby's diet. Their naturally creamy texture makes them well suited to mixing into porridges, mashing into fruit or spreading over soft toast fingers. Packed with essential nutrients like zinc, iron and omega-rich fats, seed butters support brain development, immunity and healthy growth. Best of all, they're free from added sugar and salt, making them a gentle and wholesome choice for developing tastebuds.

1 cup (160 g) pepitas (pumpkin seeds)

½ cup (80 g) sunflower seeds

¼ cup (30 g) hemp seeds

1–2 tablespoons melted coconut oil (optional, for a creamier texture)

In a dry skillet, toast the pumpkin and sunflower seeds over medium heat, stirring frequently, for 3–5 minutes, or until lightly golden and fragrant. Remove from the heat and allow to cool slightly.

Transfer the toasted seeds to a food processor or high-speed blender. Blend for 2–3 minutes, or until the mixture starts to break down into a coarse meal, scraping down the side once or twice to help blend evenly (see tips).

Add the hemp seeds and continue blending. Scrape down the side of the blender, as needed.

If the mixture seems too dry or isn't blending smoothly, add 1 tablespoon coconut oil at a time, blending after each addition, until you achieve your desired consistency.

Stir into mashed banana or porridge, or offer as a dip for soft veggie sticks.

For toddlers, use as a sandwich spread or drizzle over pancakes for a nutrient boost.

Tips Toasting the seeds enhances their flavour and helps release natural oils, making the butter smoother and richer. Be careful not to over-toast, as this can result in a bitter taste.

Blending may take longer, depending on your food processor or blender. Pause occasionally to scrape down the side and avoid overheating the mixture.

Make it ...

Sweeter Add 1–2 (15–30 g/½–1 oz) pitted soft medjool dates to blender.

Nutty Add 1 tablespoon unhulled tahini or a drizzle of pure maple syrup (for 2+ years).

Pantry friendly Swap hemp seeds for flaxseeds or sesame seeds (if sesame free isn't necessary).

Family friendly (2+) Add a spoonful to smoothies, stir into overnight oats or dollop onto baked sweet potatoes for a savoury twist.

Leftovers Store in an airtight container or jar in the fridge for up to 2 weeks.

8+ months

Makes 1 cup

Prep 5 mins (+ cooling)

Cook 15 mins

Wholemeal sourdough breadcrumbs

 Vegan

 Dairy free

 Egg free

 Fish free

 Peanut free

Sesame free

 Soy free

 Tree nut free

Skip the unwanted extras in packaged breadcrumbs – preservatives, artificial flavours and hidden nasties, like added sugars, excessive salt and even questionable oils – by blitzing up your own! Elevate the dinnertime meal with a fresher, more wholesome crumb with a deliciously tangy flavour and satisfying crunch. Plus, it's a fantastic way to reduce food waste by using up bread that has lost its freshness.

- 4 slices stale wholemeal sourdough bread
- 1 tablespoon olive oil (optional, for extra crispiness)
- ½ teaspoon dried herbs (such as oregano, thyme or rosemary, optional)

Preheat the oven to 150°C (300°F). This low temperature helps dry out the bread without burning it.

Tear or slice the sourdough into chunks.

Spread the bread over a baking tray and bake for 10–15 minutes, or until it feels dry and crisp. (If the bread is already very dry, you can skip this step.) Allow to cool completely.

Transfer to a food processor and process until fine or coarse crumbs form (depending on your preference). (Alternatively, place the bread in a sealed plastic bag and crush with a rolling pin.)

Toss the breadcrumbs with oil and herbs (if using), then return to the tray and bake for another 5 minutes for extra crispiness. Allow to cool completely.

Use the breadcrumbs to coat soft-cooked pieces of sweet potato, pumpkin (squash) or zucchini (courgette), then bake for soft veggie fingers. For protein-rich bites, coat strips of soft-cooked chicken or fish, then lightly bake or pan-fry until tender and golden. For baby-led weaning, create easy-to-grasp pieces by coating small vegetable sticks or mashed potato patties with the breadcrumbs and baking.

Leftovers Store in an airtight container or jar at room temperature for up to 2 weeks or freeze for up to 3 months.

Make it ...

Gluten free Swap wholemeal sourdough for gluten-free sourdough.

Family friendly (2+) Use as a crunchy coating for homemade chicken nuggets (see page 160), fish fingers (see page 132) or veggie burgers; sprinkle over pasta bakes, salads or roasted vegetables for added texture and flavour.

8+ months

Makes 2¼ cups

Prep 5 mins

Vegan

Dairy free

Egg free

Fish free

Gluten free

Peanut free

Sesame free

Soy free

Tree nut free

Gluten-free crumb mix

Forget bland, gritty gluten-free coatings; this crumb mix brings flavour, texture and nutrition. Designed with little eaters in mind, it's made from brown rice puffs and nutrient-dense seeds, like pumpkin, sunflower and flax. The result? A naturally crunchy blend that bakes beautifully without added oils or fillers. Coat veggie fingers and nuggets or sprinkle over pasta bakes for all the crispiness without the ultra-processed extras. It's a pantry essential you'll turn to again and again, especially if feeding children with food sensitivities or looking to boost meals with extra fibre and healthy fats.

- 1 cup (20 g) unsweetened brown rice puffs
- ½ cup (80 g) sunflower seeds
- ¼ cup (40 g) pumpkin seeds (pepitas)
- ¼ cup (45 g) golden flaxseeds
- ¼ teaspoon freshly ground black pepper (optional)

Optional extras

- Chia seeds
- Sesame seeds (if sesame free isn't necessary)

Place all the ingredients, including the optional extras (if using), in a food processor. Pulse until the mixture resembles coarse crumbs (not too fine), scraping down the side once or twice to help blend evenly.

Store in an airtight container or use straight away to coat your protein or veggies.

Use the crumb mix to coat veggie fingers (like sweet potato, pumpkin/squash or zucchini/courgette) or fish bites before baking. For a protein-rich option, coat strips of chicken or fish, then lightly bake or pan-fry until tender and golden. For baby-led weaning, create easy-to-grasp pieces by coating small vegetable sticks or mashed potato patties with the crumb mix and baking until lightly crisp on the outside but soft inside.

For babies 12+ months and family meals, use as a crunchy coating for homemade chicken nuggets (see page 160), fish fingers (see page 132) or veggie burgers. Sprinkle over pasta bakes, salads or roasted vegetables for added texture and flavour.

Make it ...

Nutty Swap seeds for nuts.

Different Add pure garlic or onion powder for extra flavour.

Pantry friendly Swap seeds for seeds of choice.

Leftovers Store in an airtight container in a cool, dry spot in the pantry for up to 2 weeks.

Rice 'breadcrumbs'

This is another simple way to make a gluten-free crumb mix.

Use 1–2 cups (210–420 g) brown rice (short or medium grain work best).

Grind the rice by blitzing in a high-speed blender, food processor or spice grinder until the texture resembles coarse crumbs (not powdery like flour). You're aiming for a crumbly, panko-like texture.

For extra crunch (optional), preheat the oven to 160°C (325°F). Spread the rice crumbs over a baking tray and toast in the oven for 5–7 minutes, or until lightly golden. Allow to cool completely before using or storing in an airtight jar or container.

Parent's guide to nutrition terms

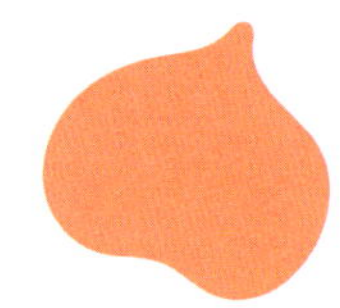

Added sugars

Sugars (and syrups) that are added to foods during processing or preparation. These can include white sugar, honey, cane sugar, golden syrup, rice syrup, fruit juice concentrate and more. Added sugars provide energy but no essential nutrients, and too much can increase the risk of tooth decay, obesity and other chronic health conditions.

Additives

Substances added to foods to preserve flavour, enhance appearance or improve shelf life. These include colours, preservatives, emulsifiers and thickeners. Some additives are linked to hyperactivity, gut disruption and allergic reactions in sensitive children.

Allergen

A substance that can cause an allergic reaction. Common food allergens include milk, eggs, peanuts, tree nuts, fish, shellfish, soy, wheat and sesame.

Antioxidants

Compounds that protect cells from damage caused by free radicals. Found abundantly in colourful fruits and vegetables.

Bioavailability

How easily a nutrient can be absorbed and used by the body. For example, iron from meat (heme iron) is more bioavailable than iron from plants (non-heme iron).

Carbohydrates

Your child's main energy source. Think of carbs as fuel for your little one's busy day! Found in fruits, vegetables, grains and legumes. Complex carbs (wholegrains and vegetables) provide longer-lasting energy than simple carbs (sugars).

Essential nutrients

Nutrients the body cannot make (or make enough of) and must get from food. These include certain amino acids (protein building blocks), fatty acids, vitamins and minerals.

Fats

Not the villains they're made out to be! Healthy fats are crucial for brain development, hormone production and absorbing fat-soluble vitamins. Good sources include avocado, oily fish, nuts, seeds and extra virgin olive oil, as opposed to less desirable fats (industrial seed oils and trans fats).

Fibre

Keeps your little one's digestive system running smoothly. There are two types: soluble (helps soften stools) and insoluble (adds bulk to stools). Found in fruits, vegetables, wholegrains and legumes.

Food sensitivity

A delayed, non-life-threatening adverse reaction to food that can cause digestive issues, skin reactions or other symptoms. Unlike food allergies, sensitivities are not life threatening and do not involve the immune system in the same way, but they can still cause discomfort.

Gluten-free oats

While oats don't naturally contain wheat, most commercial oats are processed in facilities that also handle wheat. For babies with wheat allergies, celiac disease or gluten sensitivity, choose certified gluten-free oats and always check product labels. Or you can substitute the oats for brown rice or quinoa flakes. All gluten-free oats available in Australia are imported due to labelling

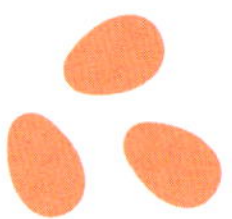

law challenges. There are now Australian producers creating uncontaminated oats, though they cannot use the 'gluten-free' label.

Gut-brain axis

The two-way communication system between your child's digestive tract and brain. This connection explains how gut health can influence cognitive development, mood and behaviour.

Inherent sugars

Sugars that are naturally present in whole foods, such as the fructose in fruit and the lactose in milk. These sugars come packaged with fibre, water and nutrients, so the body digests them more slowly and they provide more nutritional benefit. For example, the natural sugar in an apple also delivers vitamin C and fibre to support gut health. The recipes in this book only contain these types of sugars.

Iron-rich foods

Iron is essential for brain development and preventing anaemia. For babies, iron-rich foods include meat, poultry, fish, legumes, egg yolk and iron-fortified cereals. Pairing iron with vitamin C-rich foods helps improve absorption.

Macronutrients

The nutrients your child needs in larger amounts: carbohydrates, proteins and fats.

Microbiome

The community of trillions of bacteria, fungi and other microorganisms living primarily in the digestive tract. A diverse, balanced microbiome supports digestion, immune function and even mood regulation.

Micronutrients

Vitamins and minerals that are needed in smaller amounts than macronutrients but are still vital for health, growth and development.

Nutrient density

The concentration of nutrients relative to calories in a food. Nutrient-dense foods provide substantial vitamins, minerals and other beneficial components with relatively few calories.

Prebiotics

Non-digestible food components (special types of fibre) that feed beneficial gut bacteria, helping them multiply. Sources include banana, onion, garlic, leek, asparagus and many whole plant foods, such as onion, garlic, leek, asparagus, Jerusalem artichoke, legumes and wholegrains.

Probiotics

'Good' live bacteria that, when consumed in adequate amounts, provide health benefits. They help maintain a balanced gut microbiome. Found in yoghurt, kefir, sauerkraut and other fermented foods.

Protein

The building blocks for growing bodies. Essential for muscle development, immune function and cell repair. Present in meat, fish, dairy, eggs, legumes, nuts and seeds.

Real food

Wholefoods that are as close to their natural state as possible. Real food is minimally processed and free from artificial additives, preservatives, flavours and colours. Think fresh fruits, vegetables, wholegrains, quality proteins, healthy fats and homemade or simply prepared meals. Real food is the foundation for raising healthy, resilient eaters.

Real Food Rating

A parent-led movement and independent certification system designed to cut through confusing food marketing. The Real Food Rating evaluates packaged foods based on ingredient quality, level of processing and the presence of additives, helping families make informed choices and avoid ultra-processed foods. Look for the Real Food Rating on products or visit realfoodrating.com for trusted product reviews and guidance.

Responsive feeding

Recognising and responding to your child's hunger and fullness cues, rather than enforcing strict mealtimes or portions.

Ultra-processed foods (UPFs)

Foods that are industrially formulated using refined ingredients, additives and artificial flavours, often far removed from their original form. High UPF intake in children is linked to increased risk of obesity, ADHD symptoms, poor gut health and other chronic diseases. Avoiding UPFs is a key focus of the Real Food Rating movement. A long ingredients list on the packaging is a red flag. UPFs often displace wholefoods in children's diets, contributing to poor nutrient intake despite high calories.

Wholefood nutrition

Focusing on foods in their natural or minimally processed state, rich in nutrients and free from artificial additives. This means choosing an apple over apple-flavoured puffs or homemade chicken strips over processed nuggets.

References

Step 1: The Real Food mindset

- **Pages 5–11** Appetite, Volume 9, Issue 3, December 1987, Pages 211-300, sciencedirect.com/journal/appetite/vol/9/issue/3
- **Page 11** Martínez Steele, E., Baraldi, L. G., Louzada, M. L., Moubarac, J.-C., Mozaffarian, D., Monteiro, C. A. (2016), *Ultra-processed foods and added sugars in the US diet: evidence from a nationally representative cross-sectional study*, BMJ Open, pmc.ncbi.nlm.nih.gov/articles/PMC4785287
- **Page 11** World Health Organization (2022), *Global oral health status report: towards universal health coverage for oral health by 2030*, World Health Organization, who.int/publications/i/item/9789240061484
- **Page 11** Aguilera, A. C., Dagher, I. A., & Kloepfer, K. M. (2020), *Role of the Microbiome in Allergic Disease Development, Current Allergy and Asthma Reports*, 20(9), 44, pmc.ncbi.nlm.nih.gov/articles/PMC7702839
- **Pages 11–13** Snuggs, S., & Harvey, K. (2023), *Family Mealtimes: A Systematic Umbrella Review of Characteristics, Correlates, Outcomes and Interventions*, Nutrients, 15(13):2841, doi.org/10.3390/nu15132841
- **Pages 11–13** Dallacker, M., Hertwig, R., & Mata, J. (2018), *The frequency of family meals and nutritional health in children: a meta-analysis*, Public Health Nutrition, 21(1),114-127, pubmed.ncbi.nlm.nih.gov/29334693
- **Pages 11–13** Berge, J. M., Wall, M., Hsueh, T. F., Fulkerson, J. A., Larson, N., & Neumark-Sztainer, D. (2015), *The Protective Role of Family Meals for Youth Obesity: 10-year Longitudinal Associations*, The Journal of Pediatrics, 166(2):296-301, pmc.ncbi.nlm.nih.gov/articles/PMC4308550
- **Pages 11–13** Pagani, L. S., Harbec, M. J., & Barnett, T. A. (2017), *Associations Between Early Family Meal Environment Quality and Later Well-Being in School-Age Children*, Journal of Developmental & Behavioral Pediatrics, 38(1):52-58, pubmed.ncbi.nlm.nih.gov/29227338
- **Pages 11–13** Laue, H. E., Coker, H., Madan, J. (2022), *The Developing Microbiome From Birth to 3 Years: The Gut-Brain Axis and Neurodevelopmental Outcomes*, Frontiers in Pediatrics, 10:815885, pmc.ncbi.nlm.nih.gov/articles/PMC8936143
- **Pages 11–13** Lane, M. M., Gamage, E., Du, S., Ashtree, D. N., McGuinness, A. J., Gauci, S., Marx, W. (2024), *Ultra-processed food exposure and adverse health outcomes: umbrella review of epidemiological meta-analyses*, BMJ, bmj.com/content/384/bmj-2023-077310
- **Pages 11–35** National Health and Medical Research Council (NHMRC) (2012), *Infant Feeding Guidelines Summary*, eatforhealth.gov.au, eatforhealth.gov.au/sites/default/files/files/the_guidelines/n56b_infant_feeding_summary_130808.pdf
- **Page 12** Neumark-Sztainer, D., Larson, N., Fullerton, J., Eisenberg, M., Story, M. (2010), *Family Meals and Adolescents: What Have We Learned from Project EAT (Eating Among Teens)?*, Public Health Nutrition, Cambridge University Press, cambridge.org/core/journals/public-health-nutrition/article/family-meals-and-adolescents-what-have-we-learned-from-project-eat-eating-among-teens/AB59377509554C9A39FCBD29C2E3AFA2
- **Page 12** Øverby, N., Hillesund, E., Røed, M., Vik, F. (2020), *Association Between Parental Feeding Practices and Shared Family Meals. The Food4Toddlers Study, Food & Nutrition Research*, 64:10.29219, pmc.ncbi.nlm.nih.gov/articles/PMC7478118

Step 2: Starting solids

- **Page 25** Australian Bureau of Statistics (2023), *Dietary behaviour, 2022*, Australian Bureau of Statistics, abs.gov.au/statistics/health/health-conditions-and-risks/dietary-behaviour/latest-release
- **Page 29** Australian Bureau of Statistics (2022), *Key Statistics and Data About Child and Adult Consumption of Fruit and Vegetables, Dietary Behaviour*, Australian Bureau of Statistics, abs.gov.au/statistics/health/food-and-nutrition/dietary-behaviour/latest-release
- **Page 29** Maier, A., Chabanet, C., Schaal, B., Issanchou, S., & Leathwood, P. (2007), *Effects of Repeated Exposure on Acceptance of Initially Disliked Vegetables in 7-month old Infants, Food Quality and Preference*, 18(8):1023-1032, sciencedirect.com/science/article/abs/pii/S0950329307000523
- **Page 29** Birch, L. L., McPhee, L., Shoba, B. C., Pirok, E., Steinberg L. (1987) *What kind of exposure reduces children's food neophobia? Looking vs. tasting*, pubmed.ncbi.nlm.nih.gov/3435134
- **Page 31** National Allergy Council (2020), *The Learning Early About Peanut Allergy (LEAP) study*, National Allergy Council, preventallergies.org.au/the-learning-early-about-peanut-allergy-leap-study
- **Page 34** U.S. Department of Agriculture and U.S. Department of Health and Human Services (2020), *Dietary Guidelines for Americans 2020-2025*, Dietary Guidelines, dietaryguidelines.gov/sites/default/files/2021-03/Dietary_Guidelines_for_Americans-2020-2025.pdf
- **Page 34** Jenco, M. (2023), *Health officials detail proposed changes to food*, AAP News publications.aap.org/aapnews/news/27256/Health-officials-detail-proposed-changes-to-food

Acknowledgements

To my gorgeous children, Summer and Aaron, you are both my daily inspiration. This book is for you. Being your mum has taught me more than any degree or career ever could. It has grounded me, fuelled me and shown me what truly matters. You are, and always will be, my greatest accomplishment. I am so proud of you both.

To my parents, thank you for your unwavering love, support and guidance. Your strength and belief in me have been the foundation of everything I've built. I love you both deeply.

To my brother Paul, my friend, my mentor, my ally. Thank you for sharing your wisdom and walking beside me through every step of this journey. To my brother Ivan, I know you'll always have my back, and that means the world.

To my soul sister Nanda, we have laughed and cried together. The light will shine on you again, I promise.

To my grandparents and to Brett, I know you are smiling down on all of us.

To Lori, you'll always be the best listener and such a special friend in my life.

To all my dear friends and family, thank you for your support through the good times and the hard ones. Special mention to my great grandmother Bella, aunty Elaine and cousin Wallis. I love you all very much.

To Kevin, thank you for your wisdom and support, and for standing by me through tough times.

To my literary agent, Joe Boschetti, thank you for your guidance and for helping shape this book into reality. To my manager, Drew Lambert, your belief in the Real Food Rating mission has meant so much. Thank you for being in my corner.

To Keegan McLaughlin, thank you for your creative support behind the scenes.

To my team, past and present. Sandra Bendersky, you worked tirelessly with me to perfect these recipes. It has been a journey, and it's just the beginning. Thank you, Annabel Clancy, for your research assistance.

To Karli and her beautiful children, thank you for being my little taste testers. To Lisa, Amelia, Jordana, Nate, Archie, Tal, Gilad and all the amazing mums and bubs who took part in the photoshoot, your energy brought this book to life.

To my publisher, Melissa Kayser, thank you for making this book happen and believing in the vision from the start. A heartfelt thank you to Loran McDougall, Megan Pigott and my wonderful copyeditor, Alex McDivitt. To the rest of the incredible team, including Cath Muscat, Vanessa Austin, Double Slice, Clare Maguire, Sandy Goh and Natalie Crouch, your creativity and care made this book shine.

This book was created with love, lived experience and deep gratitude. I hope it nourishes your family the way it has nourished mine.

About the author

Mandy Sacher is Australia's leading paediatric nutritionist, the founder of the Real Food Rating, and a passionate advocate for children's health and wellbeing. A Sydney-based mum and author, Mandy has spent more than two decades helping families cut through misleading food marketing to make informed, nourishing choices. She is best known for pioneering one of the only independent food certification systems that assesses packaged foods based on ingredient quality, processing level and additive content, and supports parents across the nation to make better choices.

Mandy offers one-on-one consultations, runs workshops for families and educators, and collaborates with paediatricians, schools, children's food brands and healthcare providers. She developed one of the first wholefood baby weaning programs rolled out in hundreds of childcare centres across Australia, and co-developed and wrote the training manuals for MEND (Mind, Exercise, Nutrition...Do it!), a globally recognised childhood obesity prevention initiative.

Her brand partnerships span ALDI, Paw Patrol, Nourishing Bubs, Munchkin, Grumpy Bums and Bellamy's Organic. She has also worked with Elevit to create pregnancy education campaigns. Through Real Food Rating and her growing movement, Mandy continues to drive systemic change by empowering parents, supporting reformulation, and championing transparency in the food industry.

Index

D

E

F

Published in 2026 by Murdoch Books, an imprint of Allen & Unwin

Murdoch Books Australia
Cammeraygal Country
83 Alexander Street
Crows Nest NSW 2065
Phone: +61 (0)2 8425 0100
murdochbooks.com.au
info@murdochbooks.com.au

Murdoch Books UK
Ormond House
26–27 Boswell Street
London WC1N 3JZ
Phone: +44 (0) 20 8785 5995
murdochbooks.co.uk
info@murdochbooks.co.uk

For corporate orders and custom publishing, contact our business development team at salesenquiries@murdochbooks.com.au

Publisher: Melissa Kayser
Editorial manager: Loran McDougall
Design manager: Megan Pigott
Designer and illustrator: Double Slice (Amelia Leuzzi and Bonnie Eichelberger)
Editor: Alex McDivitt
Photographer: Cath Muscat
Stylist: Vanessa Austin
Home economists: Clare Maguire, Sandy Goh, Sandra Bendersky
Production manager: Natalie Crouch

Murdoch Books acknowledges the Traditional Owners of the Country on which we live and work. We pay our respects to all Aboriginal and Torres Strait Islander Elders, past and present.

EU Authorised Representative: Easy Access System Europe, Mustamäe tee 50, 10621 Tallinn, Estonia, gpsr.requests@easproject.com

ISBN 978 1 76150 121 0

A catalogue record for this book is available from the National Library of Australia

A catalogue record for this book is available from the British Library

Colour reproduction by Splitting Image Colour Studio Pty Ltd, Wantirna, Victoria
Printed in China by C&C Offset Printing Co., Ltd.

OVEN GUIDE: You may find cooking times vary depending on the oven and oven setting you are using. For fan-forced (convection) ovens, as a general rule, set the oven temperature to 20°C (25–50°F) lower than indicated in the recipe.

TABLESPOON MEASURES: We have used 20 ml (4 teaspoon) tablespoon measures. If you are using a 15 ml (3 teaspoon) tablespoon, add an extra teaspoon of the ingredient for each tablespoon.

10 9 8 7 6 5 4 3 2 1

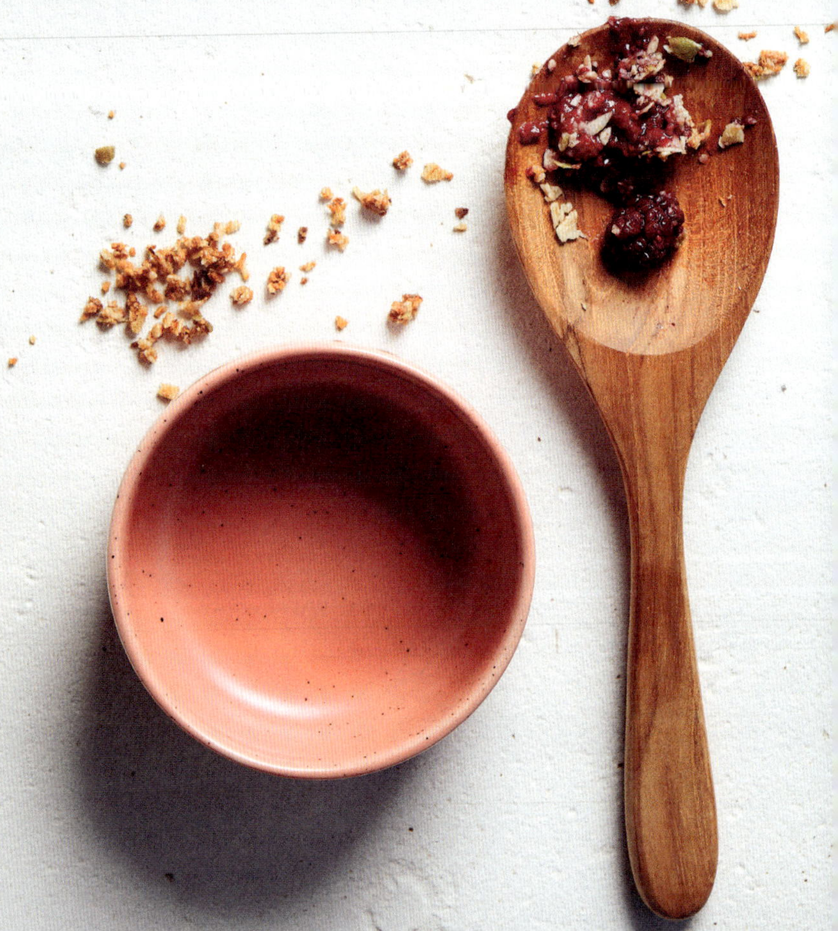